THE ULTIMATE SOFTBALL DRILL BOOK

A Complete Guide For Indoor & Outdoor Skill Development

RICHARD TRIMBLE *with* PAT BARNABA

PublishAmerica
Baltimore

First printing

PublishAmerica has allowed this work to remain exactly as the author intended, verbatim, without editorial input.

Softcover 9781629078366
PUBLISHED BY PUBLISHAMERICA, LLLP
www.publishamerica.com
Baltimore

Printed in the United States of America

DEDICATION FOR RICK TRIMBLE

To

Blake

She will be raised a

Red Sox fan, but I'll

forgive her.

DEDICATION FOR PAT BARNABA

To

my parents,

Mary & Roy

&

my Aunt Dorothy

TABLE OF CONTENTS

A Word About Structure—

Coaches crave drills, especially indoor drills. In sections of the country where the winter forces baseball and softball teams indoors, innovation and improvisation become watch words.

Wherever an indoor drill is described in this volume it is noted with a capital letter *"I"* in the upper right hand corner of the page. Of course, indoor drills can be employed out of doors as well, so pay attention to the *"I's"* even if you are planning an outdoor workout.

INTRODUCTION

I recently passed my 60th birthday and notwithstanding the sheer trauma of that milestone, I had promised myself that I would try to compile all of the baseball drills that I had used over 45 years of coaching. Yes, 45…I have always loved working with young ballplayers and did so even when I was in high school. In addition, I retired from active coaching in the same year that I became a sexagenarian. I still, and hopefully always will, work with kids in private instruction and serve as an assistant coach for my grandchildren's Little League teams (I only work the practices where I can teach; I get too competitive in games so I prefer a lawn chair in the outfield), but as for coaching a team of my own, those days are in the past.

These two events conspired to motivate me to put together my own drill book. For most of my career, I have always been an assistant coach and that has always been the way I preferred it. I was in a better position to teach. Let me have the pitchers in the bullpen or the hitters in the cage for an hour or two and I am in heaven. Moreover, by serving as an assistant coach for most of my career, I have been fortunate to have worked with some great head coaches. I have included many of their drills in this volume.

Besides the talented head coaches that I worked for over the years—Jake Landfried, Ernie Leta, Paul Murray to name a few—another source for my knowledge base has been the "Be The Best You Are Coaches Clinic" run by Jack Hawkins in Cherry Hill, New Jersey for over thirty years. It is simply a mind-boggling panoply of big-name coaches, and most importantly, excellent teachers of the game, that he has assembled over the years. He has provided softball coaches up and down the East Coast with a veritable "University of Softball." I always made it a point to purchase a systems book, a drill book or a strategy book from one of the many vendors that Jack has had on site. I have incorporated research from these literary sources as well.

Yet a final source, and perhaps the most important, has been that instinctive "feel" that all teachers have for their craft. The ability to look at a skill or a lecture topic and break it down to its component parts, and then teach and drill it through repetition and artistry. Legendary coach Jack Dunn once wrote in "Collegiate Baseball" magazine, "Effective coaching of a particular skill involves three factors: philosophy, mechanics, and drills to implement the mechanics." Teachers, be they in the classroom or on the diamond, understand this. They develop a philosophy about how best to succeed in executing a skill; they then break it down to its component parts and movements and then teach it and develop it through drills. The legendary basketball coach, John Wooden once put it this way:

1. Explanation
2. Demonstration
3. Imitation
4. Repetition

Many of the drills I have included in this volume have come from my own attempts to make my players better, to solve problems in their mechanics and to build "muscle memory" through repetition. A coach must be a teacher, first and foremost.

In these books, it was my goal to infuse drills from both softball and baseball. Coaches of these two sports teach basically the same game, yet they run in entirely different circles. I am a baseball coach at heart but in an attempt to learn more about the softball component, I still attend yearly clinics, including the aforementioned "Be The Best You Are Softball Coaches Clinic," and read coaching and drill books from what many baseball coaches would view as "the other world." There is much that can be learned from the integration of both sports. Moreover, by reading softball books I was able to add a previously untapped element of research into my repertoire of drills. The drills offered here are the product of years of reading, practicing and observing. I list a bibliography at the end of this book that contains some of the excellent literary sources that can be found in both spheres, all of which I consulted for this volume. Something written by Coach Mona Stevens struck home. She wrote, "I can't possibly gain the knowledge of all the coaches before me through my experience alone." (The Softball Coaching Bible, p. 290).

I confess that I was nervous about transitioning from baseball to softball and, perhaps presumptuously, suggesting drills for softball coaches. So I recruited an expert: Coach Pat Barnaba, a Hall of Fame high school softball coach, teaching colleague, and friend. She is my "quality control" expert and I am deeply indebted to her.

I have also coached ice hockey over the course of my long career and I was fortunate to have authored a three-volume series of hockey drill books. The final count put the total at over 400 hockey drills in what my editors called The Ultimate Hockey Drill Book. One of them called me, purely for the salesmanship impact, "a drill guru." I laugh about that now, but it is my deepest desire to bring that sense to you, the reader of these, The Ultimate Baseball/Softball Drill Books as they each contain, once again, over 400 drills.

My goal now is as simple and straightforward as it was then—to use research, coaching experience and reflective teaching to create the most comprehensive drill book(s) that is available to my colleagues.

Richard Trimble

FORM THROWING & PITCHING DRILLS

"One of the most inspiring things we can do for our athletes is to believe in them. We see what they cannot see yet. We know what they can become."

Coach Mona Stevens

The opening segment of this book contains nearly 100 drills for softball pitchers. It is not intended as a "how to" manual to instruct young pitchers in the basics, but it certainly functions as an offering of drills to enhance pitching skills.

THE "K" POSITION

SOFTBALL: BASIC THROWING—GRIP AND DRILLS

For young girls beginning their softball career, the simplest grip they should employ is a three-finger grip over a long seam on the ball. They can add a fourth finger over the top if their hands are small. They should try to keep the thumb underneath and in line with the middle finger on top.

Form throwing drills are critical with young players and are, arguably the most significant initial skill that we need to teach. It has been suggested that, as coaches, we may ask the young player, baseball or softball, to point the glove at their intended target. This has the benefit of aligning their shoulders to the target. However, I would like to take this opportunity to suggest another approach; align the front elbow to the target. Both techniques have merit, so it is up to the coach.

BASIC THROWING DRILLS: FOR YOUNG PLAYERS (UP TO AGE 10)   *"1"*

1. LONG TOSS—modified to distances of 60 feet and then 90 feet, this can have the same benefits as it does for older players;

2. "10-TO-THE-CHEST"—pairs of players are competing to see who can throw ten tosses into their partner's glove held at the chest. Have them count out loud and come up with your own reward system. Be a tough judge, don't allow cheaters to count errant throws.

3. SYNC-THROWS—Players are paired up along parallel lines. One line has the softballs. On a whistle or go-signal they throw in unison. See if they can obtain one "pop!" into the gloves with singular harmony. Difficult, but fun.

4. TARGETS—Call out throwing targets such as "Nose!", "Belly Button!" or "Glove-side Shoulder!"

5. THROW-N-GO—Use an infield and place a line of players at first, second, third and home. The player at home has a ball and begins with a throw to second base. When the throw is released, they run to first.

This first throw now establishes that each throw will have to beat a runner. Each thrower from this point will throw and then break for the next base. It looks like this:

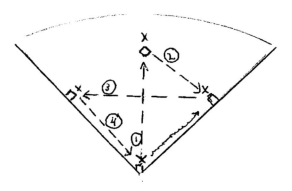

Throw #1: Home to Second
Throw #2: Second to First
Throw #3: First to Third
Throw #4: Third to Home

Repeat. Each throw is made on a whistle or command to avoid chaos.

If you wish, you can reinforce tagging techniques by having them slap down a tag. This in itself can be beneficial as young players many times are not aware of how to tag nor when and where to tag.

(I want to recognize Coach Jay Miller from Mississippi State Softball for presenting this drill series at the 2011 "Be The Best You Are Softball Coaches Clinic" in Cherry Hill, NJ).

THROWING: WARM-UPS & STRETCHING THE THROWING ARM

I have used this pre-practice throwing stretch for years, having first leaned from a college coach, Paul MacLaughlin of Brookdale Community College in New Jersey. It is particularly effective, even important, for young throwers, position plays.

Two players are involved. With the one to be stretched lying on the ground as shown, the partner grasps the throwing hand and with the elbow locked, she rotates the arm forward against mild resistance put up by the partner. This works the shoulder. An element of strength-training is involved as well.

The second stretch calls for the thrower to hold her throwing arm at a 90-degree, bent at the elbow as shown. In this movement only the lower arm rotates forward, also against mild resistance. This works the elbow.

Each of these stretches lasts ten-seconds in duration. Rotate the partners after one or two reps of each stretch.

THROWING AND ARM STRENGTHING: TENNIS CAN DRILLS

Fill an ordinary tennis ball can with sand. Tape the top on tightly. A whole routine of "loosening up" and arm strength exercises follows. It is worth noting that this routine can help position players as well as pitchers. I observed one high school team using the cans en masse';

each player had one in his glove bag and they did this as part of the stretching regimen. The player here is using a five-pound dumbbell.

a) ARM HANG—Let gravity do the work;

b) LATERAL SHOULDER LIFT—Raise the rotate the arm in small and large circles, can from the hip to the top of the head: keep clockwise and counter-clockwise. the arm relatively straight.

c) FRONT SHOULDER LIFT—This exercise d) "OVER THE TOP"—pull the can from a reportedly strengthens the rotator cuff. With "scratching position" behind the back to a the arm straight, raise the can in front of the position where you are pointing the top of body to eye level; pro-nate the hand with a the can at an imaginary someone in front thumb-down motion. of you. Feel the stretch in the triceps and be sure to turn the can over as if spinning a "yo-yo".

FORM THROWING: THE KNEE-DOWN DRILLS   *"I"*

This drill is an old standby. The player drops down on one knee, the knee on his throwing hand side. The two points of emphasis are "up and out" with the ball and proper follow through outside and below the knee. It is also a good short-order warm-up drill prior to pre-practice throwing and long toss. Some coaches prefer to work this drill by having the players face "up-field" at an angle to the receiver. In this execution, the knee that is down is the knee away from the receiver and the upper body rotation is necessarily enhanced.

This drill is excellent for Little Leaguers just learning how to throw properly and it should be part of every youth league coach's pre-practice routine. Emphasize flinging the throwing hand across the body, finishing outside and below the elevated knee.

THROWING FORM: WRIST FLICK DRILLS   *"I"*

Have two throwing partners face each other at a distance of ten feet or so. The throwing hand is elevated to shoulder height and held out in front of the body. The glove hand, with the glove on, is used to stabilize the throwing arm. The upper arm is parallel to the ground while the forearm is perpendicular as shown below.

Next, simply flick the ball with the wrist, having a "catch" as it were, with the partner.

This drill helps strengthen the wrist and forearm muscles. It also serves to reinforce the notion, inherent in both sports, of finishing the pitching motion with a snap of the wrist. In addition, wrist flick throws are used in run downs and need to be practiced for that purpose alone.

Another adaptation is to have the player lie on her back and snap the ball into the air above her, in effect having a "catch" with herself."

Some coaches make this simple drill a regular part of their pre-practice throwing routine.

FORM THROWING: Preventing Elbow Drop

Players must be taught to throw with the elbow at least as high as the shoulder, if not higher, otherwise as phenomenon known as "pushing the ball" occurs. This drill addresses inexperienced throwers who consistently drop their elbow on release of the ball.

Stand next to them, facing their "open" side or in a position to look at them face-to-face, as shown. Hold a fungo bat or a broomstick slightly in front of the pitcher's shoulder and slightly above their shoulder. Tell them to throw "over the stick" (reinforce this concept with the oft-used phrases "throw over the top" or "get on top"). Of course, there is the danger of hitting the bat or stick with their arm, so as they arrive at the release point, drop the stick.

A variation to have the player throw over a rope as indicated in the photo below.

Another simple drill is to stand next to a young ballplayer, on their throwing hand side. Elevate their elbow to shoulder height and hold it in your fingertips. Have them release the ball into a net or wall target from that abbreviated position.

Good verbal cues for young players include these: "Throw your hand at the target" and "Reach out."

These drills take constant repetition with players who have this flaw in their motion; it is not for everyone. They are remedial drills that need to be done each and every practice until corrected.

THROWING RANGE & ACCURACY YOUTH LEAGUE DRILLS

Continuing the discussion about teaching younger ball players how to catch and throw, here are two more drills. I have drawn them from Betty Hoff and Jacki Wright, one with modifications, from their chapter in <u>The Softball Coaching Bible.</u>

DRILL I: *"I"*CHEST CIRCLES—As the players are lined up to have a catch, have the receiver make a circle with their glove. They will demonstrate a circle around their upper body and torso as the target they want to receive the ball in. It is simple and provides a good visual cue to the thrower. Do this each and every time that a ball is thrown.

DRILL II: CROSS DIAMOND THROWS—Place six cones along each baseline extending into the outfield. The players begin with the shortest throw across the diamond, basically across home plate. They will work their way up to the fourth throw which sails fully across the diamond from first to third. The last two throws will be the most difficult as they will cross the deeper part of the infield, but never deeper than across second base.

How many throws you ask of each set of players at each cone is up to you. This is an excellent drill for young players and is, in effect, a form of controlled "long toss." As they progress to the longer throws, you may wish to teach them the "crow hop."

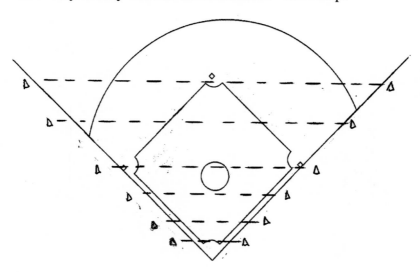

THROWING FORM & FUNDAMENTALS FOR BEGINNERS

Few introductory skills in softball are more critical than throwing mechanics. Flaws in a batting swing or improper mechanics in bunting and fielding can be adjusted later in a younger player's career, but if their throwing motion is corrupted, it stays with them for life. Here are three drills that can help in teaching proper throwing mechanics and maximizing reps needed to master the skill.

LINE THROWING DRILL # 1: Set up as many buckets of balls as you have along the foul line. Players will line up behind each bucket. Ideally, there is a bucket for each player. They can throw any type of ball—hard, softy, wiffle, tennis, etc. After teaching proper mechanics, have each player step up to the bucket, pick out a ball and throw it to a target perhaps 15-feet away. Continue until they have emptied the bucket. One school of thought is that you use parents and sibling receivers in this mass throwing drill. Another technique is to set up cones and ask the players to knock over the cone.

LINE THROWING DRILL # 2: Line the players up against a fence, a wall or the backstop and one-by-one, they approach the coach who is coordinating each line. Each player comes up with a ball in their hand and upon the coach's command throws at a target on the wall or fence. Use athletic tape, coat hangers, or even hula hoops.

LINE THROWING DRILL # 3: "The Throwing March" after having taught the mechanics of throwing, line the players up along a foul line and have them simulate a catch, step, throw and follow through. No ball is actually thrown. They will begin a march, in line, across the field using proper mechanics.

The key in each of these drills is to maximize repetitions, but with an insistence on proper mechanics. The coaches must be super-critical and pick out even tiny flaws after each throw. Teach-throw & correct...throw & correct...throw & correct.

SOFTBALL PITCHERS: FORM "3-PHASE ROUTINE"   "1"

Here is an introductory training program for softball pitchers; it emphasizes form and proper technique. It can be done on a gym floor, a formal pitching circle or even a stride rug.

PHASE ONE: "STEP & POINT: It is an axiom that when the stride foot lands, the pitching arm should be at the top of its arc. In addition some coaches feel that the arm should begin its rotation so that the ball will, at this point, be facing outward and away from the body. Drill this by simply having the pitcher curl or rock to begin their motion and then explode out with a long stride in line with the plate. As they do this, the pitching arm is raised to a point directly overhead. The palm rotates the ball so that it is facing outward and away from the body. No further motion takes place, nor is there any release of the ball. Insist on explosiveness.

Since every pitcher, has a different motion—slightly or radically—it is difficult to suggest one teaching template. Avoid "cloning" your pitchers. Therefore, these drills are drawn from several different sources and hence, different philosophies. Use what works for you and fits your teaching package.

Another disclaimer: this section is not intended as a primer on the "how-to's" of softball pitching. I merely offer a variety of pitching drills.

PHASE TWO: "DRIVE HOME"—Have the pitcher drive from her pre-set position into a classic "K Position"…and then freeze. Check her form. Next she explodes from the K to the plate. This can help arm strength as well as quickness and form. Insist on "pop;" insist on the release hand curling to the throwing side shoulder, snapping the wrist. Softball pitchers, by rule, must drag the back toe.

COACHES NOTE: For former baseball coaches like myself, there is a confusing differential in nomenclature from softball pitching to baseball pitching. When baseball coaches refer to keeping the "hips closed," they mean in line to the plate; in softball this is referred to as "open"! Similarly, softball pitching coaches want their girls to keep their hips "open," meaning along the power line to the plate. If a softball pitcher closes her hips it means that she is facing the plate. Note that the hips never fully close to face the plate. The hips remain at a 45-degree angle to the power line.

A good verbal cue came from Cheri Kempf—Start "Fat"...turn into "Skinny"...and return to "Fat." Fat would mean facing the catcher in a closed position. Skinny refers to the rotations of the hips into an open position and in line with the plate. Return to balance, facing the catcher...or "fat." Make doubly sure that your girls know that you mean when you use this nomenclature or you will have tears.

PHASE THREE: WALL DRILL: Have the softball pitcher stand with their throwing shoulder close to a wall or fence. They will step (stride) and rotate the throwing arm in its counter-clockwise arc and execute proper follow-through. No ball is thrown; however, this form drill keeps the arm from rotating off line.

This also serves as a good remedial drill for the softball player, pitcher or position player who cannot break the habit of throwing sidearm.

LISA FERNANDEZ'S THOUGHTS ON PITCHING FORM AND A TEACHING PROGRESSION

Coach Ralph Weekly from Tennessee called her the greatest female softball player this country has produced. Not only was she an Olympic pitcher, but she was also a world-class hitter. Lisa Fernandez was the total package.

FOOTWORK: SET-UP: Ms. Fernandez shared her thoughts on pitching form. She liked to begin, as NCAA rules stipulate, with both feet on the rubber and finish with a "Figure 4" or "Bowler's Release."

   NOTE: Glove-side foot back
Glove-side foot strides

Some girls prefer to set the stride foot back behind the rubber and up on the toe as shown above, but there are some conference rules that stipulate both feet begin on the rubber. There is something to be said for the increased "rock back and drive" that this staggered stance offers. In either case the weight should begin on the front foot.

RELEASE: Some coaches prefer a rear foot toe drag while others prefer a "bowler's" follow-through after release of the ball (rules stipulate that the toe must be in contact with the ground on release).

Ms. Fernandez preferred a "sprinter's stance" with hand and glove on to her side.

Caution: do not allow the head to get out over the front knee.

THE FERNANDEZ TEACHING PROGRESSION:

1. SIDEWAYS TOSSES—stand sideways with the feet and the hips in line with the plate—easy flips and high follow-throughs; no other body movement. There is minimal arm arc in this.
2. Add a full arm circle, but no other hip or feet movement.
3. Add a Figure 4 Bowler's follow-through with the back leg after the release. This helps with balance.

4. Use the karate kid stance-swing-leap/stride drill described elsewhere. Fernandez advocates initially looking downward to the spot where her stride foot will land; she also tries to stride all the way to the edge of the 8-foot circle.
5. Put it all together, aiming for spots and quadrants. "Stay Tall" on the release, the head is back and up. The stride foot should land on the inside "ball" of the foot.

SOFTBALL PITCHERS WRIST FLICK DRILL:

It is fundamental that the softball pitcher "flicks her wrist" upward on the release of the ball. Some coaches refer to the technique as tapping the shoulder with the fingers. Have the pitchers stand about five or six feet away from a fence and with no body motion or arm arc, have them simply "flick" the ball into the fence, isolating the wrist action.

I just admit that I am hesitant to teach this technique with beginning softball pitchers. I would prefer to teach them about the stride, body rock, staying on the power line and the arm arc first. The wrist flick can be a variable that causes erratic release points and thus, erratic control. As a coach, you can add this element once they have mastered the mechanics of the delivery. Some readers will disagree.

It is important that the young pitcher understands the mechanics of the arm arc and motion. As the pitching hand approaches the hip, the upper arm de-celerates and the lower arm accelerates. Thus, in using this drill, have the pitcher focus on clamping the upper arm to her side and snapping the lower arm and hand forward and upward. They can pop the ball into their glove, too, rather than into the fence as shown.

SOFTBALL PITCHING DRILLS   **"I"**

Frankly, coming from a baseball background, when I first sat in on softball pitching lectures at the "Be The Best You Are Coaches Clinic" in New Jersey, I was about as lost as a coach could be. It is so very different from anything that I knew and taught in baseball. However, with reading, video study and talking to softball pitchers and pitching coaches, I developed an understanding and more importantly, I am growing each year.

Several of the drills listed below come from Coaching Fastpitch Softball Successfully by Kathy Veroni and Roanna Brazier. Their book is one of the best in the field.

A) KNEE-DOWN DRILLS: Here are two variations of a standard drill. In the one pictured below, the player releases the ball from the position shown. Into a fence or to a partner works, either way. This drill is especially good for working on grips and spin release. The variation of this drill is as follows: place a ball on the ground at the "6 o'clock" position. The pitcher rotates the arm through a soft yet sound arm arc and slaps the ball with a cupping action into a net or across to a partner. This drill is best done on grass or on a gym floor as fingers and nails can scrap on dirt or macadam. The function of this drill is to keep the shoulders and hips aligned, to the target.

Good drill for working on grips and spin release

B) SIX CIRCLES—Have the pitcher stand in the "K Position" and rotate the throwing arm as if she is pitching. She is not to release the ball, however, until she has rotated the arm six times. The "feel" should be the same for each arm rotation and on release. Pitchers can do this by having a catch with others. A variation of this drill is to have the player set her feet, rotate the arm twice and then stride and release.

C) PITCHING FROM THE KNEES—Kneeling on both knee with the hips aligned sideways to the plate, pitchers can work on feeling the release and spin on the ball, practicing their various pitches and/or learning new ones as they isolate on hand release and spin. The aforementioned "Knee Down Drill" is excellent for working on grips and spin as they relate to different pitches.

A VARIATION: This simple drill is intended to develop the notion of rolling the ball on the release rather than bouncing it. Two players will have a "catch" in this way, working on their release. If the ball bounces it means that the ball has not been released at the hip.

D) EXPLOSION FROM THE "COIL"—Have your pitcher toe the rubber, drop down into a "coiled position" with the knees bent and the chest down and hunched out over the pitcher's plate. Some coaches have made the analogy of the pitcher in a "sprinter's stance." On command, she is to explode into the stride-out "K Position" with her hips in line with the plate (i.e. "open"). A rocking action is acceptable to initiate the explosion, but frankly, this position is the one that the pitcher arrives at when she has already tucked into following her rocker action. Thus, the drill accentuates and isolates the leg drive. Some coaches prefer to have the pitcher dangle her arms at her side; others prefer to have the pitcher grip the ball in the glove.

E) PITCHING: PITCHER'S SPEED CIRCLES: This can be a warm-up as well as a fast-twitch muscle fibre drill. It is simple: the pitcher rotates her throwing arm in windmill fashion as quickly as she can for a set of the repetitions. Do this in three or four re-sets.

F) CHAIR DRILL—Place a chair in a "tipped over" position. The legs of the chair face skyward as shown. The object here is to have the pitcher drop the ball into the back end of the chair. There are two ways to look at this: she can be merely working on throwing accuracy or she can be working on throwing the drop ball.

G) TARGET WORK—I heard renowned pitching coach Cheri Kempf talk at a coaches clinic and she uses targets such as these for pitchers to aim at within the strike zone. Moreover, in her teaching sessions, she charts her pitchers to establish an efficiency percentage. Target A is a simple pattern designed to teach pitchers to hit corners of strike zone. While target B accomplishes the same thing, it also presents another opportunity: called pitches. A coach in a game can literally signal to the catcher what zone he or she wants the ball thrown into.

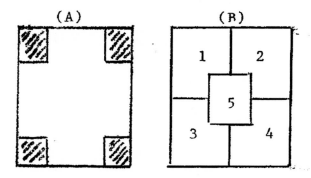

Targets such as these are available for purchase, but in my frugal mind, I am thinking of how to make one. A painted tarpaulin or a bed sheet with holes on which to hang the printed target would work. Baseball pitchers can obviously benefit from such a device, too. I made one from an old towel with clips sewn on the corners and boxes spray painted as quadrants. I would clip it on to a chain-link fence.

H) THE WRIST ROLLER—A weight training device that can help strengthen forearms and, to a degree wrists, this is another home-made device. The length of the rope should run about 4' and the weight on the bottom should be 2 ½ to 5 pounds, no more. With the handle grasped at arm length, five reps should suffice. Their shoulders will "feel the burn." Be sure to insist that they lower the weight with the same deliberate speed they used in raising it—slowly.

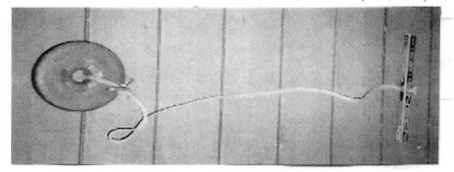

I) THE STRING LINE—Elsewhere, I have suggested tying a string across the bottom of an imaginary strike zone in the bullpen. Baseball pitchers enjoy the challenge of trying to hit the string with their fastball. Use this for softball pitchers as well, but have them "drop" the ball over the string, simulating an effective drop ball.

Why not tie a line across the top of the strike zone and have your softball pitches try to hit it with their "rise ball?"

J) ONE-LEGGED PITCHING—Upper body angle affects release point and the type of pitch one might be attempting to throw. In softball, for example, the drop ball is thrown out in front of the body while the rise ball is released from behind the midline. Pitchers, whether they have these pitches or not, should learn body control and throwing off the back foot and then off the front foot can provide an equally effective drill.

K) THE SPINNER—Cheri Kempf seems to have been the progenitor of this ingenious little teaching device for softball pitchers. It is a round plastic disc the size of a softball's diameter. It is about 1" to 1 ½ "in thickness. The pitcher grips it with two fingers across the top, or even across the abbreviated "seams" that are merely raised protuberances across the rim of the spinner. The pitcher now flings this disk using full or abbreviated motion, but with proper wrist action to achieve curving, rising, and even dropping action.

(What is shown above is actually the core of an old softball. I then trimmed the sides off of it with a table saw.) One can use an ice hockey puck, too.

L) BALL ON A CORD—Perform arm circles with a ball inside a long sock or use a ball with a hole drilled through it and a cord attached. The key is to keep the ball's rotation on a vertical axis. One can use a balled up sock stuffed on a long soccer or sanitary sock.

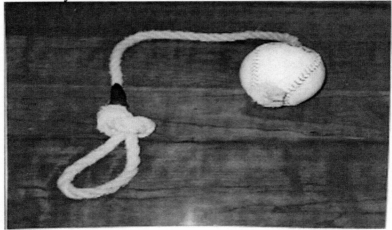

M) STRIDE CHECK—In softball, the pitcher must maintain contact with the rubber and a higher stride can facilitate this (avoid "crow-hopping," or leaping toward the plate). Have a coach kneel down in front of the pitcher, but off to the stride leg side. When the pitcher strides, they should kick the coach's hand which is set about thigh-high.

N) TOE PUSHES: Is the back foot really a "pivot foot?" Does it truly pivot on the rubber? You will see many pitchers do this so that the back foot almost seems flat to the ground, instep down. The back heel has rolled over. Some coaches even teach this. For those who teach the notion that the back toe pushes off the rubber and the heel is kept elevated to the sky, try these two drills.

   a) The FOOTBOX: Reportedly designed by LSU Coach Beth McClendon, the back foot is encased in a box perhaps 6" wide and 12-18" long. U-shaped, it is open at the front. The pitcher must push off her back toe rather than turn her heel.

b) The "FOOT BALL:" Have the pitcher stand with her rear foot on a relatively soft, flexible ball of some sort. As she pushes off, she should literally squash the ball. Remember, use a soft ball that crushes rather than something hard which can cause her to lose her balance.

c) PITCHING: FORM & RHYTHM WALK-THROUGHS: Begin with both feet behind the rubber. The glove side foot is back and takes the first stride. The ball-side foot strides next and on to the rubber. The glove side foot stride sequentially and the pitcher pitches the ball. Stride through and beyond the rubber in proper sequence as you pitch the ball. Flow and rhythm are to be emphasized.

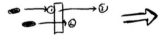

SOFTBALL PITCHING DRILLS FROM CHERI KEMPF

I heard Coach Cheri Kempf speak at a coaches clinic and read her book, <u>The Softball Pitching Edge.</u> Her book is perhaps the finest on the subject. I have infused some of her drills throughout this section on pitching, but allow me to highlight some directly from her book.

A) TEACHING THE TOE-DRAG FOLLOW-THROUGH— Coach Kempf emphasizes the rear leg toe push and to prevent a pitcher from turning her ankle over so that her push-off resembles a baseball pitcher, she places a small scrap of paper or cloth in front of the toe (on the rubber, of course). As the pitcher throws, her toe should pull the scrap of paper forward. I prefer a small strip of cloth as it will lie flat in a breeze.

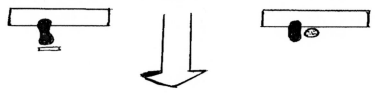

HOME PLATE

To prevent the back heel from rolling over, she places a ball beside the heel and as it drives properly forward with no "tilt," the ball does not move.

Note the use of key terms such as STRIDE LEG & DRIVE LEG. These two drills work on the drive leg (AKA the pivot foot).

B) TEACHING THE ARM CIRCLE—Coach Kempf offers an innovative drill using a swimming "noodle." Hang the pitching arm straight down, gripping the noodle so that it barely touches the ground. Now circle the arm, keeping it on the vertical line, brushing the torso with the elbow and whispering past the thigh. The tip of the noodle should not brush the ground significantly.

The ball on a rope could also be used in place of the noodle.

Note the noodle could also be used to gauge the height of the stride leg kick as has been suggested in an earlier drill using the coach's glove to tap the pitcher's thigh.

C) STRIDE LEG DISTANCES—Every pitcher's stride length, is different. There is no universal rule on this. For pitchers who may wish to lengthen their stride, a unique drill is to have the pitcher stride out, mark that spot and then string a rope four or five inches further out. Ask the pitcher to stride to the rope. You may need another "holder" for this drill, so ask an assistant coach, an on-looking parent or even jam two tent pegs into the ground to string the rope in a position parallel to the pitching rubber's edge, but perpendicular the Power Line.

SOFTBALL PITCHING: BALANCE, LEG DRIVE & STRIDE DRILLS   "I"

These drills isolate segments of the pitching motion as it pertains to the legs, hips and lower body. They enhance form, strength and balance.

DRILL #1: KARATE KID POSITION: The pitcher stands on one leg atop the rubber. Her front leg is positioned in front and elevated to a right angle toward home, just as if her front foot was resting on a chair. No throw is made, but the pitcher, from this balanced position, engages in a rocking motion, drives off the back foot and strides on to the power line.

DRILL #2: POWER LEAPS: No ball or glove is needed. The pitcher gathers with both feet on the rubber and power leaps, as in a plyometric leap, toward home. Two or three sets of five repetitions will help strengthen the lower body. A full rest of one-to-two minutes is necessary after each set. Muscle strains and groin pulls are slow to heal.

DRILL #3: ONE LEGGED POWER LEAPS: Similar to the above, the pitcher drives off the rubber with only her push-off foot. As a progression from this basic drill, add a glove and a ball and have the pitcher throw off this one-legged drive position.

PITCHING: STRIDE "THE STRIDE RUG"   "*I*"

Buy a six foot section of artificial turf. Hardware stores often sell it in three-foot wide sections. Next, paint a regulation sized pitching rubber on it near one end. From the middle of the rubber, paint a line perpendicular to the rubber and directly in line to the plate. Pitchers can be taught to adjust their stride a mere one inch to the left or right of said line to help them hit the inside or outside corners of the plate. Factor in basic geometry: one inch in the stride means six inches at the plate. As one adjusts the stride foot a mere one inch to the left or right, this will cause the ball to ride in or out to a distance of up to six inches. As Cheri Kempf has demonstrated, softball pitchers must be taught to land their stride foot slightly to the left or right of the Power line to enhance their rise ball, curve and screwball.

Shown here is a simplified, and actually more common, form of the Stride Rug.

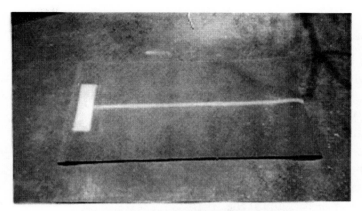

"I"

PITCHING DRILL: "ALLY'S DRILL"

As I sat in my easy chair one evening, quietly reading, I heard a rhythmic thumping from my granddaughter's room upstairs. She loves softball and had been taking pitching lessons with a private instructor. I called up to her, inquiring as to what was going on. She told me that she was practicing her pitching...red flag! A ball was being thrown in the house?

What she was doing was working on her pitching form. She stood several feet away from a large mirror and preceded to windmill a soft rubber ball with suction dimples (see photo) into the mirror. It would stick on to the glass and perhaps without realizing it she had invented a drill. If the ball stuck to the mirror in the correct spot, she could tell if she was throwing strikes.

I attended a coach's clinic about a week later and one of the speakers referred to this very drill, but for baseball pitchers and with balled-up socks.

Obviously, the "ball" (the toy that Ally used) or the socks did not need to be thrown hard; the focus is on form.

There probably is a name for the type of "ball" that my granddaughter was using, but I do not know of it. I have included a photo below.

SOFTBALL PITCHING: THROWING STRIKES—"BUCKET BALLS"   "T"

Organizing a practice is often the most challenging aspect of coaching, and frankly, some coaches never do "get it." For this drill, buy a set of soft plastic laundry buckets, as many as the number of pitchers that you have. Lean them against a fence with the bottoms facing the pitcher. Set your pitchers at a regulation distance away from the buckets and have them work on putting a pile of softballs into the bucket. Emphasize form and the avoidance of excessively arcing the ball into the bucket.

In this way, you free up your catchers and other position players for their specialized drills.

Hint: You can also use hitting nets (aka "sock nets"), taped "X's" on the wall or the fence and even painted tarpaulins hung on the fence for this mass pitching drill. Another hint: what about setting all of these up, along with stride rugs and even a live catcher in rotational stations? Each new station helps the pitcher re-focus and, given modern attention spans, that in itself can be beneficial.

Another idea: use "Incrediballs." Pitch them into targets along a wall. The bounce-back effect will increase the repetitions for each pitcher.

PITCHING: SPEED PROGRESSION

Renowned pitching coach Cheri Kempf has suggested this speed drill to train fast-twitch muscle fibers used in pitching. No wind-up is taken—just stride and throw. Use two softballs to quicken the pace. The pitcher throws and immediately upon receiving the second ball from her catcher, she throws again. The goal should be ten quick pitches in 30 seconds. The drill can be performed in sets.

PITCHING: USE OF THE BALANCE BEAM

Nothing emphasizes staying on the power line better than this drill. Buy a 2 x 12 piece of lumber perhaps six to eight feet long, depending on the age and size of the pitchers you work with. Cover it with some Astroturf carpeting that can be purchased in most hardware stores.

This provides traction as a bare board can be slippery, especially when wearing rubber cleats.

Nail a slab of wood that would replicate the pitching rubber on to the end.

Now, pitch. Watch for balance, stride length and staying on the power line.

Why not paint hash marks on it? You can challenge your pitcher to lengthen her stride by "reaching out" for a more distant mark.

PITCHING: USE OF THE SURGICAL CORD

Surgical cords for baseball pitchers are common, but we can use them to train softball pitchers as well. One technique is to wrap the cord around the pitcher's waist and have her work on "explosion from the coil," described earlier. Full body harnesses, the kind track coaches traditionally use to train sprinters, can be used in this way, too. Coaches may find these devices costly, so why not use rubber bicycle inner tubes strung around the waist? I have used these effectively to train hockey players in power skating. They are free, discarded from a bicycle shop.

I have seen softball pitchers pitch against the resistance of a weight sled, too.

Yet another technique, although caution is advised, is to wrap the cord around the drive leg to enhance push-off. Cheri Kempf also advocates using the cord with a pulling action while facing the pitchers to "assist" in driving the push-off foot forcefully.

SOFTBALL PITCHING: WALL DRILLS

The best practice area for this series is a tennis wall, those ubiquitous monoliths of smooth cement that rise near any tennis court complex. Pitchers can learn release points and accuracy against these walls. "Incrediballs" are effective here as well since pitchers can work the different grips as they pitch to different targets on the walls.

LOW RELEASE: For pitchers who "bowl for dollars" and release the ball behind their hip, have them go through the pitching motion and aim to bounce the softball high up on the wall. If properly done they will get a flyball that descends back into their glove.

HIGH RELEASE: For the pitcher who cannot get the ball "down" in the zone, have her skip the ball to a low point on the wall. The ball should be one-hopped. She has been holding the ball too long, releasing out in front of her hip and needs to get rid of it earlier.

TARGET POINTS: Because these walls are generally smooth concrete, athletic tape can be used to apply "X" targets, perhaps but not necessarily, in a strike zone. You can employ a mass pitching drill, perhaps three or four pitchers across as they aim for a series of "Xs". They can aim for the painted "net line," too.

Do not forget to use the lines that are often painted on to the pavement in front of these walls. They can be used as "power lines."

PITCHING: TOWEL DRILL

Have the pitcher execute her full throwing motion but with a towel in her hand rather than a ball. A coach stands opposite with a glove. They should be in line with the plate. The pitcher, emphasizing good form and arm rotation slaps the coach's glove with the towel. Look for the stride foot landing on the power line and the arm rotation on a good vertical axis.

While primarily a form drill there is definitely an element of arm strengthening as well.

PITCHING: "FOOTBALL THROWING"   *"I"*

Baseball pitchers often throw a football to develop arm strength. Softball pitchers can benefit from this, too, but there is a different emphasis. Have your pitchers throw a soft "Nerf" football. They are to go through their regular pitching motion, but they will notice that as they release the ball, there is a twist of the wrist that they will find advantageous when they learn to put different spins on the ball as they seek to achieve different pitches. They must try to get a good spiral in this drill. Pitchers can literally have a catch; no formal catcher is needed.

In the absence of a "Nerf" football, small, miniaturized rubber footballs can be used as well.

PITCHING AND THROWING: WEIGHTED BALLS   *"I"*

The use of weighted baseballs is a controversial topic. Some coaches reel back in horror at the very thought of using them. I, on the other hand, am an advocate. The key is that pitchers, even position players, using them must be under the watchful eye of a coach. Here are some fundamental considerations:

a) DISTANCE: Players using weighted balls should be no longer than 20 feet apart.

b) "GET AIR UNDER THE THROW": Especially with the heavier balls (10-11-12 ounces), throwers must execute their throws with exaggerated body action and arc the ball to the receiver.

c) 20 to 30 THROWS: Use the weighted balls in sequence (7-8-9-10-11-12 ounces) for 4 throws each. If you have a second pair of players throwing, then you can go "Odds-n-Evens" with one pair using the odd-numbered balls (7-9-11 ounces) and the other pair using the even numbered balls (8-10-12 ounces). These players will throw each ball perhaps seven or eight times.

I have used weighted balls for years and, knock wood, I have never had an arm injury due to their use. I have used them for baseball and softball position players who wish to improve arm strength. One can use weighted softballs, thrown underhand of course, for softball players.

In any case, insist on controlled usage—no long throws, snap throws or excessively suppurated throws. Furthermore, always begin and end a weighted ball routine by throwing a regulation ball.

Food for thought: did you ever notice how many excellent softball pitchers bowl in the off season. There's the ultimate weighted ball and the motion is similar...

PITCHING: USE OF THE RADAR GUN—CHANGING SPEEDS   *"I"*

The radar gun is a toy, but one that can be used beneficially in training your pitchers. Every pitcher needs to have two types of fastballs in her arsenal: an overpowering fastball and a "BP," or batting practice fastball.

The overpowering fastball (FB) is just as the title implies—one that can be "blown" by the hitter. Studies have shown that perceptually, a

FB thrown inside can look as much as five miles per hour faster than one thrown outside, even if clocked at the same speed.

Achieving this is easier said than done, but as a pitcher matures, it can only be hoped that their FB improves with proper training and physical growth. For the present, allow us to refer to this FB as simply the best and hardest FB he throws.

Next, take something off it, maybe just five mph. Throw this pitch with good location and control. It is the "BP Fastball" and by throwing it effectively, it can keep even the best hitters off stride. Their timing is disrupted. This can be effective for pitchers on any level of softball.

Use a radar gun to check the speed. Tell the pitcher to "gas it" and then throw "the BP." Look for a speed differential of, as suggested earlier, perhaps five mph.

The beauty of this is not only in its simplicity, but also that if a pitcher does not have her "best stuff" as she begins a game, she can still be effective by changing speed and throwing to good locations. Maybe as the game proceeds, she can recover her curve, drop, rise ball, or what ever she has.

Many softball pitching coaches emphasize speed, speed, speed under the premise that accuracy will came later. This is in diametric opposition to many baseball pitching coaches, so you need to assess, evaluate and develop your own philosophy.

PITCHING: LEARNING NEW PITCHES "PAINTED BALLS"

An innovative way to teach proper grips and spin on various pitches is to employ softballs that have been specifically painted for this purpose. I have seen three different types: painted laces, painted centerline or painted panels.

It is up to the coach as to which type of painted ball they feel produces the best result in their teaching process. With each, however, it is easy to see if the requisite spin on the ball is happening. This technique can be utilized to check not only the breaking ball, but also the fastball.

SOFTBALL: LEARNING PITCHES
I heard Coach Jay Miller from Mississippi State make the statement that grip is not important in softball pitching, getting a finger on a seam and releasing it with the twist of the palm is.

a) 4-seam b) Horseshoe

The three key pitches for a softball pitcher are the drop, the rise and the change-up. The curve and screwball are relatively easy to learn but tend to be hittable on the higher skill levels.

A) **RISEBALL**—You want backspin on this pitch, so get a seam, keep the elbow tight to the hip at release and spin it with the palm opening up to the outside away from the body. It is difficult to learn but one technique is simply to have a pitcher kneel on the ground, spin the ball like a top, palm opening outwards. Next stand up and throw with an abbreviated arm arc, perhaps beginning from a "9 o'clock position." Verbal cues to say might be "spin the dial" or "door knob" the release.

B) **THE DROP**—There are two types of drop balls—the "Peel Drop" and the "Rollover Drop."

   THE "PEEL DROP"—Get a seam. Keep three fingers together, middle finger in line with the thumb on the bottom. It has been suggested that all four fingers could be used. Release with the ball rolling off the fingertips toward the plate. Mentally picture peeling an onion. The horseshoe grip is good in learning this pitch.

   THE ROLL-OVER DROP—begins with the 4-seam grip shown above. As you release the ball, pronate the thumb in and downward; keep the elbow tight to the torso, as always. The palm will face downward on release.

C) **THE CHANGE-UP**—Set the ball deeper in the palm and use 4-seam grip—across a long seam with four seams rotating toward the plate. One can use all five fingers across the seam for what is called a "Back-flip Change." There are so many variations: use a side release with the hand slipping to the outside around the ball; use a circle-change grip with the index and thumb pinching the inside of the ball and try both of the aforementioned releases. A couple of key points to remember are these:

   1. reduce the arm whip by extending toward the plate;
   2. keep this pitch low in the zone and preferably away;

3. the palm is the last part of the hand to leave the ball, rather than the fingers as in the other pitches.

D) **THE CURVEBALL**—In this pitch, after you "get a seam" with the middle finger, at release, slide the palm to the outside of the ball pulling the hand across the body. To learn this pitch:
1. Have players sit down and practice spinning the ball to each other, using the release just described;
2. Toss a Frisbee with an underhand; and "over the top" released;
3. Toss softy balls or even nerf balls to create spin;

Items #1 and #2 can be done standing up; the key is to feel the release. Be sure to have at least one finger under the ball. Some coaches say to finish with a "round-off" over the top.

E) **THE SCREWBALL**—Get a seam with the middle finger. Release this pitch with the palm sliding to the inside of the ball, palm out. One of the ways to teach this is to place a batting tee in front of the release point. The pitchers must then "throw around the tee," opening the ball in the process. Some coaches have their pitchers open the stride foot slightly. Other coaches warn of exaggerating the hooking motion of the arm suggesting that it may lead to elbow injuries. As with anything, moderation is the key.

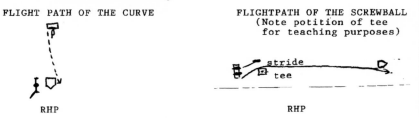

FLIGHT PATH OF THE CURVE

RHP

FLIGHTPATH OF THE SCREWBALL
(Note potition of tee
for teaching purposes)

stride
tee

RHP

DROP BALL—"Peel" off the forefingers and/or place deeper in hand

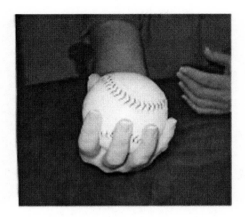

CIRCLE CHANGE UP

KNUCKLEBALL—This photo does not do justice to the proper grip—the pitcher cannot allow any finger prints to make contact with the ball.

REMEMBER: Unlike baseball, the grip is less important than the turn of the wrist.

RISEBALL GRIPS—as advocated by Coach Mike White, University of Oregon

Cheri Kempf's Rise Ball Grip:

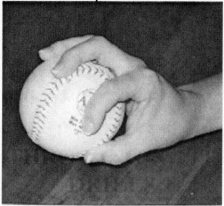

OTHER EXPERIMENTAL GRIPS:

CIRCLE THE HORSESHORE:

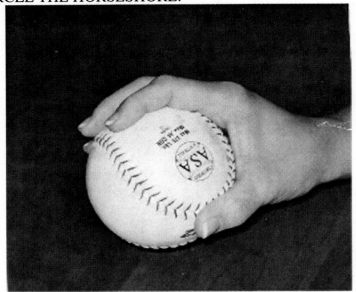

TWO-SEAM WITH THE NARROWS:

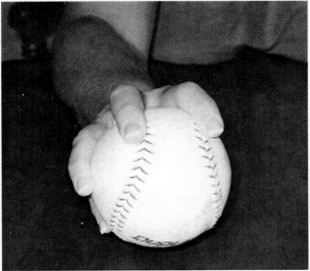

PITICHING: THE "FOUNDATION PITCHES"

The three "foundation pitches," in the words of Arizona coach Mike Candrea, are the drop, the rise and the change-up. Grips vary, but for teaching purposes, have your girls begin with the four-seam grip illustrated elsewhere. The key is the release and wrist action.

Examine the wrist action on release of the ball—

TURN-OVER DROP:	PEEL DROP:
as if turning a door knob	roll off the fingers

 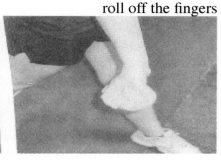

CHANGE-UP:	RISE BALL (forefinger pressure on a long seam helps; get **under the ball** as if turning a door knob)

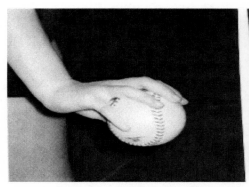 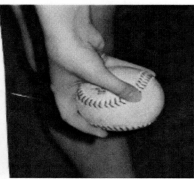

PITCHING: THE DROPBALL "CONE DROPS"   "I"

Place a series of four traffic cones between the pitcher's rubber and home plate. Have your pitchers work on the drop ball by dropping the ball over each cone, increasing their distance and release each time. This is especially effective in learning the "Peel Drop" as the pitchers can feel the ball roll off their fingertips. Coaching point—they may find it helpful to place a bit more weight on the front foot.

PITCHING: ROUND-OFF HANG TOSS   "I"

Much of pitching is "feel." Getting the feel of the release of the curve and/or the turn-over drop-ball can be learned in this simple two-person "catch." The pitchers bend over, standing perhaps five to ten feet apart. Their pitching arm hangs down, dangling loosely. Have them roll their arm in a clockwise direction and release the ball to their partner by spinning or "rolling" the palm over the top of the ball. They will realize that by standing upright and actually pitching, the feel of the release is the same.

USC BULLPEN GAMES:

Coach Beverly Smith of the University of South Carolina recently presented these drills at a coach's clinic:

A) **LADDERS:** Work within a countdown mode: 1-10 or 10-1. Be creative.

Here are two examples:

10 fastballs	1 first-strike pitch
9 drops	2 inside FBs
8 curveballs	3 outside FBs
7 riseballs	4 0-2 pitches
6 pitches called by the catcher	5 breaking balls
5 screwballs	6 low and away
4 changeups	7 wherever the catcher sets up
3 0-2 pitches	8 whatever the catcher calls, but no FBs
2 pitchouts	9 riseballs up and out/up and in
3-2 pitch	10 drop balls

B) **TARGETS:** Place some water bottles atop two batting tees, one on either corner of the plate. Challenge your pitcher to knock them off the tee.

C) **MULTIPLE PITCHERS WORKIN' THE COUNT**

Let's say you have three pitchers, all of whom happen to be in the Pen today. A fun and challenging game can evolve like this:

Pitcher A throws a strike…count 0-1.

Pitcher B throws a ball…count 1-1.

Pitcher C throws another ball…count 2-1.

Pitcher A throws a strike…count 2-2.

Pitcher B throws a strike…at-bat over.

Begin again.

D) **HUSTLE DRILL:** The pitcher throws to her catcher, but the latter does not return the ball. The pitcher must race to the plate retrieve the ball as they round the catcher and then recover to throw another pitch. As Coach Smith pointed out, the catchers love this drill; the pitchers hate it. This can be used as a disciplinary drill, a conditioning drill or a drill to force pitchers to re-focus on each pitch. Challenge them. The drill stops when the pitcher throws ten consecutive strikes or something like that.

E) **SIMULATED GAMES:** The pitcher must throw 63 strikes in her bullpen work (seven innings times nine strikes per inning) or 54 if you play six-inning games.

ARM STRENGTHINING & GENERAL THROWING: ARM STRENGTH THROUGH "LONG TOSS"

All baseball and softball players can benefit from a long toss program. I have implemented long toss programs for athletes in all levels of play from youth league softball to college players. I have seen results on all levels, but problematically, I have seen coaches who employ long toss without fully understanding how to coach it most effectively.

Long toss programs vary according to a coach's philosophy, so needless to say, there is a great variety in these types of programs.

Over the years I have read of many, heard of many and seen many such programs. Here are some considerations that you, as a coach, should think about in designing a program for your players.

1. Everyone benefits from some type of long toss program. It is not just for pitchers, so incorporate long toss in your team's general warm-up.

2. Distances: I would suggest something along these lines—
    Softball distances
    60' (normal warm-up distance)
    90'
    120'
    150'
    180'

    A convenient way to measure and mark these distances is by referencing the infield baselines. By having players throw in a formation parallel to one infield baseline, they simply double the distance to achieve throws of 180-feet.

    Another method of measurement can be to paint a small discreet mark, a dot or line on the base of the outfield fence or on the yellow "fence-cap" that adorns many ball fields with chain-link outfield fences.

    Yet another way to mark long toss distances is to have your players work through their program on a football field. Even if unlined because football is out of season, you can still discern a perspective.

3. Number of Throws: Suppose that you have warmed your team up with throws from a conventional distance of 60 feet. The players will tell you when they are ready to expand the distance. You cannot dictate the number of 60 foot throws, but once they expand the field, then an acceptable number for each subsequent distance generally falls into the range of five to ten throws each.

Some coaches call for a "warm-down" approach where the players throw, say, five long tosses fading away from each other at the prescribed distances, and then repeat the same number of throws as they walk back toward each other, but always at designated distances. Obviously, this would double the number of throws, so factor that in.

4. Form and Format: Position players should always initiate their long throws with a crow hop. This puts less strain on the arm as the body is brought under control. It is also more game-like, as players should rarely throw "flat-footed."

Another approach, which has merit in my mind, demands that players throwing and catching in a long toss program be able to make each of the throws, at least on one hop. If a player is simply incapable of reaching a partner at 180 feet, keep her at 150 feet until her arm is strengthened through training and it enables her to complete the 180-footer with some degree of consistency. When young players strain to throw distances that they are not capable of, form goes out the window. The head pulls out, they run to throw, and they open up and even fall down. Is this what you want? Good form and proper body mechanics count.

Whatever you decide to do for a long toss program, it is always better to outline a prescribed, controlled program rather than just send the players out to "long toss." Training is best achieved under controlled, prescribed circumstances. Go to the point of even having an assistant coach monitor their throwing in long toss.

PITCHING: ARM STRENGTHENING PITCHER'S LONG TOSS

Notwithstanding overhand long tossing described above, pitchers can apply the concept to their trade as well. Begin at normal distance,

35-feet to 43-feet, depending on the league you play in. Throw strikes. Next, move back to a spot halfway between the circle and second base. Throw strikes. Now move back all the way to second base and continue to throw strikes. If possible, move out on the edge of the dirt or even into the outfield grass. Keep throwing strikes. You may wish to telescope back in to the circle. Maintain good pitching form throughout this drill. Be sure to keep the weight back.

PITCHING: FORM ASSESSMENT USE OF VIDEO CAMERA & STILL PHOTOS   "I"

In this day of modern technology, we need to make as full a utilization of the available technology as we can. Having said that, not everything is practical. Video cameras are fine, but not every coach has access to them or to a monitor or "screening room" to examine them.

Being somewhat "old school," I still use a small hand-held camera to take still-shots of my pitchers. I will take about six-to-ten photos at various points in the set-up, stride, k-position, release and follow through. Not every photo will capture what you hope for, but if you array them in line, as shown below, they can produce the desired results.

At the end of the day, it is a simple and inexpensive way to analyze your pitcher's form. I have included an example:

PITCHING: CONTROL "IN & OUT DRILL" "I"

You have a young pitcher with a live arm. But she's wild. How many times have you seen this? Here is a simple drill to help her learn how to control her pitches.

First of all, insist upon, and teach, proper form. Drill, repetition and "muscle memory" are the keys. The form drills and the towel drill suggested earlier in this volume are means toward that end.

Set up a home plate about 10-15 feet away from the pitching rubber. Get a catcher or become one yourself (I use a chair or a ball bucket these days). With an exaggerated focus on proper form, the pitcher is to go through her mechanics—from "rocker" stride, release and to follow-through and throw a perfect strike into the catcher's glove at what amounts to half-speed.

Ask her to throw ten such strikes and then move the chair back to 30-40 feet. She then throws ten more strikes, all fast balls. No "experimental" pitches.

To conclude the drill sequence, work back in toward home: 10-15, and so forth. Emphasize form and focus throughout.

This drill can be applied to young softball pitchers in particular. Plus, it is an excellent way to learn/work on new pitches. Distances as short as 10 feet are acceptable.

PITCHING: TARGET & PURPOSE "I"

Hall of Famer Tom Seaver once wrote about "pitching in sequences." In the bullpen, and particularly during pregame warm-up, if a pitcher throws, for example, five fast balls, five changeups, five curves, and so on, she can immediately see what is "working" and what is not. Moreover, the catcher and bullpen coach can make adjustments or at least know, going into the game, what the pitcher "has" that particular day.

I apply "sequencing" to both bullpen practice sessions and pregame prep. Many people do, so here's the twist. Apply it even to targeting work. A pitcher entering my bullpen first performs her standardized form work routine. Next is sequencing. I ask the pitchers to throw five pitches in sequences (a) and (b) and one final pitch in (c).

a) 5 "1st—Pitch" strikes (they are to imagine a different hitter with each throw) Get ahead in the count; many hitters take the first pitch.

b) "In & Out" (the catcher sets up on the inside corner of the plate for two pitchers, then the outside for two more location fastballs, followed by a third of choice)

c) "O-2"; Low and in, up and out (preferable), or a breaking ball—each pitch has a purpose;

I do not believe in bouncing one in the dirt or "waste pitches" as all this does is elevate the pitch count and it signals a mental surrender in the pitcher's mind.

We, of course, work on our other pitches, again in sequence, but teaching location and purpose is essential to pitcher focus and true bullpen "work."

I usually close with a 0-2 pitch to create an aggressive mindset as the pitcher strides from the pen to the circle. Other location and targeting sequences include:

d) "Put her in the Book!"—Throw to an imaginary hitter for an entire at-bat. Name her, often their big gun; create a scenario of 2 outs, runner on second, Suzie is their number three and a lefty—get her. This puts the pitcher and the catcher on the same page and creates that aggressive mindset referred to above.

e) Pitchouts (we as coaches do not work on this enough and it must be drilled like any other pitch—have the pitcher use a new target, not the catcher's glove but rather a link or pole on the backstop).

A further word needs to be said about the necessity of emphasizing "First Pitch Strikes." Studies have repeatedly shown that when pitchers "work ahead" they are more effective. Major league pitchers threw the first pitch to hitters as strikes 57% of the time (2007). The batting average for hitters with a 0-1 count was .248 while hitters facing a 1-0 count rose to .340. (0-2 dropped to .206 while 2-0 rose to .388, and so forth).

PITCHING: TARGETING TOOLS   *"I"*

Gimmicks abound. There are painted tarpaulins, cloth strike zones, bungee cord string targets and so on that can all serve to help pitchers with their control. Many of them are simple home-made devices that any handy, creative coach can make in their workshop.

a) Cut out **plywood home plates** and paint, with different colors, the inside 1/3, the outside 1/3 and the "dead red" middle. Have the pitchers work in and out.

b) **Bungee cords** stretched out on a chain link fence can serve as a quick, handy strike zone, easily portable as well.

c) Cut an old **towel** into a rectangle about the size of a strike zone. Sew hooks on to each corner and hang it up on a chain link fence. You may wish to paint four quadrants on it and have pitchers throw to different locations such as down and in, up and out, etc. Colorize each quadrant to enhance mental imaging.

d) Hang a full-sized **tarpaulin** on a chain-link fence. Paint a strike zone on it, or even a batter for the more artistically inclined. This "target tarp" serves the same purpose as that above, but is more durable.

e) Buy a **blow-up clown or doll**, a child's toy. Set this up as a batter with a catcher prepared to handle the pitch. With this drill you are teaching your pitchers to throw inside and they can do so without a fear of hitting a teammate.

f) **Target cups**—stuff a batch of Styrofoam cups into the gaps in a chain link fence. Place them in various spots within a strike zone. Next, have the pitchers knock the cups through the fence. This is a fun drill.

g) Would you like to train your pitchers to throw "in and out" to both edges of the plate? Try using **two catchers,** one on edge of "the black." Issue a command on each pitch, "in" or "out."

h) **Live batters** standing in are obviously effective as they create game-like conditions. Do not allow them to swing, merely "stand in." They may keep a bat on their shoulders or they may wear their glove as a protective shield if the pitcher buzzes one in tight. To add an interesting twist, place two batters "standing in" (most assuredly with their gloves for this drill), one on each side of the plate. The pitcher must focus, throw the ball down the middle and be good at doing it or she will be sure to incur the wrath of her teammates.

i) How many **throwing blind?** I have read of several coaches who experiment, even advocate this technique. (No live batter is standing in for this drill!). After a pitcher has thrown a bit, working on location and such, have her close her eyes and attempt to hit the same spot. At first the pitcher will look at you like you have three heads and the catcher will pop up to make a plea for sanity, but try it. It may be only marginally successful, but it can help sharpen a pitcher's focus. It has been suggested that the pitcher can "feel" her body motion more acutely. One of the advocates of this drill is major league pitching coach Rick Peterson. Michigan State's legendary and equally innovative coach Dan Litwhiler used an eye patch over the "dominant eye" to improve the accuracy of one of his pitchers. Dominant eye can easily be tested. You can do it right now. Hold your thumb out over a distant object; your arm is extended at arm's length. Close one eye. Did the thumb move off of the object? If not, then the open eye is the dominant eye. Test the other eye to be sure. Generally, the dominant eye will be the eye on the same side as the dominant hand, right or left.

j) **H.O.R.S.E.:** The game is simple. It replicates the old schoolyard basketball shooting contest done with two pitchers competing against each other. One pitcher "makes" her pitch by calling location or type. The other girl must match her pitch. If she misses, she gets and "H." If the first girl misses with her called pitch, the other girl gets to initiate the contest. It's fun.

PITCHING: FOCUS & TARGETING "THE LATE TARGET DRILL"   *"I"*

When I teach proper pitching focus, I tell my players to "see the whole catcher" as they begin their motion, but when they arrive at the release point, they must fine-tune their focus to a tight, even tiny, focal point. For instance, see the whole catcher and then zoom in on a lace on the catcher's glove or a logo on the mitt.

To facilitate this I will tell my catchers not to set a target at all until the pitcher comes to her release point. The "late target" helps the pitcher focus as Mel Gibson told his sons in the movie, "The Patriot."—"aim small, miss small,"

This drill is, of course, bull pen work, but I wonder if it could be used in a game...?

PITCHING: CONTROL "THE DOT DRILL"   *"I"*

Here is another way to enhance the fine-tune focus: buy a packet of orange or green stick-on tabs. They are inexpensive and can be picked up at any stationary store. Stick one in the pocket of the catcher's mitt. It is highly visible to the pitcher and hence, effective in tuning her focus. It is easily peeled off after one-time use.

PITCHING: "BP COMBAT" LIVE PITCHING/HITTING*"I"*

Pitchers and hitters need that taste of reality—live game-conditions in one is trying to beat the other. This can be set up in miniature, in the batting cage.

The drill, perhaps "game" is a better word, is simple; place a pitcher in the batting cage along with a catcher and a hitter. The hitter gets a full at-bat while the pitcher/catcher battery uses everything they have to get her out. A coach can call the pitches from outside the cage and, in addition, she will call the "shots"—when the batter makes contact, the coach assesses location and quality of the hit to call out "single up the middle" or "ground-out 6-3." The drill may last for just one pitch; it may be true "battle" with the count running to 3-2 and pitches being fouled off. This is a great preseason drill and there is always a winner and a loser. But isn't that what baseball is all about?

If you have a pitcher coming back off an injury and she has not seen the circle in several weeks, this drill can help sharpen her edge for true game conditions. This drill can be inefficient, however, as there can be a lot of "standing around" if you make it a full-team drill. That said, there can be a lot of cheering and "jeering" if you set it up properly, perhaps moving imaginary base runners along or determining the number of team sprints based on who "wins" each at-bat. Yet another option is to use the entire pitching staff versus a group of hitters, perhaps the outfielders, while the infielders are working drills on the diamond.

What about a "warm-down" or "cool down" after throwing a bullpen session of this intensity? Some coaches advocate perhaps twenty pitches at half or 2/3 speed following their hardest throwing.

PITCHERS: GAME PRESSURE PITCHING "THE PRESSURE COOKER"

One of the most difficult aspects of coaching, in any sport, is to create game-conditions and teach mental toughness within such conditions. The drill suggested here is not for every athlete and it is certainly not for the younger levels of play

Put a defensive team in the field. Put everyone else in the dugout. Run a single pitcher out to the mound for one at-bat. Tell him what the situation is and have her pitch through it. Do not use a batter in the first round, hit fungoes, but definitely send a batter up in the next rounds of this drill. Put base runners in place, too.

You will find that some kids wilt under the pressure; others thrive. You can at least get your pitchers accustomed to it all. Have both "teams" yelling, screaming and chattering. Perhaps make the number of conditioning sprints depend upon the pitcher's effectiveness in the initial round.

    a)   Set up situations like this:
    b)   Runner on third, 0-out
    c)   Runner on second, lefty hitter, 0-2 out

d) Bases loaded, 0-out, 3-0 count

Be creative. Sometimes you will call for a single pitch to be thrown. See what the pitcher throws and where. Hint: if you have a kid with a fragile ego on the mound, expand the strike-zone a bit for her. You, as the coach, are calling the balls and strikes, so you do have a modicum of control.

Believe it or not, the first round goes fairly quickly. Since most high school teams have only two or three pitchers on their staff, there is not a lot of standing around. In the second round, the pitcher may throw a hittable pitch, but the defense is there to help her out.

There is a lot of high-fiving and glove-slapping if you set this drill up properly. Everyone cheers when the pitcher breaks off a nasty 0-2 curve to "get" the imaginary hitter in the opening round; watch her fanny-slap the left fielder when she throws a runner out at the plate, knowing that she "laid one in there" and grimaced.

This drill is actually a twist on the old "situational batting" drill described elsewhere, but the focus is entirely different. All eyes are on the pitcher.

This is a good preseason drill as you prepare for the opener and you need to not only induce game-pressure situations in you practices, but also assess what pitchers can "get it done."

This is also an exceptional drill for pitchers that you intend to use primarily in relief roles.

PITCHERS: CONDITIONING

Traditionally, pitchers run distances. The thoughts behind this are that they need well-conditioned leg strength and stamina to get them through seven innings of pitching. If a pitcher throws 100 pitches in a game, it is measurable that she has "exploded" 100 times toward that end.

Hence it is assumed that pitchers need to run distances longer than those needed for position players. Pitchers, when they finish their bull pen work, or are off duty on a non-throwing day, might adopt conditioning modes such as these:

a) Run the **warning track**, circling the outfield, back and forth, five times or so.

b) Run **"poles"**—each field has some sort of marker that can generically be termed a "pole," light stanchions, chain-link fence posts, a scoreboard and flagpole combination, anything to designate a prescribed distance. A coach can even use particular outfield fence ads or distance markers from home plate. The program might then call for "run-jog-run" or "sprint-walk-sprint" between the designated markers. Back and forth three, five, or seven times can be strenuous.

c) **Line-to-line** dashes are also employed to get pitchers' legs into shape. They would run the entire outfield perimeter, along the warning track and skirting the grass, from the right field line to the left field line. Pause, regroup and do it again. Again, perhaps three, five or seven times.

Other types of pitcher conditioning drills would include riding the stationary bike and running the stadium steps. The former has the advantage of being "kind" on the knees, but the stationary bike program takes a long time to reap physical benefits. Running is more efficient, but for a pitcher with sensitive knees, there is a toll to be paid in the repetitive pounding. Running the stadium stairs is exhausting, hence time efficient in terms of conditioning, but this, perhaps more than any of the programs cited can wear down the knees. Moreover, you must factor in whether or not your facility can accommodate this.

Ron Wolforth and Eric Cressey both came out with treatises decrying the hoary traditionalists who advocate long-distance running in the January 23, 2009 issue of "Collegiate Baseball." Pitchers need to develop explosiveness and fast-twitch muscle fibers in their legs, not the slow-twitch fibers of marathon runners. They called for sprint work. Wolforth's article was a bit vague in terms of a specific program, but he seemed to advocate up to nine or ten sets of 15-20 short explosive sprints with 20 seconds of rest between each sprint. Cressey's piece was very specific and supported by research data. Basically, he called for a combination of 10-30 sprints of 10-15 yards, although on some days he sprinted his pitchers for top speed at 50-60 yards. His rest intervals varied from ten seconds to a full minute. This was to be done twice per week.[1*]

Put it another way: incorporate variety in your pitchers' conditioning program. Include both sprint work and distance runs on varying days or even on the same day.

PITCHING: FIELDING THE POSITION "PFP"

Pitchers' fielding practice is another old standby, but, having said that, it is often overlooked on the weekly practice plan. When does it "get remembered?" When the pitcher throws the ball away on a routine play and the result is a big inning for the opposition.

Line the pitchers up around the circle area first. Hit soft fungoes to them, one right after the other; keep the line moving. Here are the plays that must be practiced:

a) Pitchers throwing to first base on come-backers or bunts;
b) Pitchers covering first base on balls hit to the right side of the infield;
c) Pitchers spinning on a come-backer or bunt and throwing to second base;
d) Pitchers fielding a bunt and throwing to third base;
e) Pitchers fielding a bunt and throwing home;
f) Pitchers covering the plate, and applying a tag, when the ball gets by the catcher with a runner on third.

Communication must be reinforced. Calls such as "Ball! Ball! Ball!" need to be instilled, particularly between pitchers and corner infielders and pitchers and catchers. Insist on verbal calls during these drills.

There are some other subtle aspects of PFP that could be incorporated into the aforementioned drill sequences, but they need not get the same degree of attention as they arise less often in games:

1* Source: "Leave Distance Running to Marathoners," by Ron Wolforth and "Cressey Outlines Better Plan Than Distance Running," by Eric Cressey. Both articles appeared in the January 23, 2009 issue of "Collegiate Baseball."

g) Ball bunted on the left side of the infield—third baseman and pitcher both go for the ball; third baseman calls for it, so the pitcher must continue to third for coverage

h) Ball hit to the right side; pitcher covers first, but as the first baseman has been drawn out of the play because she went after the ball, the pitcher must receive a throw from the second baseman.

i) Pop-ups back to the pitcher—spin and throw to a called base in an attempt to get a double-play. (The catcher makes the call; make them randomly for this drill).

j) The 3-6-1 double play combination

PITCHING: PFP—A VARIATION   "I"

Line your pitchers up behind the circle, but off to one side to keep them out of the throwing lanes. Place four or five balls on the ground in front of the circle or have a coach or catcher roll them out as if they were bunted balls. With fielders standing at first, second and third bases, call out where each throw is to go, "1!", "2!", or "3!". You may wish to add "4!" (home) for an additional wrinkle.

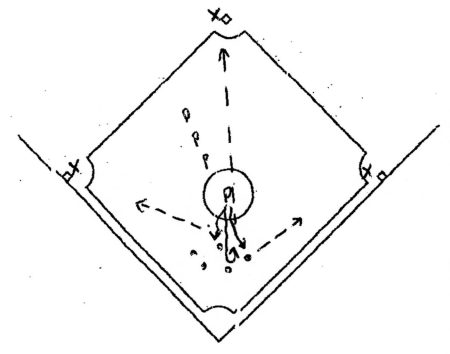

THE BULLPEN BAG

This goes where I go. The Bullpen Bag is as integral to my coaching as a bat bag is for my players.

The contents of the Bullpen Bag are as follows:

- Radar gun
- Weighted balls (6-12 oz.)
- Towel (for "towel drills")
- Hockey puck
- Surgical cord(s)
- Tennis can filled with sand
- Rubber medicine ball (ball)
- Two or three "pearls" (new softballs)
- The "Spinner" described elsewhere
- Oversized softball

I have a football in each bag, perhaps a foam "Nerf" ball.

By the way of explanation for some of the trinkets in each bag, many involve drills described elsewhere in this book, but here is a quick overview for some of the more curious items.

The HOCKEY PUCK helps softball players develop the notion of spin. They have a catch with two fingers aligned on the edge of the puck and throw it underhand, attempting to create slice and rotation.

The "SPINNER" is the softball-sized disk that players use to learn the proper wrist action for various pitchers.

OVERSIZED SOFTBALLS—You can purchase 14" and 16" softballs. Use of these can train your pitchers to enhance spin on their release.

The Nerf Foam FOOTBALL training program has been outlined earlier.

HITTING DRILLS

"Hitting is like shaving. If you don't do it every day, you look like a bum."
Coach John Scolinos

This chapter deals with hitting. It begins with bunting—form and drills—and then proceeds into hitting fundamentals. Drills that address bat speed, tee work, short toss, and correcting hitting flaws are addressed in over 135 drills. Also included are teaching tools and "gimmicks," cage games and even organizational formats for team "BP."

One disclaimer: the old way of teaching women and girls to hit, namely to bar-arm, flatten the bat and swing with a sweeping motion (i.e. "sweep the glasses off the kitchen table") is old hat and completely out of date. Women hit using the same techniques as men.

HITTING: A TEACHING PROGRESSION FOR BUNTING "1"

They say that "bunting is a lost art" and this is probably true, but nonetheless, it is fundamentally necessary for young hitters. Not only does bunting teach the art of "tracking" the ball, and thus makes for better hitters, but also effective, skilled bunting can have a positive impact on a game. Furthermore, I would suggest that bunting is even more essential for girls to learn as it is even more integral in softball.

Here is one way to teach this "lost art:"

DRILL #1: FOOTWORK: Line the players up and have them work on the heel-toe pivot. For some, balance may be a factor, so I allow a small 2-3 inch "balance step" with the front foot stepping to the outside. No more than 2-3 inches, as it can effect plate coverage with the bat head. (Note: I have gotten away from teaching the double-hop-turn method, or the old technique of "squaring up" to the ball. It seems to be used nowhere anymore and, frankly it can be intimidating for players to face up against a speeding pitch)

DRILL #2: HAND POSTION AND BAT ANGLE: Teach them to "slide." In this technique, they are to slide their top hand up to a point about midway up the bat.

Although some coaches have gotten away from it, I still teach the "pinch grip" on the bat for (safety reasons primarily). Moreover, I do insist that the bat barrel is angled upward approximately 45-degrees.

A good verbal cue of young hitters is "shoulder to hip" in describing bat placement from barrel to handle.

Have the players literally hold the bat out in front with one hand—in the middle of the bat, just below the beginning of the "sweet spot" and using a balanced pinch grip.

Insist that they extend their arms with the bat out over the plate.

Now, put it together with these commands: "Pivot!", "Slide!", and then "Pivot & Slide!", all with one motion. Next, have them read the proper timing for when to pivot and slide. Say nothing. Just go through a pitcher's motion and have them "pivot & slide" as the pitcher's arm arc comes to the release point.

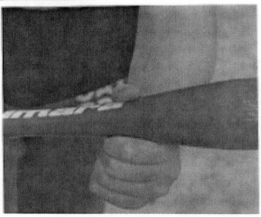

A good way to isolate on the proper footwork yet still is to see a live ball coming at them so have each player approach the plate with the Fielder's glove on they hand—no bat. Pitch to them; they pivot properly and catch the ball in their mitt.

DRILL #3: FROM THE KNEE   "I"

Good bunters "sink down" from the knees to bunt the ball; they do not "reach" down for the ball. If they do the result invariably is a foul ball. To teach this concept, have the batters assume their pivot and slide stance described in the first two drills. Then they simply drop their back knee down until it touches the ground. Since this drill, or any drill done on one knee, can be uncomfortable, you may wish to have the batter-bunter place her glove on the ground to cushion the knee.

Players can work in pairs in this drill—one bunter working with an underhand tosser. Switch up after perhaps ten bunts. Work on "aiming" the label at the shortstop or the second baseman (imaginary, of course) to bunt to the right side and to the left side.

As some late model bats may not have traditional "labels," another way of teaching the same concept is to have the bunter point their top hand, or "slide hand" at the shortstop or second baseman.

Next, have them rise up slightly so that they are in a crouched position, half way between fully down on the knee and fully upright. Continue bunting. Admittedly, this is uncomfortable, so this phase of the drill cannot be prolonged.

Insist on the bat being held at a 45-degree angle in their initial approach. There is a tendency to drop the bat barrel down when executing a bunt. Hence, if the bunter assumes a flat-bat stance, she will drop the barrel down below the horizontal line and the result is a foul ball or an easy pop-up. If they begin at an upright angle, then the barrel drops to parallel.

DRILL #4: "WALK THE LINE"   "I"

To maximize repetitions, line your players up along a fence or sideline. The coaches will then slide along the line, soft-tossing underhand pitches to each player. They do not linger if a player is having difficulty. They pitch, give feedback, and then slide down the line to the next bunter. The more coaches you have, the more reps the players will see.

BUNTING: PLACEMENT DRILLS "THE FORBIDDEN ZONE"   "I"

Many coaches, when teaching about proper bunt placement, lay out traffic cones, bats and gloves or some other kind of markers. They want to create "target zones" up the baselines where the bunters will hopefully place their bunts. Look at this from another perspective—where you do NOT want the hitter to bunt the ball. Defining this as "the forbidden zone," place cones, markers, bats, even chairs or benches out in front of the pitcher's circle. Tell the batter that they must avoid getting the bunt down in that zone, shown below as Zone B.

Traditional Bunt Placement MarkersThe "FORBIDDEN ZONE" (B)

Another good way of designating and visualizing bunt zones is to lay colored blankets or sheets on the ground indicating areas where you want the ball placed or where you do not want it to go.

How about using small hockey goals arranged on strategic locations in your infield?

Yet another technique is to place traffic cones in various locations in the infield and have the bunters knock them over.

BUNTING: DIRECTIONAL CONTROL DRILL   "I"

Basically stated, this is an "aiming" drill. Place a bunter against three fielders arrayed thusly: (10-15' from B to F-1)

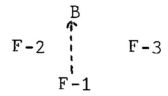

In effect, this is the old game of "pepper." Insist on proper form and bat control. Have the bunter bunt the ball back to the player who initially threw them the ball, F-1, F-2, or F-3.

After teaching the bunter to angle the bat so that the shortstop (F-3) could read the label in order to make the bunt go in that direction, or toward the second baseman (F-1) to angle the bunt toward the right side of the infield, have F-1 soft-toss balls at the bunter (B). They must use proper set-up ("Pivot & Slide"), angle the bat at the proper fielder and bunt away. Rotate the players in a clockwise manner after five bunts.

Coaching Point: Have the players keep the bat still—no movement. I have even discouraged the time-honored practice of "giving with the pitch" (to deaden the ball) to achieve less bat movement and increase efficiency.

An enjoyable way to make this drill competitive is to have the players add in the traditional basketball game of "HORSE." When a bunter fails to lay one down in the directions called for, they get an "H", then after a second failure, an "O" and so on. Once they have failed enough times to spell out "H-O-R-S-E," they run a lap and then get back on line. They will learn to focus.

In teaching directional control, another technique involves using verbal cues. Use a tri-colored plate. Toss balls into all three zones—inside, down the middle and away. For the inside pitch, the verbal cue is "Attack"...for the pitch down them middle, tell them to "Wait"...for the pitch away, it is "Wait; Wait."

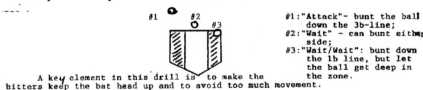

#1:"Attack"- bunt the ball down the 3b-line;
#2:"Wait" - can bunt either side;
#3:"Wait/Wait": bunt down the 1b line, but let the ball get deep in the zone.

A key element in this drill is to make the hitters keep the bat head up and to avoid too much movement.

BUNTING: GIMMICKS—FLAT BATS, HOLED BATS & LAX STICKS   "J"

A) FLAT BATS

Cut the barrel of a wooden bat so that the entire barrel is flat. Bunters can learn to "catch" the ball on the "flat" of the bat. I have even used bats with the flattened barrels widened with a 4 inch slab of plywood screwed on to it.

As a cautionary point, use softy-balls ("Incrediballs") as a regular softball can break these types of bats.

Another use of the flat-bat is to teach the bunter to "get on top" of the ball. Here referring to the regular wood bat that has been cut along the barrel (with no supplemental slab of wood added), have the bunter go after the ball with the flat part of the bat facing skyward. He must then bunt with only the bottom half of the bat. This works, but be careful of strange deflections and errant rebounds. Again, use softy balls.

B) "HOLED" BATS   "I"

As the reader can see in the photo below, this paddle-like bat can be very effective in teaching the art of bunting. The bunter tries to allow a tossed ball to pass through the hole unencumbered and untouched. This is not easy, but there is a definite benefit in enhancing focus. Use tennis balls or softy balls. Do not allow the bunter to "punch" at the ball, as many young bunters seem to want to do.

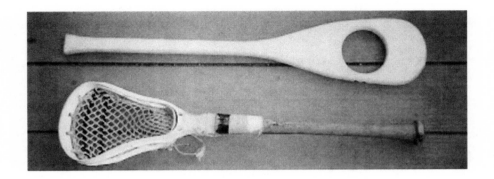

C) LAX STICK BATS   *"I"*

We want to teach our young bunters to "catch the ball" on the head of the bat. Try this method: I attached the head of a lacrosse stick to the handle of a wooden bat. Simply using a conventional lax stick would probably be just as good, but as you can see, I love "gimmicks." Use tennis balls or, preferably, softy balls.

HITTING: BUNTING "BUNTING ROUND ROBIN"   *"I"*

Use the full diamond for this creative drill. Place four "throwers" around the circle area. They could be coaches or players; they need not be formal pitchers. A batter/bunter will stand at each base, using the base as a home plate. It would be a good idea to place a "catcher" behind each hitter/bunter to retrieve missed balls.

This is a "do-or-die" drill in that the bunters will each see only one pitch. They must execute the bunt and then break for the next base. If they have missed the bunt, then they must see this as a dropped third strike. Emphasize proper footwork coming out of the box; emphasize explosiveness and demand good base running technique as they "beat it out" to first.

Rotate around the infield twice before switching the groups. In this way, each player will get eight live bunt attempts plus an element of conditioning.

Key: T=Thrower
      B=Bunter
      R=Retriever/Catcher

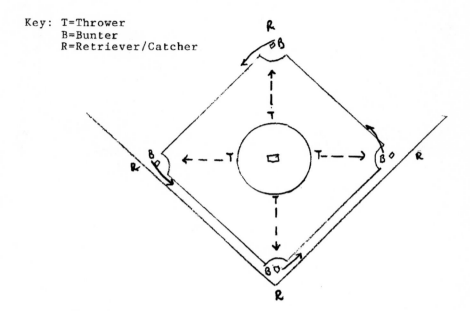

Coordinate this drill. Have each "thrower" simultaneously pitch the ball on a whistle or a set command.

BUNTING: "GAMES"   "I"

Brian Shoop, Head Baseball Coach at the University of Alabama, Birmingham literally painted lines on his game field to set up competitive bunt games. Points were awarded for placement in designated areas.

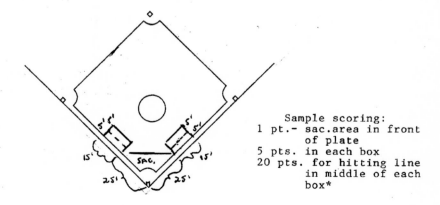

Sample scoring:
1 pt.- sac.area in front
       of plate
5 pts. in each box
20 pts. for hitting line
       in middle of each
       box*

Although not shown in the diagram above, Coach Shoop also drew a box on the right side of the field for right-handed batters to push bunt and for lefties to drag bunt.

He also spoke of having a special miniaturized field within his complex that is specifically designed and designated as a "Bunting Field." The beauties of a big-time program.

*There is a reason for aiming for the line inside of the baseline and in the 15' boxes. As Coach Shoop explained it, too many players aim for the baseline lines and the bunt goes foul. Aim inside.

Note: This drill was designed for a 90' baseball diamond, modify the distance for the 60 foot softball infield.

BUNTING: STRATEGIC BUNTING   "I"

The concept underlying this drill can be utilized in both softball and baseball. Just modify the type of bunt. Described below is a round-robin sequence specific to softball.

Each hitter will place four bunts during their at-bat. The first one is a slap-bunt to the left side (lefty hitter) or a conventional drop-bunt for a base hit (right-handed hitter). The second bunt is a sacrifice to move the runner from first to second (bunt to the left side). The third bunt is to the right side to move the runner from second to third and the final bunt is a suicide squeeze.

Each bunt is a "do-or-die" to keep the drill moving. You may wish to include base runners, but this is not necessary.

Coaches can incorporate the push-bunt if they wish.

BUNTING: EXECUTION OF VARIOUS TYPES OF BUNTS
"POINTS"   "I"

This is a great indoor drill. Basically, divide your squad into two teams (or even four for a mini-tournament). Go through the line of each team four times, calling for a different type of bunt on each go-through: slap, drag, sacrifice, suicide. (Add the fake-bunt-and-hit if you prefer).

Points are awarded for each bunt and the team with the highest total wins.

If you do elect to run a mini-tournament, the structure is simple: Team A vs. B and Team C vs. D. The winners play off against each other and the losers run the bases.

This game can be effective in teaching and drilling hit-and-run settings as well.

BUNTING: SQUEEZE PLAYS "DO-OR-DIE"   "I"

Line your base runners up near third base. Choose one or two plays to work on—safety squeeze or suicide squeeze. They will read and execute their proper keys as to when they must break for home. In clarifying, the runner breaks on a suicide when the pitcher releases the ball. The runner breaks on a safety when the ball is actually bunted on a downward trajectory. There is a batter (bunter) and an on-deck hitter. The pitcher, preferably a coach, throws home and the hitter must execute the squeeze play, safety or suicide. One pitch; one bunt. Execute the play—do-or-die. The runner goes to the on-deck circle or end of the line the on-deck hitter moves up to the plate and the bunter runs all three bases to get on line at third. This can even be used as an end-of-practice conditioning drill.

Upset at my team's lack of execution one game, we did this drill in the pouring rain the next day—100 suicide squeezes!

BUNTING: BUNTING SCRIMMAGE   "I"

This drill, actually a game, can be done indoors or outdoors. It can be looked upon as an offensive drill as well as a defensive one. It is simple: place an infield out on the diamond or on the floor. Have a line of batters ready to go at home plate. The pitcher throws, the batter bunts and the defense tries to get them out. You may prefer to have a coach serve as the pitcher—it saves arms and produces more strikes, especially if you have a young team. If you do, be sure to have a player standing beside you to field the bunts and cover bases.

Insist on execution and bunt placement from your offense. Insist on proper coverage and communication from your defense.

BUNTING: BUNT-RUN OFFENSIVE MINI-SCRIMMAGE
"I"

This drill can be practiced on a full diamond or in a corner of the gym.

Set four bases in an infield pattern. Line your players up at home. The coach can serve as the pitcher. The batter at the plate lays down four bunts:

1. Bunt for a hit;
2. Run & Bunt with a runner on first;
3. Sacrifice bunt with a runner on second;
4. Suicide Squeeze.

Both the batter and the runners will apply their proper reads and rules. Note that there will be no runner on the first bunt, but after that the same base runner works his way around the diamond from first to second, third and then home, applying proper reads all the way.

Elaborating on the reads and rules, in bunting for a hit, insist that the batter get a good pitch to hit. Too many young players will go after anything thrown their way. In the second bunt, with a runner on first, the bunter should cover the runner who is essentially stealing on the pitch. In the third bunt, she must go after only a strike; she does not have to cover a breaking runner because the runner goes only when she reads the downward trajectory of the bunted ball. The bunter should square around early as this is a sacrifice situation, as is the final bunt, a do-or-die suicide squeeze play. Following the execution of this final bunt, the bunter runs to first and execites her role as the next base runner.

As good as this drill is, there tends to be some degree of standing around so I often divided my squad up into two or even three units executing the drill in various areas of the field or the gym on miniaturized infields.

HITTING: BUNTING "BUNTING VS. THE MACHINE" *"I"*

Your team is preparing to face a pitcher with overwhelming speed. One of the ways your team can "solve" this pitcher or "get to" her is via the bunt game. But you must prepare. Crank the pitching machine up to an appropriate velocity and have the kids bunt against it. At first they will falter, even be intimidated, but as repetitions mount, they will get used to the speed.

Once accustomed to the speed, you can even play a scrimmage game—utilizing only the bunt—against the machine and an infield positioned to work the proper bunt defenses. Your emphasis may be on the offense, but your defense can benefit equally. Why not add this novel idea. Coach Michelle Gromacki from Cal State Fullerton wrote in <u>The Softball Drill Book</u> about how she had her infielders call out which type of bunt the batter was about to execute. They were to read the hitter's feet and hands. Interesting idea.

HITTING: SOFTBALL "SLAP HITTING" A TEACHING PROGRESSION   *"J"*

The art of slap hitting is all but unknown among baseball coaches, although it should be noted that Japanese players, even in the Major Leagues (Suzuki Ichiro and Matsui Hideki) regularly execute slap hits. Generally speaking, it is a technique most commonly found in softball. I wonder if we should teach the technique to our left-handed baseball hitters…for lefty softball hitters it is a must.

All that being said, first of all, consider the two basic technical coaching points: the cross-over step and the throwing of the hands and bat head at the ball. While good "slappers" can even slap the inside pitch, it is most effective with a pitch on the outside one-third of the plate. The hitter has the clear intention of driving the ball through the hole between the shortstop and third baseman.

A suggested teaching progression might look like this:

    a) Footwork: Line your lefty hitters at the plate and have them walk through the cross-over step. A good "aiming point" for the rear foot is the upper left corner of the batter's box.

Technique A:
Pivot & Cross-over

Technique B: Drop
Step & Cross-over.

The slapper can use either of two techniques. Technique A: calls for a simple front foot pivot and then a cross-over step with the back foot. Technique B: calls for the slapper to take a slight drop-step with the front foot and then followed by the cross-over.

Timing is crucial in either case. Begin the steps once the ball reaches the release point from the pitcher's hand—no earlier. In slapping, being late is better.

A mirror set in front of the hitter can be an effective teaching device. No ball is thrown or hit, but they can check their footwork.

b) Throwing the hands at the ball. This implicitly means throwing the bat head at the ball, so have the hitters line up, cross-over and then literally fling their bats at an imaginary pitch low and away just to learn the "feel" for doing this. Work on keeping the bat head above the hands and the hands behind the bat head.

c) Use of the batting tee: have your hitters line up against a tee and slap the ball off it using proper hand action and cross-over footwork. For more advanced hitters, it is suggested that you place the tee at different heights and set the softballs at different locations, in and out. This is decidedly more difficult, but it is also more realistic.

d) Short Toss Slapping: Place a coach behind a protective screen in the batting cage, toss soft underhand pitches and have the hitters work on slapping a softball against the opposite wall of the cage.

Other teaching drills include bouncing tennis balls toward the hitter and have them slap at the ball as it crests after the bounce. This helps them keep their weight back and not prematurely release toward the ball. Another drill is to teach the slap hit as a "swinging bunt." Have the hitter slap at the ball and freeze their bat at the point of contact rather than follow through. You will find that this helps keep the head down and in (aka "nose to the zone").

There are some visual cues for the coach who is teaching the slap-hit technique. If the hitter is pulling the ball or bouncing back to the pitcher too often, check their front shoulder. They are probably opening it too early. Opening the shoulder brings the bat head out front too early.

Try working on "soft slapping" and "hard slapping." The difference lies in the follow through with the bat. Work this off a batting tee. In the soft slap, the hitter punches at the ball with little follow-through. In the hard slap, they follow through in a full bat swing.

In working off the batting tee, set the slapper in the foot positioning that they will be in at the point of contact. Insist that they keep their hands back, their front shoulder in, and their hands high.

Two further thoughts: One, this technique takes quite a while to master so it can be a good indoor drill begun early in the preseason or even taught during the off-season. Second, it is virtually ignored by youth softball coaches at the elementary level. More often than not, it is because the coaches themselves do not know how to teach slap hitting, thus it is not part of the agenda for young girls learning the game in Little League. Why?

A)Teach the footwork, hand positioning & bat angle;
B)Drill slapping off a batting tee;
C)Teach it live off short toss.

HITTING/BUNTING: SLASH HIT CONES DRILL

Slash hitting, or fake-bunting-&-hit, can be very effective in a game, especially after you have established the bunt attack. If the hitter shows bunt, watch the corner infielder's crash toward the plate. This opens up the infield, especially if there is a runner on first and the middle infielders are racing to cover the bag. A good way to teach the necessary targeting in the slash technique is this drill:

Teach the proper footwork (pivot technique described earlier) and the sliding of the hands. Some coaches, in teaching the slash, prefer to slide the bottom hand up the bat toward the top hand for more bat control. In effect, they are teaching their hitter to radically choke up and punch the ball.

Having accomplished that, set two cones out on the infield dirt where the shortstop and second baseman might normally play. Have the hitter show bunt early and once the pitcher begins her motion, pull the bat back, and maybe the front foot back in toward the plate, and try to punch the ball toward the vicinity of the cones. In a game, these areas are where the "holes" will be.

Good slashers create an element of fear in the minds of the crashing corner infielders as they demonstrate the capability of swinging away at a very close range.

This same drill can be used for your lefty slappers and your push-bunters.

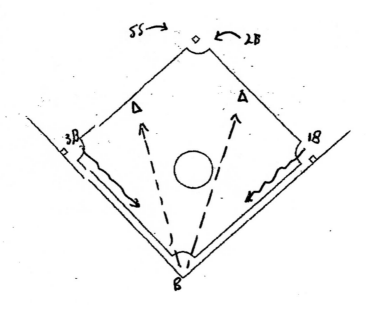

HITTING: SOFTBALL SLAPPING WITH A CONE BARRIER "I"

Many softball slap hitters burst out of the batter's box too early. For that matter, even lefty baseball drag bunters do this. Moreover, many of them take their initial step away from the pitcher when they should be stepping directly toward the pitcher.

To reinforce this notion, place a cone just in front of the batter's box. The slapper or drag bunter must actually run around the cone before re-gaining their line toward first base.

HITTING: SLAP CATCHING "I"

Try this one with your lefty slappers. They approach the plate wearing a fielder's glove on their left hand. A tosser throws underhand. The slapper uses the proper foot work but catches the ball in the glove. It helps them to look for good pitches to slap.

HITTING: SOFTBALL SHORT TOSS "I"

This is a great little drill for working on "short stroke hitting," in closed spaces such as an indoor facility. Wiffleballs are used.

"Pitchers" will toss underhand and the hitters, in sequence, will work on their various bunt techniques, slash hitting and "chop hitting." Since the throwers are at a distance of only about 12-15 feet away, all of these dimensions can be drilled.

HITTING: FORM TEACHING PROPER MECHANICS (1) "I"

When I teach hitting, I follow a somewhat traditional format in that I work with a hitter's lower body mechanics first and then re-focus into the upper body mechanics. It is a two-phase process because there is so much for a young hitter to learn.

This first set of drills is directed at lower-body mechanics, but first allow me to set the stage with an overview of proper hitting mechanics and how I approach them.

Place all of your prospective hitters in a line or semi-circle around you, the coach-demonstrator.

1. Balance: feet at slightly wider than shoulder width and knees inside the feet. One hitting coach suggested referencing the length of the bat as the distance between the feet.

2. Demonstrate the difference between the open and the closed stance. For the youngest hitters, aged four to seven you may prefer a more linear stance with the toes set on a line drawn in the dirt. They can relate to this as it is similar to "lining up" in gym class or school. Thus, there is no "closed" or "open" stance here—they can learn that later.

3. Show them where to align their front foot in relation to the plate. I use a numerical reference—points one, two and three. The youngest hitters should set the front foot on the line nearest point "two."

    4. (Coaching Point: You may tell bunters to stand with front foot near #1)

5.

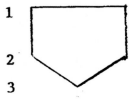

6. Stride or "Toe-Tap": philosophies vary. I have gravitated in recent years to the "toe-tap" rather than a distinct stride because young hitters tend to shift their body weight forward when they take a stride. Telling them to keep their weight back by merely tapping their front toe with perhaps a subtle lift and drop, the

toe lands with the heel elevated off the ground. The purpose of either action is to keep the weight shifted back. (In addition to a timing element) See the next photo.

7. Hip Action—Teach the batter to bring the rear hip through the ball rather than opening the front hip prematurely (although there is an element of truth in "clearing the hips" on an inside pitch).

8. "Roll the Back Heel" into an upright position, keeping the toe on the ground. To put it another way, roll the heel in such a way that the laces of the shoe will "face" the pitcher.

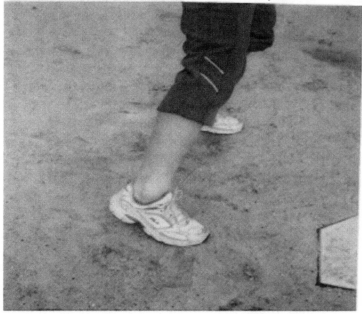

These techniques can best be taught in dry-run demonstrations. No bat is even necessary in teaching this. Have them feel the initial balance, the toe tap, the weight shift and the pivot of the hips. Have them see the heel roll (aka "squashing the bug"). As they begin the swing sequence in a balanced position, so must they end it as well. The weight shifts from the "back side" (hands, hip, knee, foot all in relative alignment) to the hips and navel, not the front foot as some coaches teach. Tell the kids that it shifts to the "belly button"—they can identify with that more easily.

Some coaches suggest that 65-70 percent of the body weight should be shifted on to the "back side" as the stride or toe tap is taken.

Balance is a crucial factor. Ty Hawkins, a friend and a hitting coach in the New York Yankees organization uses a "Hop Drill" to teach this. He sets the kids up in a good athletic batting stance in his youth clinic and then asks them to hop straight up. If they land on both feet simultaneously, they are balanced. He then has them take a dry run swing (no ball). Upon completion of the follow-through, they hold the position and then hop again. They must maintain balance throughout the swing sequence.

Again, a dry run demonstration following your talk is the best way to teach this. Next, after they have gone through the steps, literally show them pictures. Whenever, I see a photo of a major league ball player's swing or stance, I clip it and paste it into a file which I bring to the field. Show these photos to kids, let them see it to create a mental picture in their heads. Now for the next step: drill it.

a) "Dance With The Pitcher"—The players are lined up in front of you as you are giving your demonstration on the fundamentals of lower body mechanics. This simple drill, then, becomes part of that talk. It is meant to establish rhythm and timing. Your coaching cue is, "Dance with the Pitcher." As she swings her arm back to initiate a release of the ball, the hitter must also synchronize her weight shift on to the back hip and foot. To put it another way, "as the pitcher goes back, the hitter goes back." Thus, with the players lined up in front of you, become a pitcher, go through a pitching motion and have the players respond by shifting their weight back and either taking a stride or toe-tapping. Give them a sense of timing.

b) Shoulder-Touch Drill—So many players, even on somewhat advanced levels of play, allow their weight to shift forward as they take their stride. One of the simple teaching drills designed to prevent this is the "shoulder touch drill." Have the player stand in a balanced, pre-pitch hitting stance. Her front shoulder is nearest to you, as the coach. Tell her to take her stride as you gently touch her front shoulder. If her weight shifts toward you, she will feel the pressure of your fingers on her shoulder. She will learn to keep her weight back.

c) The Sun-Shade Drill—Another way to convey the same concept of keeping the weight back and allowing no "leakage" forward is this drill. You need a day when the sun is shining, however. Tell the hitter to get into his stance. Position her so that her upper body, particularly the head, casts a distinct shadow. Place your foot on the shadow of their head. Tell her to stride. If her head's shadow moves off your foot when she strides, then her weight has shifted forward. Use both of these drills (b & c); the hitter will get the picture. The latter drill also has the effect of teaching her to keep the head still.

A good verbal cue is to tell young hitters, who often dip their upper body rather than move forward, is that their head is in a "box" and as they prepare to swing and then execute the swing, the "head stays in the box."

Jeff Stitt, former head baseball coach at the University of Arizona and often spoken of as a hitting guru, accomplished the same thing by placing the palms of his hands one inch away from the ears of a hitter as he stands behind him. The hitter will swing off a tee; she can feel if her head moves on either the trigger set-up or during the course of the swing. Be careful of the backswing, however. You may get hit so time it properly and back away at the right moment.

HITTING: FORM TEACHING PROPER MECHANICS (II) *"I"*
Having discussed, taught and drilled the lower body, out next focus is on the upper body. I look for several things:

1. **The "L" Position:** I insist that the hitters keep the front elbow bent at a 90-degree angle, thus resembling the letter "L". This creates a short, compact swing.

2. **"Hands High":** Set their hands at the top of the strike zone, or atop the back shoulder. Ralph Weekly, softball coach at the University of Tennessee, teaches his hitters to set their bat in the "notch" created by the shoulder clavicle, the deltoid...then lift the hands. Maybe a little technical for young hitters, but certainly an excellent reference in terms of "setting the hands atop the shoulder."

3. **"Load & Separations":** As the stride or toe tap is executed the weight shifts back and the hands slightly elevate, maintaining the "L Position" all the while. Some coaches call this the "Trigger." The concept of "separation" comes in when the hands lift as the stride foot lands—they separate away from the body, in a sense.

   Use of the Surgical Cord to teach "separation." Often a misunderstood concept, "separation" occurs when the hitter takes her stride or toe-tap and she elevates her hands. Thus, the hands separate the distance between the feet and the bat. Perhaps a better verbal cue is the word "stretch." To reinforce this, tie a surgical cord to the front foot and hold the other end in the hands gripping the bat. As the batter "loads," she will both stride and lift the hands, thus creating separation or stretch, something she can literally feel with the surgical cord. Begin with the cord somewhat taut or at least in a straight line with no slack. This is an excellent way to teach the notion of "Triggering."

4. **Downward Approach:** The lower hand takes you to the ball. Astute hitting coaches watch the knob of the bat to see that it does not drop down or retreat backward prior to the swing. The former creates a "hitch;" the latter creates what we call "bar-arming" or flattening out.

5. **Level Through the Zone & Finish High:** Jim Lefebvre talks about the "Power Curve."
A good verbal cue to teach this notion is that of "landing an airplane." The bat, like a plane, glides downward into the hitting zone and then levels out on the runway. Then tell them that the pilot changed his mind and decides to take off again.

6. **"Nose to the Zone":** Keep the head in and the nose down to the hitting zone.

7. **"Coil and Uncoil":** A lot is made about "linear hitting" or "rotational hitting." It can be controversial. My co-author Pat Barnaba and I agree that the hip action is rotational; the hand action is linear. Good verbal cues such as "Coil and Uncoil" work here. "Hip rotation actually means turning on the axis. So many young hitters have a linear weight transfer," Pat observes. Another cue that can help emphasize this point is to have the hitter drive her back hip toward the hitting zone. "Explode to the ball."

As for the hands being "linear," have the hitters drive their hands through the ball toward the pitcher. "Stay on the ball" and "Don't pull off." This is called "extension." Driving two balls off a double-tee or having the hitter drive softballs into a suspended hula hoop keeps them on the ball and through the zone—LINEAR.

THE "DOWNWARD APPROACH" & THE "POWER CURVE"

LITTLE THINGS TO LOOK FOR REGARDING UPPER BODY MECHANICS

A) In the "Trigger Position" notice how the weight is shifted back and the front heel elevated slightly, but even more importantly, notice how the hands align with the back knee and the rear foot:

B) CLAMPING THE FRONT SHOULDER—Use a towel, wooden dowel, even a batting glove to remind the young hitter to keep the front shoulder down.

TWO COMMON HITTING ERRORS:
C) "BAR-ARMING:" Insist on the "L." Position of the front arm; use half bats and paddles hitting in side-toss drills.

D) DROPPING THE HANDS: Insist on placement of the hands up by the ear. Tee work with the instructor literally holding the bat knob up until the swing begins can help conquer this. Also insist that the hitter "throws her hands at the ball" from the "hands high" position.

Having broken down the elements of the fundamental stance and swing sequence, take your players through "shadow swings." No ball is thrown, just call out commands such as these and check the elements described:

1. "Stance!" (or "Balance!")
2. "Trigger" (as you simulate a pitcher's motion)
3. "Swing!" (Check the feet and head positioning)

WEEKLY'S DRY SWING SEQUENCE—Ralph Weekly is one of the most successful women's softball coaches in the country. His "Lady Vols" from the University of Tennessee are annual visitors to the College World Series.

Earlier, we referred to the analytical value of "dry swings." Weekly insists on a patterned teaching sequence that he calls "**The 1-2-3 Drill.**" He lines his girls up, perhaps along a foul line. On the command of "One!" they must trigger (Weekly emphasizes a soft and subtle backward movement of the hands). On "Two!" the girls take their stride, a toe touch with the heel elevated to keep the weight back. On "Three!" they take their swing.

Try the "Lift Technique" often employed by high-caliber women softball players. They stand with the bat resting on the shoulder and then, when the pitcher begins their motion, they literally lift their hands directly upward. It is uncanny how much Division I softball hitters do this. Some pro baseball hitters do, too. The key is that they get their hands high.

What follows next are drills designed to teach, train and enhance the subtle nuances within the swing sequence.

The "notch" referred to earlier.

HITTING: FUNDAMENTALS "BOTTOM HAND/TOP HAND" DRILLS   "I"

Proper action involving the hands is fundamental to successful hitting. The hands determine the swing path of the bat. There are, however, two distinct ways to look at a hitter's hands. Focused drills for each hand, and reinforcement of the principles behind each hand's purpose in swinging the bat, are essential to a hitter's understanding and adjustments.

Let us begin with this concept: THE BOTTOM HAND TAKES YOU TO THE BALL. THE TOP HAND ALLOWS YOU TO EXTEND THROUGH THE BALL.

In my teaching, I have found that too many hitters and coaches fail to grasp this concept, especially with regards to the top hand. Let me state at the onset, however, that I am a "bottom hand guy"—I emphasize the route of the lower hand to the ball and into the hitting zone. I only work with the top hand when I see a need to correct a flaw.

Let's begin with the bottom hand.

BOTTOM HAND DRILLS: In each case, position the hitter in her launch position ready to attack the ball. As a point of teaching, I never use a player's bat for these drills. Even if the hitter chokes up, the bat is too heavy for one hand, especially when you are trying to teach the proper approach path.

T-WORK: Use a sawed-off wood bat roughly ½ of the normal length;

Use a "paddle" made from a sawed-off hockey goalie's stick;

Use a ping-pong table tennis paddle;

Use a "bottle bat" available for purchase and shown below.

In each case, I suggest that you use softy balls, tennis balls, or wiffle balls since a hardball can create stinging vibrations or even break the bats shown.

Employ any or all of these drills devices to enhance the "downward approach" stressed by modern hitting coaches. The purpose is two-fold: to teach and to develop "muscle memory." What is that Japanese saying, "It takes 8000 repetitions to master a technique"?

Devices for teaching the route of the lower hand:

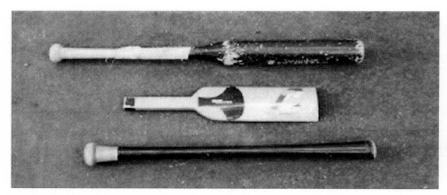

SIDE-TOSS: The hitter assumes her stance. The coach kneels or sits on a bucket in front of the hitter and to the side at roughly a 45-degree angle. The coach underhands a soft toss toward the front edge of the plate while the hitter takes the proper swing path. Only the lower hand is used. Notice how I place the top hand up by the player's ear as a reference. This helps her feel the proper placement of both hands atop the strike zone and by not using the top hand in the swing, it gives her a tactile reference point. If the bottom hand drops or travels rearward ("bar-arming"), then the hitter can feel it. She must feel the lower hand launching into the ball from its position atop the shoulder.

Again, use half-bats or paddles for this drill, hitting softy balls or tennis balls.

Yet another technique, one described by Coach Jack Perconte in his <u>The Making of a Hitter,</u> is to use a small towel. The hitter grips the towel in her lower hand and with proper load-up, footwork and swing path, she snaps the towel at an imaginary ball. This helps with the concept of "extension" through the ball as well. A variation of Perconte's drill that I have used is to place a light wiffleball on a batting tee out in front of where the plate would normally be. Ask the hitter to flick the ball off the tee by using the towel.

I have read of another coach, who used a Frisbee to accomplish the same thing. I suggest that the towel or the Frisbee can also be use to teach "top hand extension" through the ball and out toward the pitcher.

HITTING: FUNDAMENTALS "TOP HAND EXTENSION" DRILL   *"T"*

You will see many kids hitting off a "T" and executing drills with either the top hand or the lower hand. They will be slicing, slamming and chopping away with little observational commentary from a coach and even less regard and understanding for what they are attempting to accomplish. If they are older players, high school students for instance, they may be choking up on the regular bats, attempting to leverage one-handed swings. They look like they know what they are doing. Don't be fooled.

Having already described the esoterics of the bottom hand, let us examine the purpose and route of the top hand. To me, it is all about "extension" through the hitting zone." The top hand action has been described as a type of karate chop. I do not quite agree, but I will suggest that the top hand does approach the ball with the palm facing upward. To me, the crucial aspect is that the top hand "drives" into the ball and extends through to the pitcher. In some ways it resembles an awkward "belly punch."

A drill to teach this principle is cited by Jack Percante in his aforementioned <u>The Making of a Hitter.</u> The bottom hand grips the bat (or a half-bat) and swings through the ball, either side tossed or on a tee. The proper stance. As the swing is taken, the top hand, never actually gripping the bat handle pushes through the hitting zone in such a way that his open palm finishes toward the pitcher.

Jerry Stitt has used this extension drill: the hitter swings off a tee, but in slow-motion. The coach holds his hands, palm toward the bat path about 6-8 inches in front of the tee. The hitter's bat must slap into the coach's palm.

HITTING: ITCHY JONES BALL TOSS DRILL   *"I"*

Former Illinois Coach Richard "Itch" Jones always swore by this simple hitting drill. It teaches the approach to the ball and the notion of inside, middle field, and opposite field contact.

The player wraps her fingers together, the bottom of the top hand and the top of the lower hand intertwined. The batter holds a ball in the top hand. She replicates her swing by loading and striding, "swinging" without a bat and then flinging the ball in a predetermined direction, right, center or left.

Try it. The hitter really does get the feel of a pulled ball, one driven up the middle and one hit to the opposite field.

HITTING: EXTENSION "THROWING THE BAT"

Frankly, I have reservations about this drill, but it is one that vividly illustrates a key point—extending the hands through the ball.

Line the players up along a foul line. With bats in hand, they assume a batting stance and then, as they swing on your command, they release the bat head out on to the field. The key aspect is that the bat should land in line with their feet, validating that they did not over-rotate or "pull-off" or "fly-open."

My reservations about this drill are that with younger players, in an effort to throw the bat farther than their teammates they will drop their hands, bar-arm and fling rather than maintain good form. I have done this in camps, but I do not like the result. With older players—

high school varsity or collegiate—it may have value as a one-time instructional drill, however.

One of the benefits of having two authors for this drill book lies in the differences of opinion that can emerge. Pat Barnaba noted that she always liked this drill. In her words, "it made a big impression on my players. The cue was to "throw your hands at the ball" and release the bat as the hands moved through the hitting zone just before rolling the top hand over."

You try it. You decide.

HITTING: FUNGO HITTING   "I"

Too many young players, even up to the high school level, do not know how to "fungo" balls out to other fielders. This does help with eye/hand coordination and bat control. Teach your players how to properly hit out of their hand.

To be honest, I've seen too many Little League Dads, and fewer Moms, who cannot hit fungoes. You will see many weird techniques. Teaching your girls the proper technique can help them now and in the future.

HITTING: SHORT TOSS DRILLS   "I"

A) SIDE TOSS—Sitting on a bucket or kneeling, feed balls to a hitter aligned at a plate. Insist on proper mechanics, load-up, swing plane and follow-through. This is an excellent drill for maximizing repetitions. One can even work inside and outside pitches by tossing toward the front knee of the batter (inside pitches) or the back knee of the batter (outside pitches).

Another good side-toss drill is to toss two balls (out of the same hand) at once. Command the hitter to go for the high one or the lower one. This is a good lower hand adjustment drill that also helps keep a hitters' weight back.

Yet another technique is to "hold the toss." Begin the motion of tossing the ball underhanded, but hold it, do not release it. The hitter will set up, load up and then be forced to hold her weight and hands back. This helps not only to teach that concept, but also can help remediate a hitter who "leaks forward" in her stride or is too quick and lunge to the ball. Release the ball after a one-second hold.

B) SHORT TOSS—Throwing from behind an L-screen from a distance of 20-30 feet is another excellent method of maximizing hitting reps. As a coach, most of us can throw strikes from that distance and with little or no strain on the arm. Look at major league pre-game batting practice or Homerun Derby at the All-Star Game—the pitchers all throw from abbreviated distances.

Another thought. Got a sore arm? Can't throw strikes? Toss underhand. There is absolutely no arm stress and you will be more accurate, guaranteed. Young hitters may see this as juvenile, but I heard New York Yankees hitting Coach Kevin Long advocate this at a coaches clinic. He will toss underhand in many drills...and to hitters like A-Rod and Jeter. That's good enough for me. In deference to release-point principles, you probably should stand up if you employ the underhand motion.

C) DROP TOSS—Stand on a bucket and drop balls into the hitting zone. This is a very difficult drill and one that can frustrate hitters. Frankly, I feel that it is of marginal value, but it can help hitters keep their weight back and avoid lunging.

D) BACK TOSS—A variation of side toss, this drill is very effective in teaching three successful components of hitting:
   a) Extension through the ball
   b) Bat speed
   c) Avoid dropping the hands & "looping" the bat

Have the hitter stand at the plate in normal fashion. The feeding coach, however, stands behind the hitter. Allow the hitter to look back at the feeder. With an underhand toss into the hitting zone, the hitter will find that she must "catch up to the ball" in order to hit a line drive up the middle. This alone helps her bat speed. She will also discover that the quickest route to the ball is directly at it—no drop, no loop. Ultimately, this drill helps her understand "extending through the ball" or "driving the hands to the pitcher" before rounding off on a follow-through.

E) BOUNCE TOSS—This drill can be as difficult as it is important. Many hitters "leak forward" in their stride. They must learn how to keep their weight back until they explode into the swing. This drill can help accomplish that feeling. The batter assumes her stance, loads into her triggering sequence and then waits before lashing out at the ball…which is a tennis ball that is bounced toward her. Bounce the ball about three or four feet in front of her at such an angle that it crosses into the strike zone belt high. The hitter will experience some frustration at first, but she will get the picture and the feeling.

This drill can be frustrating for the thrower as well. If the ground surface of the cage is uneven with dirt patches, depressions and grass clumps, getting the ball to bounce "true" is difficult. Suffice it to say, then, that this drill is best done indoors on a flat, smooth floor. If this is unavailable, you may try bouncing the ball from a side-toss position.

HITTING DRILL: RHYTHM ROWSON'S 5-BALL DRILL
"T"

James Rowson, a hitting coach in the New York Yankees organization, uses this drill to impart rhythm; side toss five balls in a row. Do it slowly and rhythmically, but do not allow the hitter to stop his or her motion. Toss…swing…hit…recover to shoulder height… toss again. No stopping. Feel the flow. Three sets of five tosses works well.

HITTING: FOCUS DRILLS "SEE IT & HIT IT"   "T"

Seeing the ball, keeping the head down, "nose to the zone" at the point of contact—these are all keys to hitting success. And as such, we can drill them.

A) Hit color-coded balls—Paint a colorized dot on each ball and as the batter hits the ball, she must call out the color;

B) Hit number balls—A variation of the aforementioned, have the hitter call out the number written on each ball;

I keep separate bags for each of these "drill balls;" I also like to use soft pitching machine balls as they are easy to color code or write numbers on.

C) Hit wifffle golf balls—The concept here is simple: if you can hit a small object, you can hit a bigger one. This drill can be made more challenging by using a broom handle or stickball bat. Another advantage to this drill is that it can be done in a compact area.

Hitters need to take controlled, fundamentally sound swings and they can literally see the ball hit the bat. This drill can also be used as pre-game batting practice if league rules, time or field availability inhibit or prohibit conventional "BP."

D) Hit marbles into a tarpaulin—I heard Coach Rod DelMonico speak about this at a coaches' clinic. Side-tossing marbles can really make a hitter focus on the task at hand.

Of course, the "ping" may give you a headache! I once tied this with grapes, but the juice got all over everything...

E) "Sweet Spot" stick bats—You can go to a vendor or look through a catalog and purchase one of these for $40 or $50, or you can make one from a broom handle and a section of pipe insulation. The purpose is to focus the hitter on hitting the ball squarely on the "sweet spot" of the bat head. Use wifffle balls. This is a great indoor drill.

F) Candrea's Tracking Drill—University of Arizona softball coach Mike Candrea uses a variation of the Itch Jones Drill mentioned else where. With the bat held behind the back, he has his players hit numbered balls. However, they go after only the balls with numbers that he calls out. Suppose he is prepared to toss five balls, each with a number. He will tell the hitter to bunt only numbers two, five and one…pull back on the others. An interesting variation to say the least. You can use colored balls, too. Have the kids swing at only the red ones, for example. This concept can be used in other hitting drills as well.

HITTING: SWING STRENGTH & BAT SPEED 2-MAN ISOTONICS   *"I"*

This simple drill is one that I always included with young players upon conclusion of their pre-practice stretching and agilities.

Have them partner up; one player assumes a batting stance. The other grips the bat head and provides resistance as the batter goes through the swing pattern.

Use a verbal ten-count to time the drill properly. Two or three reps should suffice and then switch positions.

The resistance is moderate. Players should not "muscle up" and break down their swing mechanics in a straining effort to push the bat head through the hitting zone.

A modification of this drill is to use the surgical cord that is employed by pitchers. Attach it to a fence at shoulder height. The hitter, with either her lead arm or with two hands, replicates the swing motion holding the unattached end of the cord. Two or three sets of ten reps should suffice.

How about a five-pound dumbbell? Have the hitter lie on her side on a bench. She holds the dumbbell across her body. The dumbbell is held in the hand of the lead arm only. With the proper right-angle flexion of this lead arm, she pulls the weight upward, again across the body and then straightens it out pointing the dumbbell skyward. Two or three sets of ten reps are again suggested.

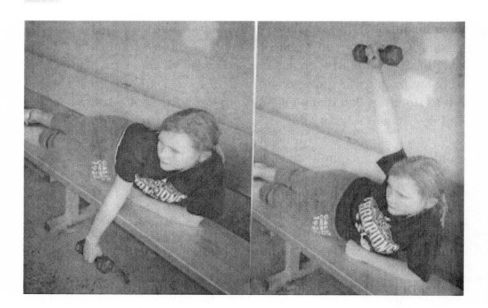

HITTING: BAT SPEED DRILLS   *"I"*

A) THE BROOMSTICK: Speed in any athletic movement involves the fast-twitch muscle fibers. Power comes from utilization of the slow-twitch fibers. The appropriate muscle fibers, then, need to be trained in an appropriate way. Take a broom stick or even a wiffle bat. Have the hitter swing it back and forth as fast as they can, repeating this action. Employ three sets of ten to twenty reps. It will enhance bat speed. Interestingly, some recent studies have demonstrated that the age-old practice of swinging a heavy bat in the on-deck circle may actually slow down bat speed by as much as four or five mph! Try selling that to baseball traditionalists!

Coach Ralph Weekly uses this drill and emphasizes that the hitter must stop and re-set after each swing to work on explosiveness from the "triggered position."

B) THE HANGING TIRE: Suspend an old car tire from a tree branch, batting cage support or some other appendage. Have the players swing, with good mechanics, into the tire. It will move as they not only strike the tire, but also as they drive the bat head and hands "through the hitting zone." Do not allow them to "muscle up" and push the tire. Tell them to trust their mechanics, assuring them that the tire will move or at least rotate on contact and follow-through. This helps develop bat speed.

C) WEIGHTED BATS & BALLS OFF A BATTING TEE: Self-explanatory, this drill can also help develop upper body strength and bat speed. One must be careful, of course, to use old bats rather than new ones if they are hitting weighted softballs as they are larger and will call for more force from the hitter than conventional weighted baseballs. Consider using rubberized medicine balls, too.

D) THROWING BATS: Described elsewhere, this drill can also help with not only bat speed, but also linear mechanics and extensions. The difference here, however, is rather than throwing the bat up a baseline or into an open field, have them throw the bats into a batting net.

E) THE RAPID-FIRE DRILL: Using a quickly re-loaded batting tee or side-toss in quick succession, this drill is described elsewhere.

HITTING: CORE STRENGTH "MEDICINE BALL TOSS" "1"

Power in hitting a softball emanates from many components: bat speed, hips and legs, and upper body strength. The latter is the focus here as two players face each other perhaps 5 feet apart. They will hold a medicine ball in their hands as if it were a bat. They assume a full and proper batting stance. Then have a catch.

Form must never be sacrificed for distance. Employ all the intricacies of a fundamentally sound swing. Have the players work on exploding the upper body, emphasizing quickness. Insist they keep everything in line—the ball and the hands should finish in a line toward the receiver. Also check their feet. Is the front leg stiff? Has the back heel rolled? Are they balanced and is the weight centered in the middling of the body?

Another good "core development" drill using the medicine ball is to have two players stand back to back, passing the ball around behind their back to the receiving player. Round and round they go, the ball circling their bodies. The feet never move, only the torso. Reverse the direction after a minute.

HITTING DRILL: RHYTHM "THE ELEPHANT TRUNK DRILL"

I took this drill from Ty Hawkins, a hitting instructor in the New York Yankees organization. It helps a hitter develop rhythm in her swing. Use a batting tee. The hitter initiates the drill by properly gripping the bat with two hands. She then leans forward on the front foot and points the bat at an imaginary pitcher. She then draws the bat back in a low arc, pulling it back to the shoulder-height set-up position. Then she swings through the ball on the tee. Note the weight transfer from the front foot to the back foot and returning to the middle of the body in good midline balance. You can even use commands with young hitters: "Forward"…"Back"…"Balance." Another coach in the Yankees' chain advocates the use of three rhythmic swings, back and forth, before actually launching into the tee. Reminder; do not allow the hitter to stop during the course of the draw-back or the swing rhythm is the key…flow.

An interesting variation of this rhythmic drill can be found in Jack Perconte's book, <u>The Making or a Hitter.</u> Standing in front of a batting tee, he has the hitter lean forward with her weight on the front foot. The back foot is literally off the ground. She then rocks back so that the weight transfers to the back; the front foot is off the ground. Next, she strides and transfers the weight on to the hips as the swing takes place. Both feet will be firmly on the ground, the body is balanced and the hitter feels the weight centered at her "core," the hips and navel.

HITTING: VISUALIZING & MENTAL IMAGING   "I"

A lot of research has been dedicated to vision, reading the seam-rotation on the ball and even improving eyesight. Much as it is beyond the comprehension of young hitters and with the time constraints imposed on the typical high school coach, all this stuff becomes nebulous and a luxury that few coaches can afford.

Here are some drills and techniques that coaches everywhere and at every level can infuse into their program.

In my section on pitching, I spoke of the use of a camera to take still-shot photos of athletes. The same can be applied for hitters. Take a picture of the hitter's set up, her "trigger" and launch, her point-of-contact swing and then her follow-through. I generally take about five-to-eight shots in hopes of getting three good pictures that I can teach from. Pay particular attention to head movement, gauging it against some object in the background of the photo—a portion of the fence or a tree perhaps.

Another technique is to assemble a photo file of major league hitters. I have done this with pitchers, too. You can find these pictures anywhere: newspapers, magazines, even baseball cards. Clip, cut and paste. In this way you can literally show the young hitter what it means to roll the back heel, brace up the front leg, set the hands high and so on.

How about bringing a large dressing mirror to practice? As hitters take "air swings" (no tee or ball to hit), they can check themselves in the mirror. Have them look at their balance, their hands, their back-heel roll and so forth. You may wish to stick small pieces of tape on the mirror, replicating softballs that they can "aim" for.

As your young hitters mature, have them build in their minds a mental photo album, a "mental highlight film." Have them picture the perfect swing, as they have seen it and felt it. Tell them to mentally "feel" that laser line drive jumping off the bat and perfectly timed up the middle. As many sports psychologists have suggested, ask them to "see the result before it happens."

By the way, this is a good mental exercise for a hitter waiting on deck. As hitters mature, they can "picture success," success that they enjoyed in some previous game or some lower level of ball. A game-winning hit, the double that they crushed into the gap last week, and so on.

SWING ANALYSIS:

A) The hitter needs better knee flexion, more extension through the hitting zone and she needs to keep her head in and down to the tee (hitting zone). She has "leaked" forward a bit too much on her weight transfer, too.

B) This hitter's hands are too far back; she needs to lift them on top of her shoulders. The footwork is solid—front heel elevated when "loaded up" and her back heel roll is well done, too. Her weight transfer is fairly good. Good balance. She could keep her head down and in longer.

HITTING DRILL: PITCH SELECTION STITT'S SELECTIVITY DRILL   *"I"*

Jerry Stitt, renowned hitting coach from Arizona, advocated this unusual drill for hitters who chase balls out of the zone or even go after pitches in the zone that are not good ones to hit. Have the hitter set up a batting tee on one side of a screen or cage. She is to set the tee, with a ball on it, at what she feels is her optimal zone—her favorite spot to hit. Have a coach stand on the other side of the screen or cage wall and simulate a pitching motion. She throws the ball at the screen wall. Her aiming point is the ball on the tee. If she hits the "spot," the hitter can swing. If not, no swing.

HITTING DRILL: STITT'S FOCUS DRILL   *"I"*

The aforementioned Coach Stitt once described a "Command Drill" to improve hitter's focus. Throwing in a cage or even in conventional BP, have the hitter call out "Ball!" when she first sees the pitch coming at her. Then she calls out "Hit!" when she strikes the ball (actually when she begins her swing sequence). This is a great focus drill.

HITTING: FUNDAMENTALS & INTRICACIES T-WORK VARIATIONS   *"I"*

The batting tee is an old standby. Young hitters sometimes view it as "baby-ish" because they first learned off the batting tee in instructional youth leagues. This mindset must be broken as it is a fundamental tool used even at the highest level of ball.

Here are some uses of the batting tee that can help focus the hitter, break the aforementioned mindset and allow them to work on some of the esoterics of hitting.

A) **Conventional Tee Work:** Check stance, approach, swing plane, weight transfer and follow-through. As mentioned earlier, I like to use still-shot photographs to analyze hitters' technique and on the tee is where I photograph them.

B) In-Out Tees: Place the tee on the inside 1/3 of the plate and out in front of the hitter to work on pulling the ball. Insist on "clearing the hips" and getting the bat head out in front. For outside pitches, place the tee in the outside 1/3 of the plate and deep in the hitting zone. In this instance, the batter must "lead with the hands" (i.e. the bat head is actually behind the hands) and drive the ball to the opposite field. The diagrams below illustrate this concept.

RHB inside/outside tee placement

Legendary Coach Dan Litwhiler was known for his innovative teaching techniques and "gimmicks." Amplifying this drill, he developed a three-ball batting tee for players to work on inside, outside and pitches down the middle. Coach Litwhiler's tee is shown on the right.

A good drill that emerges from all of this is the **Double Tee.** While there are manufactured batting tees created for this very drill, it can be replicated by placing two batting tees side-by-side. The inside tee will be located on the inner 1/3 of the plate while the outer tee is set up on the outer 1/3. The outside tee should be about four to six inches lower than the outer one. Both are loaded with a ball. On command, the hitter triggers into her set-up position, holds and then waits for the command on "In!" or "Out!" before swinging at the appropriate tee. This teaches the hitter to keep their hands and weight back. It also teaches them to adjust to the inside and the outside pitch. For the sake of time efficiency, once the hitter has driven a ball off one tee, then set up and drive the other.

How about setting both tees at the same height in line with the plate and ask the hitter to drive one ball into the other? This teaches the hitter to stay "long through the zone." If you really want to challenge them, place the second ball on another tee ten, twenty even thirty feet away and then see if they can hit it. This is a great drill for teaching extension and driving the middle. You can also use the conventional double tee with both balls at the same height and have the hitter drive one ball into the other. For the hitter who "flies open" or "pulls off the ball," this is an excellent drill. A simple verbal cue might be to tell the hitter to imagine hitting three balls in a row.

C) **HI-LO Tees:** So many hitting coaches talk about the "downward approach" of the bat head into the hitting zone. Jim Lefebvre referred to this "The Power Curve" and it is discussed earlier in this book. An observant coach will focus on the knob of the bat to see that this is pulled down into the hitting zone by the lower hand. Note how the hitter "finishes high" rather than chops downward.

To work on this concept, one can use Hi-Lo tees specifically designed for this drill. One is shown below. One can also place two hitting tees, one behind the other with the one behind being slightly taller, perhaps 3 inches or so, than the one in front. I have seen other coaches use a chair instead of the rear tee.

D) Close Your Eyes: After a series of legitimate open-eyed cuts, have the hitter close her eyes and swing for the ball on the tee. There are studies that suggest that this helps focus and mental imaging.

E) Short-Bat Training: Use the batting tee in conjunction with half-bats or paddles to work on lower hand approaches or top hand extension described elsewhere.

F) Line Drive "Tunnel Hitting": Place a ball on a tee and have your hitters work on driving the ball directly back through the batting cage. This emphasizes "drive the middle" hitting and the hitter must really focus on hitting the ball squarely (not pulling off the ball) and driving it hard. Coaches may also opt to put an "L" screen about ten feet in front and have the batter work on hitting the upper squared portion of the screen.

Elsewhere in this book, I show a drill using a hula hoop suspended on the rear panel of a batting cage. Players are to drive the ball through the hoop. Tee work can be done in this fashion as well. How about stuffing a cluster of Styrofoam drinking cups in a chain-link fence have the hitter try to knock them through?

G) Tee String Drill: Tie a light string near the top of the tee and run it out perhaps 10-15 feet to the end of the batting cage. Tie it there, too. The hitter gets a visual image of line drive hitting. Tell the kids to literally "hit a frozen rope."

H) "Happy Gilmore" Drill: If you have seen the Adam Sandler comedy about the hockey player turned golf pro, then you know this drill. Gilmore would approach his tee shots by striding into them, much like a hockey player taking a slap shot. The ball would soar for miles. You can use this by having the hitter assume her batting stance a full step deeper in the box than she normally would. She then takes a cross-over step with the back foot crossing over in front of the front foot. The front foot then strides in front, recovering the stance. The hitter drives the ball. This has some benefits for teaching weight transfer, but mainly it helps with balance. It is also a fun drill.

Footwork for the "Happy Gilmore Drill"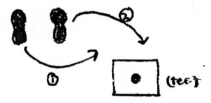

I have seen this drill done off front toss and side toss, too.

How about reversing the steps? Stand closer to the tee. Step behind the front foot and then stride into the tee with the front foot. Notice how it keeps the front shoulder down and in.

"Happy Gilmore Drill" Variation: Keep the front shoulder in.

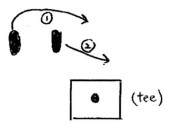

I) Knee-Down Drill: One way to isolate the upper body in hitting (and to emphasize the "downward approach" of the bat into the hitting zone) is to have the batter place her back knee on the ground as her front leg is fully extended in front. Keep everything on line to the pitcher as per normal. Have her hit tennis or wiffle balls off the batting tee from this position.

Insist that they extend the lead hand through the ball and actually point the paddle at the pitcher to create extension. (Some coaches may prefer to insist on a high follow-through, re-creating the Lefebre "Power Curve").

The hitter in this photo is not using a tee; she is preparing to hit off a short toss, but the drill position is identical.

J) The Roaming Tee: Be sure to set your batting tee at various heights and varying locations, in and out, within the strike zone. Hitters can work at these different locations as they focus on the proper hand mechanics to effectively hit pitches thrown to these spots. Make no mistake; there are subtle hand variations in the swing approach.

SET UP OUT SIDE: lead with the hands, dragging the bat head through the zone;

SET UP INSIDE: get the hips open and the bat head in front, pulling ball, in effect;

SET UP HIGH: get the hands on "top of the ball;"

SET UP LOW & IN OR LOW & AWAY: hitters may not always be comfortable hitting pitches thrown to these areas, but you must make them work on it.

The "Stacked Tee": You are working with a high school or college hitter and you want to get her to "get on top" of the ball. Place a batting tee on top of a cinder block or small garbage pail. The ball will be up around the letters of her uniform and hitting it will make her elevate her hands and elbows to "get on top" rather than upper cut a fly ball.

L) Soccer Ball Tee-Work: Balance a soccer ball on top of the tee (you may need to insert a bathroom plunger in the stem of the tee to get the soccer ball to rest on top). Obviously the hitter will be able to hit this massive object, but can they drive it with authority? That is the purpose of this drill—to drive the ball hard.

In teaching your hitters to work off a batting tee, did you ever stop to think about what their aiming point should be? Rather than just "aim for the ball," tell your hitters to cut the ball in half or, according to one theorist, have them strike the ball at the spot where it rests on the tee. This helps create the prized "back-spin line drive."

M) Swing Path Track: This is actually an outstanding teaching device, but it can be expensive. There are two parallel metal bars sloping downward toward a batting tee. They are spaced about 12 inches apart. Resembling a tuning fork, the track begins at shoulder height and the batter "slots" the bat head into the track. When she swings for the tee, she should strike no metal portion of the tracking device. This reinforces the "downward approach" very effectively. Insist on a high follow-through.

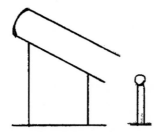

N) VOLLEYBALL BETWEEN THE KNEES—Have the hitter clamp volleyball between her knees to prevent over-striding. Set it high up in the upper thigh area (or better yet, let the hitter place it in there. We don't need lawsuits!). Note that the ball will drop out just prior to contact, but it certainly makes them aware of the concept. This can be done off side-toss, too.

O) **FRANK THOMAS DRILL**—Remember how Frank Thomas, "The Big Hurt" would hit off his front foot? His back toe was actually off the ground. Something that we do not want to teach beginning players, but we can use this as a corrective device. Set the ball on a tee and have the hitter stand on the front leg, back foot in the air; lock the front side (hence the lesson) and swing. There are young players who just cannot seem to bring their weight forward when they swing (no back heel roll; no weight transfer to the belly-button) and this drill can help that, but remind them that this is only a corrective drill, not a hitting fundamental.

P) **TEE ON THE MOUND**—One aspect of this was referred to earlier, but this version is for the hitter who collapses his back side. Set a tee on the downward front slope of a baseball pitcher's mound. When they swing, they will have to bring the weight forward and, moreover, they WILL brace up the front side or they will fall. Be forewarned—a mound is not that easy to find in a softball complex, so you may have to be creative.

HITTING: FUNDAMENTALS SUPPLEMENTAL STATIONARY BALL DRILLS   "T"

The batting tee is of course the most ubiquitous form of stationary-ball hitting work, but others exist.

A) **THE HITTING STICK:** Probably a trade marked name, this devise is essentially a hand-held rod with a ball at the end. It allows the coach to check everything that he or she would look for when their hitter works off a tee, but because there is no constant re-loading of the tee, use of this device is simpler and easier. Timing and separation can be examined as well. Have the hitter "load-up" on command; the "Hit-n-Stick" is down, the "ball" resting on the ground. The coach raises it to the hitting zone and only then does the batter swing to strike it. (Figure A)

B) **ROTATING BALL DEVICES**: There are simple devices that can be purchased and all of these can offer the coach additional hitting stations. Tony Gwynn's "Solo Hitter" and Derek Jeter's" Hit-a-Way" are two such devices. There is a ball that is suspended from the end of a short cord and attached to the chain-link fence of a backstop. (Figure B) There is a framed device in which the hitter attacks a ball situated on a bungee cord it springs back into place after contact. The former device has a downside in that the hitter must reach out and "settle the ball down" as it will keep vibrating in place after being struck. The latter can be a bit expensive. (Figure C) There also exists a batting tee that allows a rotating ball to return back to the hitter after it has been struck. On contact, the ball ricochets around in a circle. Some of these devices are made so that the hitter must reach out and stop it, settle it down and then swing again. (Figure E) Others operate with a spring-like attachment that allows for the ball to rebound back into position. A primitive, home-made type of rotational hitting tee can be this simple: the holder swings a ball attached to the end of a rope. Perhaps of minimal value, it can be a way to help teach a hitter to wait and read a curveball. Conversely, Coach Barnaba incorporated this drill into her station work. She believes that it not only helped her hitters to wait on the curveball, but it enhances focus as well.

C) **THE HITTING TREE:** This novel device can be made at home. Take a five foot length of either PVC pipe (perhaps 6-8" in diameter) or a 4X4 wooden piece of lumber (decorative "railroad ties" or two 2x4's fastened together. Drill holes at various heights as they would resemble spacing in a strike zone: knee high, belt high and up). Affix a flat base that will enable the "tree" to stand upright. Slide 3-foot sections of foam rubber pipe insulation (1/4" pipe insulation is actually 1 ½" in diameter and perfect for this device). Tape the ends with duct or athletic tape. These serve as targets. By having the pipe insulation hanging out from either side, two batters can work simultaneously. The hitter sets up, loads up and launches her swing into any of the three zones, whatever she needs to work on. A type of reaction drill can be developed with the "Hitting Tree" as well by having the hitter load up and wait for a command from his partner—"Up!", "Down!" or "Middle!". (Figure D) Two additional notes: a) the PVC pipe "tree trunk" can be damaged when a young batter inadvertently strikes it with her bat (why and how, I don't know...) and b) the pipe insulation cross pieces (i.e., the "targets," can frazzle, split and break down). Keep a few extra on hand; they are inexpensive.

Figure A—The Hitting Stick

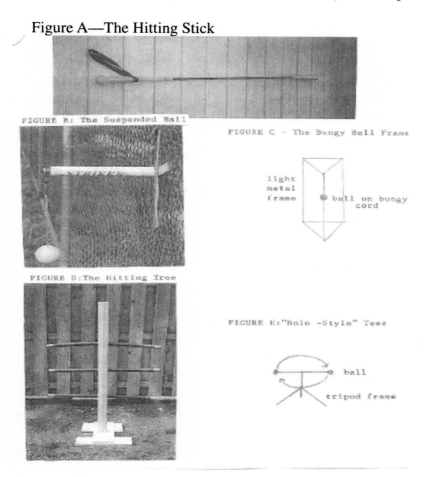

FIGURE B: The Suspended Ball

FIGURE C - The Bungy Ball Frame

light metal frame   ball on bungy cord

FIGURE D:The Hitting Tree

FIGURE E:"Bolo -Style" Tees

ball

tripod frame

HITTING: MISCELLANEOUS HITTING DEVICES & GIMMICKS   *"I"*

A) **SNAP CORDS INVOLVING A WIFFLEBALL**: A coach holds two nylon cords, one end in each hand and the other end is anchored by a clip against a fence. As the coach separates his or her hands with a quick snapping motion, the ball travels down the line toward a hitter near the fence. The batter hits away. (Problem: storage—the cords get maddeningly tangled!)

B) **SNAP CORDS AGAIN:** In this variation of the aforementioned drill, the coach holds a single nylon cord anchored at the other end by the fence. The ball is on the line, but near the hitting zone of the batter. They hit the ball back toward the coach; it travels down the cord. Re-set and repeat. We know of at least one D-1 college who swears by this drill.

C) **CHAIN BATS:** To instill the notion of snapping the bat head through the hitting, I have seen wooden bats sawn in half but connected with a chain. Hitters then fling the top half of the bat through the ball sitting atop the tee. Questionable value, not to mention safety.

D) **FLAT BATS:** Unlike the flat bat used for bunting, which has been described earlier, this bat has only about one inch of flattened surface. Thus, the bat remains strong and can be used for tee work and even live hitting. The object, of course, is to drive the ball off the flattened "sweet spot," thus increasing focus. Expensive unless home made.

HITTING & PITCHING: THE 3-COLOR PLATE   *"I"*

A good way to teach the concept of "in and out zone hitting," not to mention pitching, is to spray paint a portable home plate with three distinctly colored zones. Paint the inside one-third of the plate one color, the middle one-third another (preferably red so the hitter can relate to the notion of "dead red") and the outside one-third yet another color.

Teach the hitters to get the bat head out in front when the ball is short-tossed into the inside zone and to wait on the pitch when he or she reads it as an outside pitch. A respected coaching colleague, John Musolf from Manchester (NJ) High School, used to harp on his hitters, "React in, wait away!"

Teach your pitchers to throw into these zones as well. The painted plate gives excellent visual imagery cues.

HITTING: HITTING CURVEBALLS "SPINNERS"   "I"

Hitting the breaking ball is perhaps the most difficult aspect of an inherently difficult art. Hitting coaches can use these two simple devices to help their hitters "wait on the curve," read it and hit it.

Use plastic coffee can tops or the lids of Gatorade bottles. Flip them at the hitter—angle the top away from a right-handed batter and it will come in as a sweeping curveball from a right-handed pitcher. Reverse the wrist angle for a lefty pitcher's breaking ball.

I must give credit here—the coffee can lid idea came from Coach "Towny" Townsend (www.hittingdisc.com)[2] while the Gatorade top has been attributed to former LSU Hitting Coach Henry "Turtle" Thomas. Be forewarned—there is a technique to throwing these things that must be mastered, so you need to practice, Coach. Moreover, the Gatorade tops can get your attention if they are squarely hit and driven right back at you.

This is an excellent indoor drill that can be done in a confined space.

HITTING: SUPPLEMENTAL DRILLS TO ADDRESS HITTING FLAWS   "I"

Every hitter has her own way of doing things and this is not wrong. There is no universal template for hitting success. There are, however, certain absolutes that cannot be violated if a hitter is to enjoy success. We have already addressed many of them in this volume and have

2 Note that Townsend's tops are slightly larger than coffee can lids and are, arguably, a bit more effective (shown in middle).

suggested appropriate drills. For instance, if a hitter does not roll her back heel, put them through the "Itch Jones" Drill. For a player who "bar arms," breaking the "L" position in her front arm as she approaches the ball, we have suggested the use of the short bat or paddle in side-toss drills.

Here are some other remedial drills for hitters with flawed mechanics.

A) **Dropping the hands:** Besides using the short bats and paddles suggested earlier, try this simple method: Stand behind the hitter as they prepare to hit off a batting tee. Hold one hand on the knob of the bat, elevating it to the proper height and stabilizing it as the batter begins her swing. On the command, "Swing!", she must drive the bat head into the ball on the tee without dropping her hands. You are there to prevent exactly that. This drill gives them a good "feel" for what you are trying to teach. Be sure to back out of the way as the swing begins! Another technique calls for the use of the "doubletee" described earlier. Have two hitters swing through both balls set at the same height on the tee. This keeps their swing on a linear plane.

B) **Over-striding:** There are a couple of ways to address this flaw. Tying a young hitter's shoe laces together is an old standby. It can produce amusing results as well and it certainly gets their attention. The "stride board" is another method. One may purchase these commercially, but a home-made stride board can be easily constructed. A wooden board with a wood-block crosspiece will suffice. I have seen coaches place a brick on the ground so that the hitter's stride foot lands touching the edge on it.

C) **Poor Balance:** Make a balance beam. This simple 2 x 10" wooden board is perhaps 4-5' in length and covered with some sort of rug or Astroturf carpeting to prevent slippage. It can address two distinct hitting flaws. The "bucket-strider" who steps away from home plate and even out of the batter's box is common place in young hitters. By having them stand and stride on top of this board, they get the idea of striding toward the pitcher. The second issue is balance and the stride board certainly addresses that. In addition, the board reinforces the concept of "staying linear" within the line to the pitcher rather than rotating off line. If truly efficient, a coach could nail a crosspiece block of wood to help hitters who might have over-stride issues, as noted above.

The balance beam can also be useful in teaching a hitter to avoid chasing outside pitches. If they do, they fall off the board. And how about throwing pitches (short toss, of course) on the outside one-third of the plate? The hitter learns to wait and avoid lunging.

Stride Board/Balance Beam with Crosspiece:

If the balance beam is a little too hi-tech for you, simple draw a line in the dirt, parallel to the inside edge of the plate and in line with the pitcher. Besides having an effective tool with which to teach young hitters the concept of open and closed stances, you can also impart the principle of staying in line to the pitcher throughout the swing. I have seen some coaches place rope on the ground to assist in visualization.

A good teaching device that can serve both as a balance beam and as a tutor inhibiting the elongated stride is shown below. It is made up of 2 x 4's. The front crosspiece should be adjustable to accommodate differing sizes and strides, but a creative coach with a good workshop can build these using pegs to adjust the front board.

A variation of the same thing and simpler to make, is Jerry Stitt's "Stride Box" shown on the right. 2x4's or 4x4's nailed together at a right angle and place in the batters box. Note the holes. They are drilled so that you can anchor the Stride Box into the ground with long nails or spikes.

D) Not Setting the Weight Back: Some young hitters have a difficult time grasping this concept. First off, check their stride foot—is the front heel elevated? This is the simplest adjustment. Here, however, is a drill to get "the feel" of keeping the weight back. Bring the player in question out to a pitcher's mound if one is available. Have them assume a good balanced stance on the edge of a baseball pitcher's mound. Next, have them take their stride on to the slope of the mound. They will feel what it means to keep the weight back. Again, however, be sure that the front heel is elevated. Hint: use the back of the mound as the slope is greater, hence the "feel" of keeping the weight back is more pronounced.

E) Shoulder-to-Shoulder: For the hitters who turn their head out, another common problem, I would prefer to use numbered and colored balls, as described in the "focus drills" cited elsewhere. The simple drill described next is one that many coaches have employed over the years. It may be unrealistic in game conditions, but it can help a young hitter grasp the concept of keeping her "nose to the zone." Have her, in her balanced stance; place her chin on her front shoulder. Tell her that, as she swings, the chin must end up touching the back shoulder. As stated earlier, in a game this will not actually happen, but teaching through exaggeration can be of benefit.

F) Half-Swings & "Pepper": Here are two more drills for hitters who turn their heads out. One is novel; one is as old as the game itself. "Half swings" are exactly that—drive the bat head into the hitting zone, make solid, "on the screws" contact with the ball, but do not follow through on the swing. Frankly, this little drill technique is quite impossible to do if the batter turns his or her head out. It is analogous to "punching" the ball. Next, "Pepper," an old standby, but still valid as a hitting drill, even as a pre-game batting practice if time, space and league rules prohibit actual BP before a game. The problem is that too many kids just turn it into a haphazard slapping contest. No! Proper footwork, hand positioning and downward approach— not to mention "in and out" concepts of bat control—are to be emphasized and monitored coaches during this drill. Break your players up into "pepper groups" or four or five players, but have your coaches keep a sharp eye as to technique.

G)No Weight Transfer: Refer to the "Elephant Trunk Drill" described elsewhere.

H)Slow Bat: Simple maturation can help overcome this, but coaches can work to quicken their player's bats with the weighted bat, traditionally use by hitters on deck, or they can use the "Back Toss Drill" described elsewhere. "Dry" swings with a weighted bat can be helpful, perhaps in three sets of 15-20 swing reps. Keep in mind that what I have suggested here is for younger players, undeveloped in terms of physical maturity. For older players, there is some research that suggests using light broomstick handles to work on fast-twitch muscle fibers. Another simple method of developing swing strength is a two-man isotonic drill in which the batter assumes a stance and slow-motions her swing with a partner holding the barrel of the bat. The latter provides the resistance through the entire swing sequence. Yet another method is to employ "rapid fire" swings off a batting tee or off side-toss drills. Quickly feed and re-feed the hitter who must swing, recover and swing again and again. Perhaps twenty rapid-fire repetitions are a suggested rep-set.

I) **Fear of the Ball**: **Often** corrected through maturation, you can still teach young players to "roll" inward as they tuck their front shoulder inward. Use tennis balls for this drill. Having said that, isn't this a skill that players of all ages must learn? Line 'em up and "drill 'em" with tennis balls...obviously adjusting the force of your throw in accordance with the age of the batter.

J) **Upper-cutting:** (aka "dropping the hands") A good corrective drill for this is to have the hitter take side toss drills with their back knee down on the ground. Use a half-bat. They will find that if they drop the hands and upper cut the swing, they will be off balance and may actually fall backwards. Another corrective drill for this problem is the "Stacked Tee" Drill described elsewhere—placing a batting tee on top of a pail or cinder block with the ball at the very top of the strike zone, maybe even slightly out of it. This can help players "get on top" of the high strike.

K) **Improperly releasing the top hand on the follow-through:** Despite controversy, I admit to being an advocate of the one-handed release. I do not, however, teach this as part of my "fundamentals" package to young hitters. I use it primarily as a remedial device for hitters who turn their head out. (Look at major league hitters today—most of them release the top hand!) Young hitters learning this technique need to know exactly when to release the top hand. It is after the ball has left the bat and the bat head has passed the "front side" of the body. To teach this, have the hitters assume a stance, load up on command and then swing with no bat. Rather, the bottom hand is grasping the wrist of the top hand. They release the bottom hand only when they have driven both hands through the hitting zone. Insist on high finish.

L) **Front Foot Hitting:** Too much weight has dissipated forward when a hitter does this. The cue for the coach is to look at the hitter's front knee. If it is bent, the hitter has "lunged" at the ball and she has failed to "brace up" the front side (i.e. the front knee should be stiff and the front foot closed to a 45-degree angle inward). The hitter suffers from improper weight transfer. There are several drills that can teach this, drills such as the "Elephant Trunk Drill' off the batting tee, especially. The next drill, however, is designed to get the hitter to "feel" the front side brace-up. Set her up against a batting tee. Place it out in front a tad further than usual. Place the feet slightly wider apart than usual, too. Give her the command of "Brace up!". She straightens the front knee. With the next command of "Turn!", she rotates the back heel, "squishing the bug" as it were. No swing of the bat has yet occurred. Her feet are in the finished position and she should be perfectly balanced. Now she swings. She can feel the brace up, the balance and she can drive the ball off the tee. A good verbal cue is to have the hitter press their front heel into the ground as the back heel rolls.

Good coaches can see the finished product before the start. This drill was created with that in mind. The hitter is "finished" with her foot work and weight transfer before she has begun her swing. It is an excellent "feel" drill, but admittedly a bit awkward at first.

Described here are but a few of the remedial drills you can employ to help hitters with problems. In camps or in team practices, I have utilized station work in which one station is set aside as a "remedial station." Each hitter arriving there under goes a diagnosis from the coach and then the proper drill is prescribed and worked on.

HITTING: REMEDIAL DRILL FOR PLAYER WHO "FLIES OPEN"—   "I"
"DUSTY BAKER DRILL"

Dusty Baker, in his excellent book, (<u>You Can Teach Hitting</u>, Bittinger Books, Carmel, In, 1993), described a unique drill that can teach a hitter to keep his or her front shoulder in and prevent them from "flying open" or "pulling off the ball."

Have a player stand at the plate in a regular batting stance, but with both feet facing toward the pitcher. She is in the ultimate "open" stance, actually perpendicular to the plate (see diagram (1) below).

With her feet in this position, have her close her upper torso so that it is turned toward the plate. Her lower body is open, but her upper body is closed! Short toss her balls. She must try to hit them, which is going to be difficult at first. Once mastering this, now close her feet up so that they are parallel to the nearest baseline, or roughly at a 45-degree angle in the batter's box. (2) She continues to hit. Finally, line her feet up as if she were facing home plate and hitting normally. Notice how the front shoulder, if all went well, is staying closed now. (2)

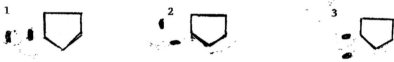

The "Happy Gilmore Drill" described elsewhere also helps keep the front shoulder in.

HITTING: KEEPING THE FRONT FOOT CLOSED "CINDERBLOCK DRILL"   *"I"*

One of the many "cues" for a hitting coach is the hitter's front foot. At the point of contact, the toe should be "closed" inward at about a 45-degree angle. If the front foot (aka the "stride foot") flies open so that the toe points toward the pitcher, then the hitter's entire front side has opened too early. Keeping the front foot and toe "closed" keeps the hitter from "flying open."

Here is another subtlety to look for: does the hitter spin open, after contact, on her front heel. While you will see many big leaguers do this very thing, it can be symptomatic of the hitter utilizing too much "spin" and not "staying on the ball" long enough. The hitter needs to stay closed as long as possible and drive her hands through the hitting zone, extending toward the pitcher. Spinning as a hitter is common, but it can cause problems.

To correct this problem, have the hitter stride or toe-tap into a cinder block placed where her stride foot would land. Hint: this can also be used to prevent over-striding, too.

How about this simple idea: smooth out the dirt and have the batter look at her footprint after each swing.

HITTING: FUNDAMENTALS DRILLS TO IMPROVE BACK HEEL ROLL   *"I"*

Everyone has their own way of saying it—"Rotate the back heel!", "Squash the bug!" or "Put out the cigarette!" (undoubtedly the most politically incorrect). Rotating the back heel ("Let the pitcher see the laces on your shoe!") is essential for weight transfer, getting on top of the ball, and power generation from the lower body. Every hitter must do this; it is one of hittings absolutes.

Many young hitters fail to do this, however. Here are some drills that can help:

A) **"Quick Draw":** With no bat in hand, both the hitter and the coach should face off against each other in their batting stances. The top hand on their imaginary bat is held up by the ear, atop the shoulders and in a simulated launch position. The coach counts "One, two, three—DRAW!" Upon this command, both the hitter and the coach will slice the top hand down to the rear hip as it rotates to another cliché—ridden position, with "the belly button facing the pitcher." Quickness is key as they slap their hip, pretend it is a gun being drawn as if in an old western shootout. Look at the result—the heel will have rolled into the proper upright position.

B) THE "ITCH JONES HIP DRILL": Legendary Illinois baseball coach, Richard "Itch" Jones often spoke at Jack Hawkins' "Be The Best You Are" Baseball Coaches Clinic, held every year in Cherry Hill, New Jersey. One of the many drills that he demonstrated was this one designed to enhance back heel roll. He placed a fungo bat against the small of his back, holding it in the crook of his elbows, as shown below. The bat barrel thus protruded out over the plate extending from the back hip. The player assumed a batting stance with the feet properly aligned. The coach tosses softy balls in an underhanded fashion toward home. The batter would swing, attempting to hit. Try it. You cannot hit the ball without proper hip and rear leg action.

This drill is particularly good for female hitters as it emphasizes hip and leg action. According to some studies, women have 65% less upper body strength, hence the need to emphasize hip and leg action. To put it another way, in women's softball, the power comes from the legs and hips.

   C) KICKBALL DRILL: Place a soccer ball near the back heel of the hitter. As they swing, the ball will roll away as the back heel rolls, bringing the hips through the swing. A subtle yet effective reminder as a reinforcement drill for young hitters.

HITTING: SETTING THE WEIGHT BACK "THE BACKWARD STRIDE DRILL"   *"I"*

I picked up this drill from a long-forgotten softball coaching book and have used it often for young hitters who do not get enough power off the back side.

The hitter assumes a balanced stance; the bat head is pointing straight up to the sky. On command, the player takes a stride with the back foot toward the catcher. In doing so, they now "load up" on the back leg and "trigger" the hands, "stacking them on the shoulder" and with the bat in a good, cocked position.

HITTING: THREE DRILLS FOR KEEPING THE HANDS "INSIDE THE BALL"   *"I"*

Good coaches "see things." They recognize flaws and make corrections. In a sense, a good coach is like a doctor—they diagnose the problem and prescribe a remedy. One aspect of hitting that many coaches do not often see is when a hitter, particularly a young one, "loops" her hands, holds them too far away from her body and fails to "keep her hands inside the ball." For instance, take a look at a hitter's back elbow when she swings. It actually clamps against her abdominal flank. Now, this is something that you may not literally teach, but it is something to look for. If a hitter fails to do this, she is opening her hands and creating a "hole" in her swing.

A coaching colleague, Kevin Oberto, describes the action of the back elbow in this way:

"Ask players if they have ever skipped a rock across a pond. Have them demonstrate how they did it. Point out back elbow. To skip a rock, back elbow must come into their side. Explain that's where the elbow goes during the swing."

DRILL # 1: "THE BELLY BUTTON DRILL"

A good drill to teach a hitter to keep her hands "inside" and relatively close to her body is this one:

a) Have the hitter stand facing a fence or wall, or even the netting on a batting cage,

b) She is to hold a bat out from her navel (hence, the name of the drill) perpendicular to the ground and straight out; the bat head touches the wall; the bat handle touches the hitter's stomach,

c) The batter sets up in her stance, loads up properly and then swings, all within this confined space. If she grazes the fence, fine, but the loop in her swing will become abundantly clear if she pounds the fence.

Something else to look for: young hitters will compensate by looping the bat head downward when they do this drill. Insist that they stay reasonably level through the hitting zone.

DRILL # 2: "CLAMP THE BACK ELBOW" DRILL

Place a rolled up towel or pad of some sort under the back elbow so that the hitter must keep it clamped against her side as she swings. If she opens up the swing, or "loops" it, the towel will drop out.

DRILL # 3: "BACK TO THE WALL" DRILL

Have the hitter stand inches away from a fence. The back foot may even rest in contact with the bottom edge of the fence. Have them take "air swings" or work off a tee hitting into a portable "sock net". This drill teaches the hitter to take a "short" approach to the ball and prevents "bar-arming" back away from the ball.

HITTING: HANDS INSIDE & STAYING LINEAR "LONG'S SHORT TOSS"   *"I"*

This drill is a variation of the "Belly Button" and New York Yankees hitting Coach Kevin Long is a big advocate. You need a left-handed "pitcher" (any lefty can throw) against right-handed batters and vice versa, RHP vs. LHB.

The hitter stands one bat length away from the edge of the screen. The coach stands along the same side of the screen and underhand tosses to the batter. A tall screen is necessary (the vertical or higher side of an L-screen is fine). This is a "live" hitting drill. Notice how their swing is compact, their hands are "inside" and they are staying on the ball longer. Their footwork stays linear, too. It's all good.

Coach Long said that he did this drill with Alex Rodriguez as they entered the 2009 playoff series against the Angels. It helped A-Rod handle the inside pitch.

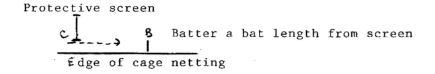

Protective screen

c⌐¯   ß   Batter a bat length from screen

Edge of cage netting

HITTING: BATTING PRACTICE IN THE CAGE   *"I"*

Too many inexperienced coaches, not to mention "Little League Dads," think of "batting practice" as one kid is hitting, someone pitching and everyone else are standing around. Even for those who love The Game, this can be stultifying in its boredom. The message here is simple: Be creative.

Many of the focus drills listed in this volume are actually best employed in the batting cage. Here are some other drills that can be utilized to make "BP" something special.

SHORT "MOUND:" Never pitch from a full 43' distance in the batting cage or on the diamond. Shorten it up; you will be able to throw more strikes Justify it, if you must, by telling the hitter that the ball gets "in on her" more quickly from this distance, thus appearing as a faster pitch.

Furthermore, what is going on when you are throwing in the cage? If you have your entire team present, think of other options:

    a) Drape a net down the middle, splitting the cage in half and have two batters, hitting simultaneously, back-to-back from the middle of the cage.

    b) Set up batting tees, Hit-n-Sticks, and side toss stations along the outside of the cage so that more kids are getting more swings. Set up a "Bat Tree" or have kids hitting wiffle-golf balls.

    c) Work other aspects of skill development—a fielding station, a weighted ball throwing stations, a wall-drill station, etc., etc. Again, be creative.

Keep the stations brief, under ten minutes. With young softball girls in a practice I ran just recently, they were paired up for six stations that ran only three minutes in length. If you understand young attention spans, you will know why.

TENNIS BALL "DART TOSS": Kids love to hit tennis balls. They jump off the bat and even the youngest hitters can "crush" them. Go with this. Since tennis balls are smaller than softballs, it helps tighten their focus. Moreover, they are easy to throw. Use a dart-like throwing motion from a short toss distance and you can throw to different parts of the strike zone, perhaps even an area where a hitter is not particularly efficient.

IN & OUT: Hitters of all ages must be taught how to recognize and adjust to pitches thrown on the inside and outside edges of the plate. Short toss, especially with tennis balls thrown in the "dart-like" fashion described above can help facilitate this. Throw a series of pitches on the outside one-third of the plate and then a series on the inside one-third. Each requires a slightly different hitting adjustment. For the outside pitch, be sure that they "let the ball get deep," lead with the hands and drive it against the opposite wall of the cage. For the inside pitch, they must "clear the hips" and get the bat head out in front of the hands, hitting the ball early and pulling it. You can use the batting cage walls as your reference points.

CAGE GAMES:
A) **"Line Drive Derby":** I don't teach the uppercut swing, hence traditional "Homerun Derby" is, to me, counter productive. I teach line drive hitting, thus the name of this cage game. The coach simply counts the number of line drives a hitter will produce. Set a goal of "20 smokers in 5 minutes" or award some recognition for whomever can hit the most LDs in 15 pitches.

B) **"Hit a Hundred":** Do-able particularly if you are working with one hitter in the cage for an extended period of time, this is an excellent confidence-builder. You have a young hitter who is struggling at the plate. Identify what she needs to do mechanically to get things right and then set a goal of 100 base hits in the cage. It really does not take as long as you might think. Count every hit, even though some (many?) might not actually go through for base hits on a diamond. Obviously foul balls do not count. For some hitters, a realistic adjustment of this game might be "Hit 50" or "Gimme 25."

C) **"Back Through the Box":** Set a goal for the hitter to drive a set number of line drives directly back up the middle. Each hit must strike the upper protective square on the "L" screen or it must hit the back end of the cage. This drill helps hitters with their timing and focus.

D) **"Tracking":** Admittedly, this is not so much a game as a teaching drill. For a hitter who lacks "strike zone discipline" and chases everything, have them assume a hitting stance and not swing at any balls. Rather, she simply calls out "Ball!" or "Strike!" identifying the pitch.

Another type of "tracking" can be utilized if you have a sufficiently skilled pitcher. Have her throw her rise ball, drop, change-up and so on. The batter reads the spin and calls out what pitch has been thrown. I have often though of producing a training video for this...any takers?

There is yet another tracking drill that can help with pitch location identification. Cut a piece of plywood into the shape of a home plate. Paint seven baseballs across the top of it, each with a number, one through seven. Underhand toss to the hitter who does not swing. Instead she calls out the number of the painted ball over which the thrown ball travelled. This is good for focus and reading the inside/outside pitch.

E) Situational Hitting: This is an excellent drill for more advanced hitters and it can provide a productive variation in the cage. In the first "situation," have the hitter look for "her pitch." Tell the batter that they have no strikes on them—they are to look for their optimal pitch on the first strike, the one that they most prefer and the one that they know they can drive. It generally will be a belt-high fastball. Have them swing only at this pitch, even if the pitch is a strike, but not in the hitter's preferred zone. In this situation, the count is 0-0 or 2-0 or even 3-0 and you have given her the "green light." For the second situation, have the hitter look for a pitch that she can drive to the right side of the infield as there is a runner on second base. Teach them to go the "opposite way" and hit behind the runner. She is obviously looking for something on the outside one-third of the plate. The third situation has a runner on third base with less than two outs. Teach the hitter to look for "something up in the zone," a pitch that they can hit out of the infield. They look for something at the belt or above so they can drive a base hit or lift a sacrifice fly to get the runner in. They must avoid going after the low pitch, even if it is a strike, since that will generally produce a ground ball which may not get the runner in. Other situations that can be incorporated into this drill could include the hit-and-run or the suicide squeeze bunt. New York Yankees hitting Coach Kevin Long advocated this one: two outs, runner in scoring position. Get a hit. Prolong the inning.

F) **Play a Game:** A particularly effective approach with young ball players is to award points for the quality of each batted ball and after having set a goal of, for example, 50 points. Another variation is to pit two imaginary teams against each other. Assess each batted ball as a single, double, triple, fly ball out, or ground ball out based on pre-set demarcations on the cage. All runs must get "forced in" and runs are tallied against innings where the batter does not score any runs, thus awarding a run for the defense.

I know of one creative hitting instructor who had made up laminated cardboard signs attached to coat hangers. They designated doubles, triples and homeruns. She hung them on the outside wall of the batting cage and kids played a game accordingly.

G) **Simulated Game:** Professional hitters on rehab assignment often resort to his drill, so it is much more serious and workmanlike than the "game" noted above. Real pitches are thrown, there is an "umpire" either in the cage or outside of it, a count and score are kept and imaginary runners are on base. As a hitter may get three, four or even five at-bats in a game, so be it here as well. The hitter must be "convinced" that everything happening is "live." Think about adding in live signs, too. The batter steps out, checks the sign and then bunts, hits-&-runs, whatever. This can be a good review.

H) **Live in the Cage:** This was written up as a drill for pitchers. Refer to "BP Combat" in the pitching segment of this volume.

I) **Two-Strike Hitting:** Teach bat control and prolongation of at-bats by having the hitters face two-strike situations. Simply tell them that they "stay alive" in your batting practice if they manage to drive good pitches, foul off marginal ones and lay off pitches that are out of the strike zone. You can make it into a game by lining hitters up at home and parade them to the plate with the admonishment that the length of their stay at the plate depends on how long they can "battle." There will be a lot of quick outs, cat calls and good natured ribbing during the course of this drill.

J) **DiMaggio Drill:** What everyone most remembers about "Joe D" is the remarkable 56 game hitting streak. The drill that emanates from this is particularly good for young hitters. Have them try to piece together their own hitting streak. Foul balls do not count against them, nor do called strikes. This makes them more selective and it helps focus them. If they swing and miss, the streak ends and a new one begins. This is a good drill for building consistency.

K) **The Line-up Game:** Again, for younger hitters, this is a drill they enjoy. Ask them what their favorite major league team is. Hopefully, it is one that you and your young protégée know the batting line-up for, or at least the key hitters. Then pick the rival opponent—you as the pitcher is that rival, even to the point of naming a key pitcher on the opposing team. Set up a challenge: name each hitter in the batter's line-up, throw strikes, have them hit away, call the shots as a single, double in the gap or down the line, homer, etc., etc. And always let the batter win...

L) **Round the Clock:** Begin with a short toss. Ask the hitter to time her swing so that she hits one ball pulled foul, another down the line, another in one gap followed by another directly up the middle. Then shoot the other gap, then down the line and finish with another foul ball. This is very difficult, but it does teach bat control.

M) **The No-Hit Cage**—Technically a misnomer, but why not set up one cage or one circuit through the cage when the hitter works only on strategic bunting (sacrifice, bunt right or left, suicide bunt, but-for-a hit or slash)? Great focus and technique work.

As many of these "Cage Games" can be utilized by coaches giving private batting instruction, as I do, allow me to suggest the following formula when dealing with hitters under your tutelage:

1. Assessment
2. Remediation
3. Visuals
4. A Game

By assessment I mean looking at the hitter's swing without saying a word. Many coaches prefer the tee, but I like the hitting stick. I spot what needs to be worked on and then I apply the appropriate remedial drills to correct their flaws. I then go to visual drills, one or two, as described earlier in this volume (I prefer the numbered balls side-tossed and/or wiffle golf balls). Then I close with a contest or game, especially if I am dealing with younger hitters, perhaps in the seven to twelve age range.

Here is another point to consider: if you have access to multiple hitting stations, do you have enough live arms to throw BP? There is a talent pool out there. In the community, you might have former players and even ex-coaches who might welcome a call from you to come in and throw.

I will never forget the day that a coaching colleague, Art Gordon from Manasquan (NJ) High School, set up a four-station batting practice in which his hitters saw nothing but lefties. I was called in, and actually left my team's practice early to assist him, as I am a lefty, too. His team was facing a talented left-hander the next day in a game with league championship implications, so he wanted to throw mostly curves in my station…my arm hurt for a month afterward.

HITTING: INDOOR GAME "TENNIS BALL WORLD SERIES"   *"I"*

Snow covers your field or perhaps it's been raining for several days. You have taken your team through day after day of indoor drills. They are getting stale; they need a change. Here it is.

Throw a set of bases out on the gym floor and choose up teams. Maybe it's pitchers against position players or infield versus outfield. Flip a coin to see who hits first. Everyone plays defense, so you might have seven, even a dozen players scattered around your make shift "diamond." Pitchers "pitch," players catch and throw—everything goes, including bunts.

The difference is the ball—it is a tennis ball and what kid does not like to crush tennis balls? You may prefer to use a stickball bat, turning your game into a "city game." Set markers and ground rules— off an overhead light is an out, off the right side wall but above the flag pole is a double in the gap, off the basketball backboard is a homerun—whatever suits your facility. Runners run the bases, but no "pegging" is allowed. Three outs per inning as per normal. Make it raucous and make it fun.

HITTING: LINE DRIVE DERBY

This is a fun, competitive game that can not only break up "BP" but also keep your hitters focused on what they are taught to do: hit line drives.

Remember the numbers (in professional softball)—17 percent of all pop-ups fall for base hits (that's a .170 batting average) while 40 percent of grounders go through for base hits and 80 percent of line drives are hits…that's hitting .800!

Divide the team in three squads. This will be a round robin tournament. Team One plays vs. Teams Two and Three in the field, followed by 2 vs. 1 & 3 and then 3 vs. 1 & 2. The defense can position themselves anywhere they wish.

Each team goes through the order twice and all line drives are counted, even soft liners. No balls can first strike the infield dirt, however. Hard hit liners that are caught will count. Each hitter gets three-to-five pitches.

Rewards can be fewer sprints, or no equipment pick-up, even a large watermelon. Yeah, did that one and then gave in, giving slices to the other two teams. I had to do something to brighten the long faces.

HITTING: COMPETITIVE GAME "BARNABA-BALL"

Coach Pat Barnaba got very creative one day and thought this one up. Divide the squad into three teams as indicated above. Two teams will be on defense while a third hits. It becomes a game of points. She says that it also "gets very competitive."

Each batter stands in with a 3-2 count. They will earn points if they "keep the line moving" with a walk, base hit, sac-fly, sac-bunt, stolen base, hit behind a runner, getting hit with a pitch, scoring a run—just about anything that is positive from an offensive standpoint. If they fly out, ground out or strike out, no points are allocated and the outs count toward a six-out inning.

Defensively, the teams get points for making plays—put outs, strike outs, etc. and spectacular plays can be given extra points. In recording the points on a groundball put-out, remember that there is a point for the assist and appoint for the actual put-out.

This can be done indoors, but it takes even more creativity as you must assess points for tennis balls hit off lights, walls, and so forth. But like any coach, you can certainly make it up as you go along... Be sure to reward the winning team and remember that there are three scoring totals as there are three teams.

HITTING: ORGANIZING YOUR BATTING PRACTICE

It has often been noted that one of the things that turns kids off to the game of softball is the boredom of standing around during team batting practice (BP). The coach must overcome this with organization and creativity.

Organize BP into small-team units, perhaps positional. In this way, you will have two, three or four kids hitting, perhaps another group running the bases and two others fielding, one unit on the right side and another on the left side of the field. Rotate them into the hitting station.

Place a screen by the first baseman and another, if you have one, out behind second base. Have two fungo hitters working each side of the field. Ideally they will hit between pitches, but realistically they hit a couple of fungoes in between batters, during ball retrieval, and during other times when there is a break in the action. They can hit fungoes when the batters are bunting, too. If you wish to have the fielders on the left side throw to first, the screen protects the first baseman. The screen out behind second also has a bucket behind it and this is where balls hit to the outfield are fed for re-feeding the pitchers. You will, therefore, need a girl "working the bucket."

Remember, softball is a game of repetition; the fielders need "reps" and you can provide them during BP. Just time them properly. Moreover, get the players moving, working and involved. Eliminate the boredom factor.

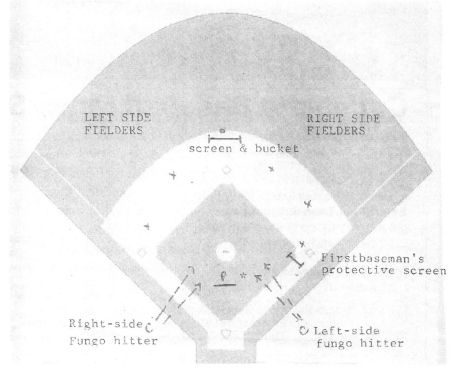

LEFT SIDE
FIELDERS

RIGHT SIDE
FIELDERS

screen & bucket

Firstbaseman's
protective screen

Right-side
Fungo hitter

Left-side
fungo hitter

Pitcher throwing from an abbreviated distance.

HITTING: A 4-STATION HITTING CAGE
Would you like to economize your hitting area? Who wouldn't? Try this one—I saw it on a Little League field and love the concept.

Place four square screen in a "plus sign" arrangement (the field I saw this on had four permanent screens):

Think of the possibilities: a) corner one has side toss
b) corner two has bunting
c) corner three has wiffle golf ball hitting
d) corner four has tee work

Or any combinations thereof…

HITTING: BATTING PRACTICE "BIG LEAGUE BATTING PRACTICE"
Divide your squad into three groups—one shagging in the field, one at the plate and one running the bases. It is obviously preferable to place the defensive unit in their proper positions in the field, but this is not always practical. Your groups should be five or six players, but another way to make this work with an eye toward realistic defensive alignment is to divide the team in two groups. The defensive team will be comprised of players who actually play those positions while the offensive group is sub-divided into hitters and base runners.

Allow me to focus on the hitting group. Give each hitter five pitches. On the first round, they simply hit; no one runs the bases yet. But on the second round, the runners are lined up, as a group, at first base. The batter bunts them to second (sacrifice) on the first pitch; she works on "hitting behind the runner" to get them over to third on the second pitch and then lays down a suicide or safety squeeze bunt to get them in from third base. The runners jog around to first again. The fourth pitch becomes a hit-and-run and with the runner either on second, or preferably third, the batter drives them in with a sac-fly or base hit. In every instance, the runners are executing proper reads while the batter is working on various dimensions of bat control. There is a good conditioning element to this drill, too.

Variations of this form of "BP" certainly exist. You can break the aforementioned into two at-bats if you prefer. I do suggest that you allow at least a third round of free-swinging BP so that the kids get a sufficient number of "cuts." Another variation is to have a fourth group of players in the batting cage getting their swings as you work directly with those on the field. Think it through, but be sure to include these elements:

- Bunt for a hit
- Bunt-and-run
- Sacrifice bunt
- Lefty slap/Righty push-bunt
- Hit behind runner at second
- Sac-fly with runner on third
- Suicide or safety squeeze

Keep the at-bats to a mere five swings as this not only keeps things moving but it also replicates a true time at bat (statistics indicate that a batter faces something just a little over four pitches per plate appearance).

This type of BP keeps everyone moving and everyone thinking. And that's a good thing.

Another hint: We all want our base runners reacting aggressively on a "dirt ball," so why not throw one every now and again in this type of BP? See if your runners react properly and break for the next base.

HITTING: "DOUBLE-TIME BATTING PRACTICE"

I once observed Keystone College in eastern Pennsylvania take their pre-game batting practice in this fashion. There were two home plates, two batters separated by an upright screen, and two pitchers behind two L-screens. They threw alternately so rarely, if ever, did the two batters hit a ball simultaneously as this would constitute a potential hazard to fielders. In addition, when an infield pop-up was hit, the pitcher would hold off on throwing so as to allow time for the fielder, whose attention is focused skyward rather than toward home, to catch it. It was unique and it was efficiency in motion. I think softball coaches can work this system, too.

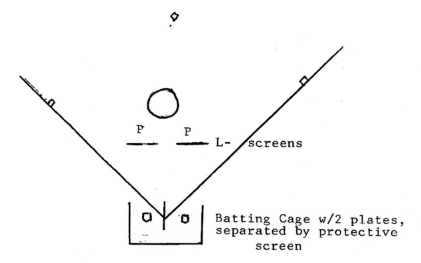

"Showcase" and tournament directors take heed. You can run a lot of kids through "BP" in a short period of time using this format.

HITTING: CREATIVE BATTING PRACTICE "RBI BATTING PRACTICE"

A good way to create some excitement in batting practice is to place a runner on second and spread a defense out on the field to try to prevent her from scoring. The batter gains a heightened focus as she seeks to drive the run in. The defense works on cut-offs and relays.

Make sure that this is a hitter's game—have the coach do the pitching. You want the ball hit somewhere. In addition, you may find that the hitter only succeeds in getting the runner over to third. So be it—the next hitter gets to drive her in.

Bring the infield in. Work on pressure situations. How about bringing the outfield up as if it were a tie game in the bottom of the last inning?

Chart this type BP. You can find out who drives in runs when you are making your preseason player evaluations. I have even used this drill with youth league teams.

HITTING: CREATIVE BATTING PRACTICE: "CONE DRILL"

Statistically, most base hits go up the middle. Studies done on the major league and collegiate level verify this. Another way to structure your batting practice is to place two traffic cones in the right-centerfield and left-centerfield gaps, roughly behind the shortstop and the second baseman. Have the batter work on hitting it between the cones. In this way, they will "drive the middle." You can randomly station shaggers out the "cone zone" or place a defense in formal, assigned positions to work on that aspect of the game. I would not suggest using base runners for this drill. This is a repetition and focus drill. With an element of creativity, you can turn this into a game by awarding points for the quality of the hit or allow a hitter to remain at the plate as long as she keeps driving base hits up the middle.

HITTING: USE OF THE PITCHING MACHINE

Pitching machines can be a source of controversy. I would never use them in youth instructional leagues below that of Little League "majors." However, pitching machines do have a use. They can be great equalizers for try-outs. Every kid attempting to make the varsity sees the same number of strikes. They can be useful out of doors for fielding drills as well, as topic to be discussed elsewhere. A good coach can show breaking pitches to her hitters. I have often felt that a station of nothing but curveballs from a righty or lefty, depending upon who your team is facing the next day, can be very effective. Pitching machines can help save arms during pre-season workouts, too. They definitely have their place in your program.

However, there is a school of thought that tells coaches to shut down the pitching machine once the regular season gets underway, lest hitters lose their sense of timing. I also suggest a simple technique in feeding machine. Replicate the pitching motion. Give the hitter a full arm arc as you feed the ball into the machine. This simple device helps with timing.

Pitching machines today come in every variety. Yet still, there are players who shun them. True, the ball arrives in the hitting zone as planned, generally speaking, but hitters complain that there is just not the same "feel" and that they cannot get their timing down against a machine.

FIELDING & DEFENSIVE DRILLS

"For me, winning isn't something that happens on the field when the whistle blows and the crowds roar. Winning is something that builds physically and mentally every day that you train and every night that you dream."
NFL HOF Running Back Emmitt Smith

Fielding is multi-dimensional. There are nine defensive positions on a softball diamond and each position has its own nuances and techniques. We open this segment with the catcher, offering techniques and drills to enhance her performance. We then move to the infielders to discuss their techniques and particulars, everything from fundamentals to positional techniques. Then, it is the outfield. Footwork drills are included for each position.

FIELDING & DEFENSIVE DRILLS: PART I—CATCHERS
"I"

CATCHERS: STANCE CHECK BASIC SET-UP

Begin with the simplest notion: What is the most efficient stance a catcher can assume? There are basically two types of stances, depending upon the game situation. With no runners on base, I allow the catcher to sit, squat, even kneel—whatever is comfortable and allows him to present a properly placed target. Remember Tony Pena? He would kneel down on his left knee with the right leg extended out to the side. Purists cringed, but with no one on base, what is the difference? The only thing I would insist upon is the placement of the throwing hand in a protective, out-of-the-way position. Keep it behind the back or underneath the thigh. A foul tip can cause not only a painful injury but also a season-ending one. The stance referred to here is "The Receiving Stance."

Everything changes when a runner is on base. The catcher should drop the right foot back slightly and open it a bit, perhaps to a 45-degree angle. Her butt should be on a plane parallel to her knee. The target is presented with the throwing hand balled into a fist just behind the glove. The catcher must be able to explode out from her crouch and into a solid, efficient throwing position. She must be quick on the transfer of the ball into the throwing hand and everything—throwing hand, ball, back elbow and even the glove are elevated to shoulder height and in line with second base. The stance referred to here is "The Block/Throw" Stance.

Be sure to check how your catchers present the target. Look for a subtle bend to the elbow and a relaxed glove position. Have them point the fingers in their glove hand toward the pitcher. This is much easier on the forearm than a taut, tight, vertically aligned glove.

There is another item to check when you examine your catchers' stances: giving the sign. Teach them, as part of this drill, to give their signs so that the fingers are not below the butt and thighs. The right knee points to the first baseman while the glove, set in a relaxed position outside and below the left knee, blocks the view of the third base coach. Also, there must be minimal arm and elbow movement. As a long-time first base coach, I was often able to pick signs and location by simply looking at the catcher's elbow movement as she gestured for an inside or outside pitch.

CATCHERS: DRILLS TO IMPROVE FUNDAMENTALS *"I"*

A) FOOTWORK DRILLS: Catchers need quick feet. Let us examine the footwork involved in the throw to second base. From the block/throw stance, the catcher can adopt any of three techniques:

- Pivot on the right foot
- Jump-pivot on the right foot
- Forward step with the right foot

The coach can easily check these things by "shadow' drills included in an agility series specifically designed for catchers. Emphasize quickness. The drill can involve a whistle signal, a "Go!" call or even an underhand ball toss. All are designed to have the catcher explode into her launch position for a throw to second base. The latter can be a particularly effective drill if the coach stands about ten feet in front of his catcher, tosses a ball underhand and then watches as the catcher executes the proper technique.

Coaches can easily transform this drill to teach the footwork involved in the throw to third base and the pickoff throw to first base. Teach the right knee drop technique for pickoff throws to first and any of a couple of footwork techniques for the throw to third:

- Step behind the batter
- Jump-pivot
- Right foot replaces the left foot in a step-and-throw sequence.

    Note that none of these drills involve actual throws; hence they can be done in confined spaces.

B) CLOSING UP: Ancillary to the footwork drills, but equally important to a catcher's efficiency ratio in throwing out runners going to second, is the "close up." The essential purpose is to get the shoulders directly in line with the second base. Look for three components:

- Right foot directly on the throwing line to second
- Ball drawn back to a throwing position in a line rather than a circular arc
- Glove drawn back toward the rear shoulder.

Again, no throws are necessary to practice this technique. Make it part of the footwork check and put it all together, emphasizing quickness.

C) TRANSFER: The transfer of the ball from the glove to the throwing hand is another skill that can be improved with practice and drills.

The "Pop Drill"—have catchers work on "popping" the ball from the pocket of the mitt into their hand. With practice, they can do this without closing the glove itself, much like a middle infielder on a double play pivot. Andy Lopez, in his book, <u>Coaching Baseball Successfully,</u> suggested an excellent coaching point for teaching this to his catchers—never let the hands and glove drop below the uniform letters in making the transfer. Coaches might further consider using tennis balls with the bare hand to further enhance their catchers' focus on proper hand action.

Yet another idea: use "paddle gloves' (described elsewhere). Once your catchers learn the proper techniques involved in "popping" the ball from the glove to the throwing hand, as well as the proper footwork, arrange a competitive scenario: time them. How many throws can they make in ten seconds? Essentially having a "catch," they will compete against the clock in attempting to increase the number of throws. They will learn that efficiency equates with sound fundamentals.

"Get a Seam"—Have the catchers give the ball a slight twist with the thumb so that their index and middle fingers are on a seam. Why? The ball will have less of a tendency to "sail" as the catcher is essentially throwing a four-seam fastball rather than a breaking ball to second.

Combine these two techniques. Have the catchers simply play "Catch" from distances of perhaps 25 feet. They can work on "popping the ball" (while using two hands and aligning the shoulders, I might add) and spinning the ball to "get a seam" as another phase of the same catch.

Having stated all this, it must be added that "popping" a softball may be more difficult given its sheer size when compared to a baseball. Coach Barnaba is of a different mindset on this: she is a proponent of taking the ball out of the glove. In her view, it minimizes fumbles and helps get the catcher into an efficient throwing position. Experiment.

D) ARM STRENGTH: First of all, set realistic goals for your catchers. On both the high school and junior college level I told my catchers that I asked them for "30-70." If they could throw out 30 percent of the runners attempting to steal second and 70 percent of those going for third, I would be happy.

Arm strength as well as proper technique and footwork are all components of what allows a catcher to achieve those numbers.

Catchers can use a controlled weighted ball program exactly like the one described for pitchers earlier in this volume. Distances are no longer than twenty feet and there is a prescribed number of throws involved.

Throwing from the knees is another excellent drill. Place five softballs in front of a catcher who is on her knees. She will pick up each ball in turn and throw them 84 feet to another catcher standing and receiving. The latter collects the ball; she does not throw them back. Upon receipt of all five balls, the receiver drops to her knees and replicates the drill. Catchers must use proper upper-body "close-up." They must resist the temptation to drop the throwing arm elbow in a misguided effort to obtain distance. Tell developing catchers that it is better to skip the ball than air-mail it. Each sequence involves five throws, it is up to the coach to determine how many sets, and total throws, she will demand of his catchers. Err on the side of caution so I might suggest no more than three to five sets. They should ice their arms after a practice session involving this drill.

A developmental sequence derived from this drill is found in Winning Softball Drills by Dianne Baker and Dr. Sandra S. Cole. This book is a standard for any softball coach and has been around for a long time. Relative to this arm-strengthening drill is a progression in which catchers throw to each other from an initial distance of 30-feet and lengthen their throwing distance in ten-foot increments until they are consistent at the regulations 84-feet. Might I suggest three throws at each distance—30, 40, 50, 60, 70, 80 and perhaps 90. This would accumulate to 21 total throws and would not tax the arm too much.

CATCHERS: FUNDAMENTALS ROPE DRILL   *"I"*

Catchers with exceptional arms can simply pivot on the back foot and throw a laser to second base. The catcher in high school and even in college may not possess such a gift. It must be developed. It is my belief that a catcher should gain ground with the right foot, even if it means a few inches. Moreover, she needs to explode out of her crouch toward second base. She must avoid standing up to throw from a stationary position.

Teaching this involves a somewhat innovative drill. Set the catcher in her "block/throw" stance. Have two players hold a rope or string about a foot in front of the catcher's head and about a foot above it. This can be modified as per need and challenge.

The catcher receives a tossed ball or picks one up from the ground. She drives out toward second buts she must gain ground and clear the rope. A throw can be made or it can be a no-throw footwork drill. Remember to insist on a good front shoulder "close-up."

CATCHERS: FUNDAMENTALS DIRTBALLS   *"I"*

There are a couple of ways to approach this. Teach the fundamentals of blocking first: tuck the chin, curl the upper body, glove to the "5-Hole," lateral sliding, footwork, etc. Next, drill it. Insist on quickness.

The coach can dress the catchers in full gear and lob regulation softballs at them, to their right and to their left. Or she can use a pitching machine. One can fungo balls at their (accuracy is an issue here—unless the hitter is particularly skilled, too many balls are bounced too far in front of the plate; in addition, the catcher can read the angle and direction of the hitter's intention). The catcher must keep her head down, "tracking the ball" as it were. To facilitate this, have her point to the spot on the floor or in the dirt where the ball hit.

The coach can dress the catchers in shin pads alone and perform drops and slides with no balls being thrown, hence a mere agility drill. They must wear their catcher's mitts in every drill described here.

You can ask them to don the shin pads and mask as you throw softee balls or tennis balls to their right, left and middle. You can drill this on wrestling mats indoors, too.

Considering which drill medium you elect to choose will often depend upon space allocation, time, and whether you are indoors or outdoors. All are effective in drilling the catcher's quickness in blocking dirtballs.

Add a challenging element to this drill, especially if you are out of doors. After blocking the dirtball, have the catcher scramble to recover and throw out a runner, real or imaginary. This element applies game situation pressure.

Add to all this element of backhand catching the dirtball. While the catcher needs to employ a full body block on wide pitches, there are times when the pitch can only be backhanded. Coaches often forget to drill this. Do so by simply throwing balls a bit wider than usual to the catcher's backhand side.

Some verbal cues that can be helpful in teaching catchers to block in the dirt:

- "Fire the knee"—lead knee driven toward the ball in the dirt to the right or left.
- "Curl"—Head down and chin to the chest protector.
- "Hips around the ball"—curl the hips and shoulders "around" a wide dirtball so that when deflected it will land in front of or near home plate rather than off to the side.

CATCHERS: FUNDAMENTALS PADDLE GLOVES & CHEST BLOCKS   *"I"*

Young catchers need to be taught to block dirtballs rather than catch them. It is an instinctive thing. Having said that here are two drills designed to teach catchers to block, not catch.

Paddle gloves are often used to teach infielders to use two hands in fielding ground balls, but they can also be utilized by catchers. Using a regular softball, the coach throws dirtballs at the catcher in the manner described above. The catcher drops, slides or otherwise blocks the ball but she cannot catch it as the paddle she is using for a glove prohibits this. In this way, she will begin to use her glove as a blocker, particularly over the "five-hole" between his knees. (Paddle gloves are shown elsewhere in this volume).

Another drill, done in the same manner, is to have the catcher place both hands behind her back and block each and every ball thrown by dropping and sliding into proper position with her body, blocking with the chest.

In all of these "dirtball drills," be sure to teach "curling." Have the catcher drop her chin to her chest thereby hunching her shoulders over the ball to ensure that it lands in front of her. Similarly, on balls off to the sides, she should slide left or right in such a way that her chest is slightly angled toward the plate, again to prevent the ball from caroming off to one side.

Another simple yet effective drill is to have each catcher face a coach. The coach holds three softballs in their hand and throws each in succession, one to the "5-hole," and one to each side of the plate. The catcher should recover into a good fundamental stance before reacting to the next throw.

CATCHERS: FUNDAMENTALS "WAR"   "*I*"

This is a "juice" drill designed to create a fun, competitive atmosphere. Ostensibly, it is a reaction drill and I have done this drill, but I have doubts about its true teaching value.

The coach uses a fungo bat and drives softballs or tennis balls at fully-equipped catchers positioned about 15-20 feet away. Try to hit dirtballs and short-hops. As the catchers, with their backs against a wall or backstop, must block them. Work the catchers one at a time with perhaps twenty balls hit at them. Count the number that squirts by each catcher. With the other catchers gathered around, there is a lot of cheering, cat calling, and laughter. I have even brought the rest of the team in to "place their bets" on who is going to win. It is all in fun.

Start with softly hit balls at first because the drill can be intimidating and then pick up the pace and speed. Frankly, as the drill emerges into a rapid-fire sequence, catchers admittedly lose their mechanical base in that they begin to resemble hockey goalies scrambling and diving rather than executing classic blocks from a proper stance. They will be improving their reaction times as they have fun, however.

CATCHERS: FUNDAMENTALS "WALL DRILL"   "I"

A variation of the "War" drill described above is to have the catchers face a wall about ten feet away from it. Throw softballs or tennis balls against the wall as you, the coach, stand behind them. She must catch or block the ball. This is a pure reaction drill and, frankly, one that is very good for infielders as well.

CATCHERS: GROUP BLOCKING DRILLS   "I"

A) 3-man Drill: One catcher in position with two "throwers" (coaches or other catchers) as shown. Alternate sides & rotate after a prescribed number of blocks.

Each thrower should have 4-6

Catcher:recover & set up quickly to face the next thrower

B) Circle Drill: Although questionable in terms of effective use of team practice time, this can be exhausting for the catchers. The entire team, or a portion of them, is circled around the catchers who are themselves circled in the middle. The players throw dirtballs at the catchers' feet as they rotate around to face the next thrower. Give each "thrower" perhaps two, three or four balls, depending upon the number of catchers in the middle.

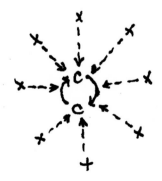

CATCHERS: FUNDAMENTALS "A CATCHER'S AGILITY SERIES"   "I"

As an old football coach, I am a firm believer in agility training. Applying such logic to catchers, here is a daily drill series that will improve "muscle memory," quickness and athleticism for your catcher. Bear in mind the rule of "6-to-10": any drill exceeding six to ten seconds will cease to be agility-oriented and will enter the category of an endurance drill.

Work your catchers through two or three sets of 6-10 repetitions of each of these drills every day:

1. Blocks—"Wave Drill"—no ball is thrown. The coach, pointing, indicates a block down, right or left and the catcher reacts with proper movement.
2. "Close-ups"—From a block/throw stance, the coach either shouts a "go" command or blows a whistle and the catcher springs into the proper position for a throw to second base.
3. "Knee drops" for a pickoff throw to first base (left knee).
4. Footwork to third base.

Run your catchers through these drills en masse. They consume less than ten minutes of practice time and they can pay dividends in the course of a season.

Anthony DiCicco from Fordham University, in an article published in the February 20, 2009 issue of "Collegiate Baseball," described an intriguing agility drill. Essentially plyomeric training, he used treaded platforms employed in step-aerobic training. He then has the catcher leap, from his stance, on to the box, re-gather himself into his stance and then pounce off the box to the left or right. Innovative and interesting.

CATCHERS: RECOVERY AND QUICKNESS "SPREAD EAGLE DRILL"

With a firm grasp of the obvious, it is a given that catchers need quickness. This next drill calls for the catchers, in full equipment, to lay face-down on the ground near home plate. Softballs are randomly spread out on the infield. On a given command, the catcher springs to her feet and pounces on the ball, firing to first base for the put-out.

I have used this drill, but as it does not truly replicate game like conditions, I have gone away from it in recent years. I have used this drill for infielders and outfielders, however, since they may indeed find themselves in such a position during a game.

CATCHERS: FUNDAMENTALS "FRAMING"   *"I"*

Framing pitches is a necessary fundamental for all catchers to learn. I have always harbored doubts about how many umpires are actually influenced by framed pitches, but the practice does have benefits in term of the catchers maintaining balance and pitchers retaining confidence.

Teach the usual basics: bent elbow, fingers to the pitchers, shifting the head and chest so as to receive the ball softly and "on top" of it. Impart to your catchers—if they can relate to this—the notion of "palming a steering wheel." They must avoid "stabbing" at the ball with their glove as this will almost certainly present the image of a marginal pitch being out of the strike zone. And that is what framing is all about—the marginal pitch. It has been said that good framers can "steal strikes." Reaching out for a lateral pitch and pulling it back into the zone is silly. It does not influence the umpire and it can make him look bad, something no one wants to do. Poor framers can cost their pitchers a strike as they sweep, stab and push the ball out of the strike zone.

I spoke to a relative from the Chicago area, Andrew Lohse, about his thoughts on the art of catching. He read over this portion of my manuscript and offered several excellent suggestions.

His thoughts on the technique of "framing" began with a slight weight shift on to one foot or the other. This would enable the catcher to "glide" and keep all framed pitches within the width of the catcher's shoulders. And rather than "stab" at the ball, his idea of framing, or "boxing" should ideally involve little arm movement, preferring to "wrap the glove" around the ball. Use the wrist, not the arm.

The low pitch is the toughest to frame, but catchers might be able to keep this pitch in the zone by extending toward the ball and tilting the thumb underneath it as the catcher pulls it in. Some softball catchers spin the glove into a palm-up position for the low pitch.

Have the catchers set up in a comfortable stance with no glove on the receiving hand. With an underhanded tossing motion, lob tennis balls at the catcher. She must not catch the ball, but rather angle the palm of her hand inward so that each ball bounces from her hand on to home plate. For the low pitch, she does grab it, but with a scooping motion, gently pulling it up and in toward the crotch.

A good way to teach this, in addition to the aforementioned use of tennis balls, is to emphasize not the receiving part of the technique, but the subtle use of the upper body. Use whiffle balls (because they move a bit slower) tossing them underhand from about ten feet away. Insist that the catcher sways her hips toward the flight path of the ball and arriving in a good receiving position before the ball gets there.

John Cedarburg, a catching instructor for the Colorado Rockies, said that if a catcher can influence five pitches a game then he has helped his team.

One final thought: why not have your pitchers, as they enter the Bullpen for a throwing session, toss 10-20 tennis or wiffleballs underhand to their catchers? It might help with "synergy" between battery mates in addition to freeing up coaching time.

CATCHERS: LIVE THROWS

At some point, you must commandeer the infield diamond to work on live throws to all bases, especially to second. You may wish to involve a live pitcher and even a base runner, but the focus here is the catcher and the receiving infielders.

The catcher must incorporate all the mechanics she has learned—a solid block/throw stance, good footwork and quickness in her close-up, arm arc and release. Teach her to aim her throws at the edge of the outfield grass as this will produce a ball that arrives at a good height for the infielder to catch and apply the tag. (You might also want to stress proper tag mechanics for your infielders—how many "outs" have been lost by infielders reaching and even standing too far in front of the bag?).

I firmly suggest using a stopwatch for this drill Make this a competitive drill. It can be fun, but monitor potential over-use of the catchers' arms.

Throw to all bases. Work "in/out" throws with the first baseman as she and the catcher coordinate on balls nubbed on to the infield grass or dropped third strikes that have squirted off into foul territory.

You can also make this a rapid-fire drill. One catcher and three tossed balls, all in quick succession. The first ball is thrown to first base as if it were a pickoff, the next toss goes to second as if defending against a steal and last to third base in the same scenario. Each throw is made from the "block/throw" stance and quickness is the key point of emphasis.

If your middle infielders are tied up elsewhere, here are two "targets" that you can set up to enhance your catchers' focus: use a batting practice "sock net" or use an old tire. The sock net is self-explanatory as it is basically an upright screen with a bag-like net built into it. The tire is exactly that: an old used car tire nailed to a flat board to provide upright stability. Set it atop a horizontally placed cinder block and fire away. Make these two "target drills" competitive—how many throws can be sent into the sock net or through the tire? Hint: there will be frustration factor here as both drills are very difficult.

CATCHERS: FIELDING THE POSITION "CFP COMBINATION DRILLS"

Besides the fundamentals of receiving, blocking and throwing, there are other elements to the catcher's game that must be worked on in combination drills, much like "Pitcher Fielding Practice" or "PFP." As outlined earlier, catchers need to work on dropped third strikes (the "in/out" call coordinated with first basemen) and passed balls in coordination with pitchers covering the plate. Here are some other suggestions.

A) APPLYING THE TAG AT HOME: Do not assume that catchers know how to do this. Teach them how to position themselves to receive an infielder's throw while blocking the plate (left foot on the third base line corner of the plate or about 18 inches up the line and on the line curling down on to the right knee in applying the tag). Work on throws from all directions. While the catcher's left foot will generally point to third base, the right foot will face the fielder (left, center, right) from which the throw originated. The catcher's weight should rest primarily on the right foot. Teach this with short-distance coach's tosses and then incorporate live infielder's throws. Infielders need to work on this as well since it is the only throw that "goes up on the scoreboard." Live base runners are probably not necessary as there can be an injury factor. A creative distraction is to roll a large medicine ball at the catcher's feet as she receives the throw. This would simulate a sliding runner.

B) FIELDING BUNTS: Work on throws to all bases. Work on the two-handed "scoop" technique with the glove and the ball—emphasize aligning the shoulders toward the intended target. Work on "reverse rounding" on bunts directly down the third base line. In this drill it is recommended that once the basic techniques are instilled, you consider adding live base runners as this heightens the urgency, speed and intensity of the drill thus making it more game situational. Teach the basics by simply having a coach, standing behind the catcher, roll balls out on to the infield. Some coaches place three balls in front of home and call out which one is to be scooped and thrown.

C) PITCH-OUTS: Another aspect of the catcher's skill package that too many coaches assume as inherent, this too, must be taught and drilled. This obviously needs to be coordinated with pitchers as they must also learn how to throw pitch-outs. This can be done in the bullpen, but pitch-outs on the diamond with live runners are more realistic if you can secure "diamond time."

D) HOME-TO-FIRST DPs: The footwork that a catcher needs to successfully complete a home-to-first double play is a bit different and must therefore be taught and drilled. In teaching this, use short tosses from a coach standing in the infield, perhaps near the mound. The catcher set to receive the throw with her right foot on the plate. Receiving the ball with two hands and "popping it" into her throwing hand, she spins off the right foot dragging the toe across the plate to quickly line her shoulders up toward first and throws a strike on the inside of the bag. Emphasize quickness.

E) BALLS UP THE LINE: The ball that squirts up the first base line can present issues for the catcher. She has got to contend with a runner sprinting toward first while she must field the ball—a bunt or blocked third strike—and make a solid throw without hitting the runner in the back. Work on "clearing" in towards the infield grass all the while emphasizing to the catcher that she has time to make this play.

Teaching this, the coach can stand behind the catcher and roll balls out into the infield or they can place three softballs out in the infield in strategically located spots. The catcher then springs out from her stance and pounces on each ball, using proper technique, and completes the play with a solid throw.

F) SOFTBALL CATCHERS THROWING ON THE RUN: There are times in the game of softball, when a runner has been picked off and the catcher must throw to an infielder on the run. The catcher must practice "leading" the fielder much like a quarterback throwing a football to a receiver.

Use a catcher-first baseman combination. Have the first baseman throw a ball home at which point the runner, imaginary or real, will break for second. Picture this as a delayed steal or the back end of a first-&-third situation. The catcher must return the throw to the first baseman as the latter runs toward second trailing the runner.

This unusual drill was taken from Coach Kelly Inouye-Perez in <u>The Softball Drill Book.</u>

G) WILD PITCHERS, PLAYS AT THE PLATE & THE "POP-UP SLIDE DRILL: The runner leads off third. A nervous pitcher throws one in the dirt that skips past the catcher all the way to the backstop. This is certainly a realistic game situation, so it needs to be drilled and rehearsed.

Stand in front of the catcher. Throw a ball past her to the backstop. The catcher scrambles to her feet, sprints to the backstop and then, to break her momentum, she goes into a conventional bent-leg slide when she arrives at the ball. Insist on a slide off to the side of the ball in such a way that the throwing hand can access it freely. Retrieve the ball and quickly throw it to a pitcher covering the plate. The catcher is generally throwing from her knees in this case, so this must be practiced. Have a line of pitchers executing this drill to maximize reps.

A good coaching point in teaching this technique is to have the sliding catcher extend the leg on her throwing hand side back toward the screen. This enables her to pop up on the other knee and brace herself for a quicker recovery.

H) CATCHER THROWS TO SECOND: You will need to work the combinations of the catcher throwing to second to defend against a steal with the middle infielders covering the bag. You will need to work on pickoff throws, too.

I) OUTFIELD THROWS TO THE PLATE: Self-explanatory, but needs to be worked on. Use cutoffs as well as "throw-throughs." And then add a secondary throw to another base as the catcher needs to recover and throw out a trail runner at second or third base.

CATCHERS: FUNDAMENTALS POP-UP DRILL

How frustrating is it when the batter pops a ball straight up and the catcher flubs it? You just gave away an out. A pop-up must be an out! But you as the coach must drill your catchers in this. They must become confident and comfortable when it comes to pop-ups.

Unless you are among the few fungo hitters who can drive baseball straight up with consistency, use a tennis racket and tennis balls. Or, better yet, there is a slingshot device that employs surgical cords attached to an armature that is especially accurate and can really "sky" them. Catchers, and for that matter, all infielders actually enjoy this drill. I once had a veteran first baseman who was terrified of foul pop flies. He simply lacked confidence. I drilled him repeatedly with the slingshot and he became totally proficient in catching foul flies. I ran into him years later and we both shared a laugh about how this drill conquered his fears.

```
       Ch          ▷C              C  C  C  C
     (coach)                       (catchers)
```

Do not forget to impact the notion of locating the ball first and then tossing the mask in the opposite direction. If your catcher uses a hockey-style goalie helmet, popular today, they do not need to remove it to catch pop-ups.

In addition to the techniques described above, teach your catchers about the spin the ball will take. A pop-up directly over their head will rotate back toward the infield grass. Catchers need to know this and they should, if possible, position themselves with their back toward the infield, just like any other infielder catching a pop fly.

CATCHING: FIELDING BUNTS "ROTATIONAL CFP"

Place three catchers around home plate, one behind the plate and one in each batter's box. A coach stands where the umpire would normally be. They roll three "bunted" balls out on to the infield grass and each catcher springs out to field it and throw to a designated base.

```
C-1: Throw to first base
C-2: Throw to second base
C-3: Throw to third base
Rotate after each throw.
```

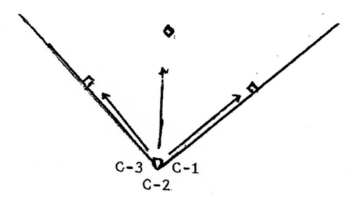

With each catcher, emphasize the "scoop" technique with the glove in front of the ball and the throwing hand "following the ball" into the glove. Teach your catchers to "surround" the ball. In taking an approach such as is described below, insist that the shoulder of the throwing hand is lined up to the target.

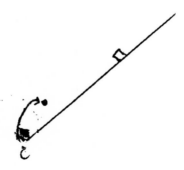

CATCHING: THROWS "FOUR CORNER DRILL"

Place four catchers around the infield. Each views the base in front of her as a "home plate." Each will throw in a prescribed direction upon a command from the coach. This drill is an excellent drill for coaches working in a "catchers' camp."

The sequence of throws is as follows:

1. Throws to second—straight across the diamond
2. Home to third base, as if on a steal attempt—each catcher throws to the left
3. Throws to first base—have each catcher drop the ball, pick it up and throw to her right.

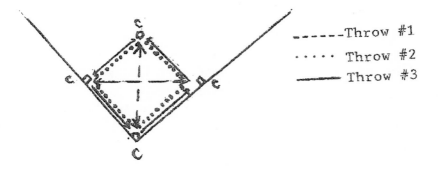

FIELDING & DEFENSIVE DRILLS: INFIELDERS

FUNDAMENTALS: "THE BASICS FOR GROUND BALLS"
"I"

A) **THE APPROACH:** Teach your players the "1-2-Spread" technique. From a comfortable preparatory stance with the feet staggered and less than shoulder-width apart, they are to step toward the plate (either foot will do, although I have heard coaches talk of a preferred foot), followed by a second step and then completed with a spreading of both feet simultaneously.

The steps occur as the pitcher winds up and the "spread" is timed so that the feet land as the ball arrives at the plate. The feet will be slightly wider than shoulder width when the fielder reaches the "spread" position. She will be on the balls of her feet with the toes pointed out slightly.

All this is designed to prepare the fielder for quick movement from an athletic position. From these initial momentum-generating steps, he can more rapidly adjust to a ball hit to the right or left. It is analogous to a tennis player swaying in anticipation of returning a serve.

B) **"PRESENTING THE GLOVE":** Too many young players receive the groundball with the glove too close to their body. They need to extend the glove out to the ball. A good verbal cue is this one, "Present the glove." Emphasize the palm being open and upward, facing the sky.

C) **"THE ALLIGATOR":** I am always appalled at how many young players emerge from Little League without the foggiest notion of what this means. If and when they field a groundball with two hands, the bare hand is either off to the side of the glove or even somehow behind it! Teach them to "clamp" down on the ball as it enters the glove with the bare hand on top, as in the photo below. Look at any professional infielder, minor or major league, and you will see this technique. Look at any sandlot or youth league player and it is ubiquitously absent.

D) "DRAW IT IN": You've heard the euphemisms—"Look the ball into the glove," and "Soften the hands." Drawing the ball into the body is just another way of saying the same thing. The infielder must "give" with the ball, "softening" her hands as it were. Tell the players that the best infielders are those from whom you never hear a grounder slap into a mitt. Coaches like specifics, so some tell them to pull the ball toward the hip on the throwing hand side while others say "draw it into the belly button." Don't over coach it, especially for young players. As long as they "give" with the ball, their technique is fine.

Drill all this with an imaginary. Have the players execute the approach, the presentation of the glove, the alligator and then the draw-in in pantomime.

Next, put them against a wall, just throw and catch, all with proper form, solid mechanics and athletic fluidity. Players of any age can do this.

FIELDING: TEACHING ROUNDING & FOOTWORK ON GROUNDERS

The coach faces the player about ten to twelve feet away in this simple instructional drill. The coach draws a line directly toward the play and then rolls a ball to the player's left. She must "get around the ball," draw it in, and then utilize the proper footwork for a phantom throw.

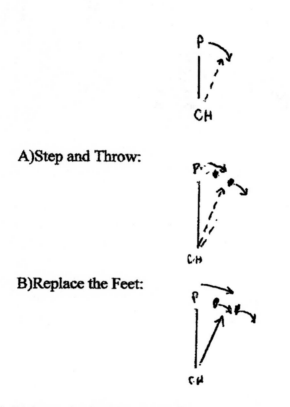

A)Step and Throw:

B)Replace the Feet:

In A) & B) keep the ball in the midline of the body.

C)Drop-Step and Throw - this technique is used on a grounder far to the fielder's left. They cannot use two hands or they will lose balance; only the glove hand is used and the footwork must change in order to get the shoulders lined up:

FIELDING: RECEIVING TECHNIQUES: OVERCOMING THE "PAN CATCH"   *"I"*

Young players, when first learning to catch a ball, often "pan catch," or hold the palm of the glove awkwardly open to the sky for every ball thrown or batted at them. You've seen it. How do we break them of this potentially injurious habit?

The traditional method is to have them stand in front of you with the glove open and the fingers pointed to the sky. Extend the hands upward and have them note how they should catch a ball with the "fingers up" on any ball coming at them above their waist. Now have them slowly move their hands downward toward their waist and the fingers will naturally rotate downward. Hence, any ball coming at them below the waist must be caught with the fingers facing down. Eventually they get it.

Another technique is to place them on one knee and repeat the same teaching concept with softly thrown balls.

Here is a good reinforcement drill for young players:

THE "GROUND BALL MARCH"—Line the players up along a foul line. They are to simulate presenting the glove, alligator the top hand, receive a grounder, draw it in, step with an open foot and then simulate a throw. As you repeat the process, they will feel the proper mechanics, build muscle memory and begin a slow "march" across the field.

FIELDING: TECHNIQUE, REPETITIONS AND REACTIONS
"WALL DRILLS"   *"I"*

This is another effective indoor drill that can also be done out of doors if the facility allows it.

A) **WALL TOSSES:** Work on proper fielding techniques— presenting the glove, "alligatoring" the top hand, and drawing the ball in—by simply having the players throw and catch against a wall. Use of the paddle gloves, as shown in the photos below, adds and additional level of skill development. Coaches can further enhance this drill by calling for a double hop-turn, or "spinning the feet" to align the shoulders as the fielder prepares to throw the ball.

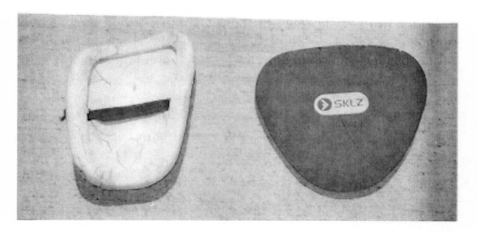

Yes, the paddle on the left is home made from an old football thigh pad and a strap laced through two holes drilled on either side. Not attractive as the store-bought model on the right, but equally effective as a teaching tool.

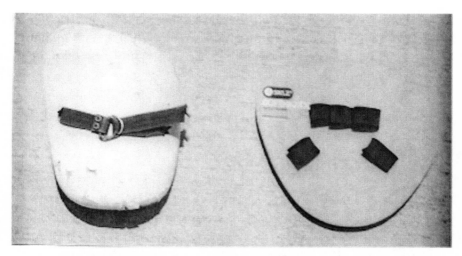

B) **OFF THE WALL REACTION DRILLS:** Similar to the wall reaction drill previously outlined for catchers, this one works your infielders. As the fielder faces the wall, about ten feet away, her partner throws a ball against the wall and the fielder reacts to it. Creative coaches can make this a one-handed receiving drill as the fielder must work forehand, backhand, short hops, etc., all with the glove. They field with their throwing hand behind the back and this will teach them to "soften" their hands.

   By way of clarification, fielders are using their regular gloves for this and for all "Wall Drills" subsequently described. They are not using the paddle gloves shown above.

C) **NO RETREAT:** Some young players will back up on ground balls, probably out of instinctive fear of the ball or at the very least, a lack of confidence. With their backs to the wall and their buttocks literally touching the wall, throw or fungo baseballs at them. Simply put, they cannot back up.

D) **SHOVEL FEEDS:** Teach infielders, particularly shortstops and third basemen to stay low and shovel the ball, almost with a bent-over sider arm action, in their throws to second. Here are two drills, both using that invaluable wall, to work on this skill. In Drill A, the fielder either replicates drawing a ball in and throwing to the wall or she has a teammate roll a ball to him. In Drill B, she throws to the wall, receives the ball, stays low and shovels it to a partner who is standing anywhere up to 75 feet away.

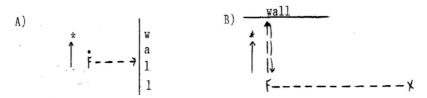

* Fielder faces this direction.

E) TURN-AROUND DRILL: While a wall is not totally necessary, it can help. Have the player face the wall, in other words with her back to the thrower. The thrower will roll a grounder at his partner, perhaps 10-12' away, as she yells "Turn!" At this point it becomes a reaction drill as the fielder hop-turns to face the approaching grounder. Check for good form.

F) "WART-BALL" REACTION DRILL: Again, a wall is not necessary for this drill, but the purchase of a special rubber ball is. I call it the "wart ball," as it resembles a regular rubber ball, but it is speckled with small rounded protuberances which make the ball bounce crazily. Players do not even need their gloves for this drill. The technique in "throwing" this ball is important. Use a sidearm fling rather than an overhand motion; underhand works well, too, but make it a speedy toss and the closer the ball lands to the fielder the better it works. The bounces are insane, but that is what makes this drill effective as a reaction drill.

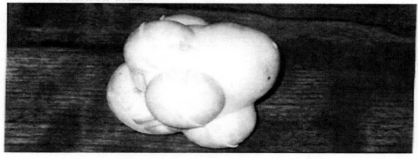

FIELDING: WALL DRILLS...EXPANDED

Coach John Cohen, currently head baseball coach at Mississippi State, produced an innovative drill video entitled "Wall Ball." On it he demonstrates some thirty drills for players seeking individual skill improvement. Here is a sampling:

1. **PITCHER'S "PFP"**—As described earlier, pitchers can enhance their skills on come-backers and bunts, develop good footwork, and even work on abnormal throws such as the 1-6-3 DP or the throw to third—often screwed up in games—by using bounce-back screens. They can receive the ball, race in and practice the glove-flip toss to a catcher as they defend against a squeeze play. Pitchers can throw a pitch into a screen set up by the plate and then, after receiving the ball, work on footwork in any direction with throws to first, second or third.

2. **CATCHER'S DIRTBALLS**—Again, as described earlier, the catcher can work on their dirtball blocking skills off a bounce-back. It might be helpful to have a coach toss the balls into the screen.

3. **OTHER CATCHER SKILLS**—Have the catchers receive a ball thrown off the screen and ask them to learn and develop their footwork on double plays in which they are pivoting and throwing to first. They can work on receiving the ball and curling down to block the plate and tag an incoming runner. Then, they can recover and throw down to second or third to get a trail runner (abbreviated distances or full distances can be set up). Catchers can use tennis balls to work on framing as the ball is tossed by a coach or another catcher. They can receive the ball off a bounce-back and work the footwork necessary for a throw to first, to second, or third.

4. **MIDDLE INFIELDERS**—Can work on double-play pivots—

5. **INFIELDERS**—in general can work on their proper ground ball technique as I have described earlier, but they can also work on the body positioning for relay throws (they themselves can throw it and set up or work with a partner throwing), charging slow-rollers, diving for the ball (use a mat and a partner tossing at an angle), shuffle-steps that are so necessary for body control (see diagram below), forehand and backhand receiving and working with or without gloves (emphasize soft hands if using no glove), paddle gloves, holding runners (receive the ball, hop step to confront a runner on third and then pivot to throw to first), double-play feeds (receive off screen and feed into a sock net or to another fielder using knee-drop, hop-turn, and flip techniques; you can get some crazy bad-angle feeds and work on them, too), pump fake throws (receive—pump fake in one directions using proper footwork and quick feet; and how about dropping the ball upon receipt, then pump faking and throwing elsewhere?), working on short hops, and soft hands drills described earlier such as the one with the glove "presented" and the throwing hand behind the back.

Receive -shuffle-shuffle-throw
To receiver or net

Receive-shuffle five/six times-throw
on command "Now!"

6. **OUTFIELDERS**—can work on rounding grounders by throwing at an angle and running the ball down, going back on the ball (play close to the screen and throw it at the base to create a pop fly over the head), and charging the ball for "do or die" plays, again emphasizing proper footwork.

7. **SPECIAL TECHNIQUES**—Coach Cohen is a bit of an iconoclast in that he teaches his infielders to draw the received groundball immediately up to the throwing hand side rather than pull it in to the belly as I have described elsewhere. To instill this, he has a drill where the player holds their throwing

hand open and up by their ear. The glove is "presented" and the ball is received, but then glove and ball are swept up to the open hand.

He also uses an effective verbal clue to teach his players to keep their head down and "look the ball into the glove"—he says, "put your face in the glove." I like it and I strongly urge that you pick up his video.

FIELDING: FUNDAMENTALS & "THE NEXT STEP"   *"I"*

Players can utilize the wall drill or simply employ the ground ball catch as two players toss grounders to each other from a short distance, always cognizant of working on good form and technique.

Have them work their feet. In fielding the grounder hit directly at them, ask them to receive the ball with two hands but slightly off the midline of their body. In this with, smooth fluidity, they will "give" with the ball, sweeping it into their hip on the throwing hand side. However, as they do this they are shifting the feet with a double hop-turn so that the feet and the shoulders become aligned toward their target. It is all done in one motion. Have the players feel their hands move in a circular fashion and they draw the ball in and then up and into a throwing position.

FIELDING: FOOTWORK "THE BOX DRILL"   *"I"*

This is a great footwork drill and one that the players will enjoy. Moreover, it can also serve to pick up the tempo of a practice session. It is also an excellent indoor drill. I have even seen teams use this in the infield prior to taking standard pregame "I/O."

Align the players in a square of perhaps 40-60 feet depending upon age, skill level and facility space. On your signal they will begin throwing the ball around the box, first clockwise and then counter-clockwise. Note that two distinct footwork patterns will emerge—a) the shuffle and b) "turning over the glove side."

In the shuffle, the feet move toward the target in a nearly simultaneous manner as the back foot "replaces" the front foot. A right-handed fielder, for instance, will employ this when he or she receives the ball as it rotates around the box clockwise. (See diagram below)

When a player "turns over the glove side," she receives the ball and then literally spins around to throw, turning in the direction of her glove hand and crow-hopping as she does so. This allows for greater balance and body control, hence a stronger and more accurate throw. Your left-handers will use this on the clockwise rotation.

Note the necessity of changing the direction of the throws from clockwise to counter-clockwise as both your lefties and righties must learn both footwork techniques. Also, be sure that the players initially receive the ball facing the thrower, squared up and with two hands extended out in front. Insist on two hands, quick transfer of the ball from glove to hand, and quick feet. Once the players become accustomed to the drill increase the tempo.

So keep things moving, you can have the players "follow their throw" and run to the next corner of the box after they have thrown the ball or they can simply move to the back of the line, remaining in their corner. Have fun with this drill. When a player drops a ball, she earns the joking moniker of "drill killer" as the teams collectively moans, "Ohhhhh!"

Yet another form of a "Box Drill" involves one player in the middle and four players arrayed about him, squared off as if in the cardinal points on a compass. Each of those players has a number. The player in the middle must quickly adjust her feet and throw to that player who will return the ball to the middle as another number is called out. Emphasize two hands in receiving the ball, quick feet, a quick exchange and speed overall.

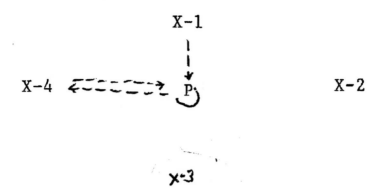

FIELDING: BOX DRILL ALTERNATIVES   *"T"*

Four players are involved in the drill. Groups of players can be arranged in squared patterns around the field, the gym or even the parking lot if the field is wet or snow-covered.

The concept is simple. Two players have bats and will hit grounders to the other two players. The fielder then flips or rolls the ball to the next fungo hitter. Thus, two softballs are working their way around the perimeter of the box simultaneously.

After a predetermined time, switch the hitters with the fielders.

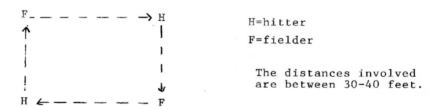

H=hitter

F=fielder

The distances involved are between 30-40 feet.

It may be advisable to have a "feeder" next to each fungo hitter. They will catch the thrown balls and feed the hitters.

Next, you can tilt the box into a trapezoid to work on fielding range. Place a line of fielders in the corners as shown. The two other corners are occupied with a fungo hitter.

The fungo hitters drive a ground ball to the fielders' right. They in turn receive the ball, continue running toward the corner fungo hitter, feed her the ball and the drill continues. It must be mirrored to work on ground balls to the fielder's left. In addition, it is a good idea to place a back-up player behind the fielders to keep errant softballs in the yard. Keep a supply of balls for the fungo hitters, too, just to keep things moving.

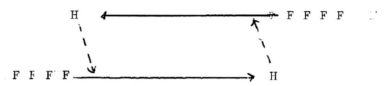

"I"

FIELDING: FOOTWORK & PIVOTS ON BALLS HIT DIRECTLY AT THE FIELDER

Station two fungo hitters about 50 to 70 feet apart and a fielder triangulated in between them as shown in the diagram below:

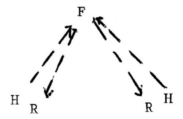

Hitters will fungo a ball at the fielder, one right after the other. In speeding up the timing of the drill, you are quickening the fielder's hands, footwork and throwing release time. This is all good. You are also exhausting them. Ten to twenty reps will do that. As soon as the fielder throws to the receiver, the second hitter drives a grounder at the fielder in rapid succession.

If you want to add another dimension to this drill, consider hitting slow-rollers at the fielder. First, have them catch and throw on the run as they return the ball to the hitter. Next, have them catch the slow-roller and throw the ball across to the receiver on the other side.

FIELDING: RANGE & FOOTWORK CONE CIRCLE DRILL   *"I"*

This drill can be done indoors or outside. Regulation softballs can be used. A further suggestion is to use soft "Incrediballs" and/or paddle gloves.

Arrange five traffic cones in a broad circle radiating perhaps twenty to thirty feet from the bucket and coach stationed in the middle. All balls are rolled out to the fielders. A fielder is stationed at each cone except for one.

The coach rolls a ball toward the open cone and the fielder to the right of that cone shuffles and crosses over, squared up at the arrival point, to field the ball and then race into the center of the circle to drop it in the bucket. The coach then rolls a ball out to the next fielder, repeating the procedure. Make this a high-tempo drill.

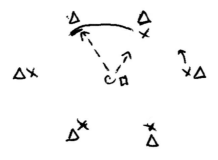

"I"

FIELDING: FUNDAMENTALS & RANGE "LATERALS"

Side hops, laterals, side-to-sides—the name for this traditional and potentially exhausting drill varies from program to program. In concept, it is a simple drill, but an innovative coach can elevate this drill into a teaching progression. Here goes:

A) **GLOVELESS SIDE HOPS:** Two players face each other about ten feet apart. One player will roll a ball to one side and then the other. The "fielder" crosses over with her feet, keeping her shoulders square to the path of the ball. She stays low, fields one ball, tosses it back (underhanded, of course) and then breaks for the ball tossed to the other side, which is already enroute. Reps can vary in accordance with the coach's whistle or even the coach's mood. See Diagram A.

Note that this is a barehanded drill. Insist on two hands being used. It can qualify as a conditioning drill as well as fielding drill.

A variation is to have both players rotate in a circular fashion as they roll softballs to each other simultaneously. Reverse the direction after a while. See Diagram B. Two balls can be used in this drill.

B) **BACKHANDS AND LEAD HANDS:** Have the players don their gloves. Although still within a set-piece structure, the throwers will roll the ball further out to the side, but not so far as to be out of reach or force a dive for the baseball. They are to roll the ball to the receiver's backhand side and then to her "lead hand" or glove hand side. With the latter, form is particularly stressed. Plant the foot on the glove side, pick the ball with backhand, spin to recovery and return the ball. To the "lead hand" side, this replicates a slow roller and the player should round the ball if possible, pick it with the glove hand only and off to the side of her body, and gather her feet for a short throw. (Note that if the player tries to use two hands when the ball is so far off to her glove side, she will lose balance— one-handed fielding is fine here, although that was anathema years back.) See Diagram C.

C) **DIVING DRILL:** Place two mats, one on either side of the fielder. The thrower in this drill tries to throw a short-hop ball to the fielder's right and then to her left. In either case, the fielder must dive for the ball attempting to at least knock it down. There will be times when you demand that your infielders "get dirt on their bellies" and keep the ball in the infield. You can practice it here. See Diagram D.

Diagrams: A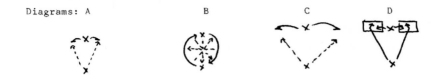

Another way to teach this is to have the player "dive" (flop, really) from one or both knees. Emphasize extension out to the ball. Next, have the player recover to one knee and make a solid throw. The later phase is particularly useful for second basemen.

D) LATERALS WITH STATIONARY BALLS: Arrange six softballs along the first-to-second and second-to-third baselines. Put a player in between each of them. Stand in the pitcher's circle and on the whistle signal right or left. Then players are to move laterally, keeping their shoulders square to the baseline, gathering each ball in utilizing the proper mechanics: glove "presented, top hand "alligatoring," and drawing the ball into the midsection of the body.

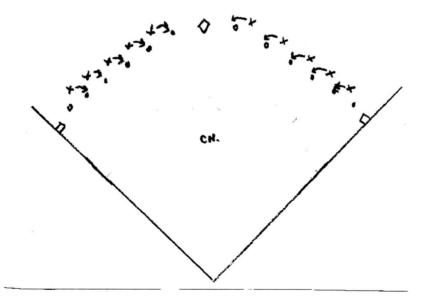

FIELDING: "SOCCER GOALIE CHALLENGE"

This is a competitive game that can liven up practice, indoors or out. Use both sides of the infield. Girls in the middle of the diamond will throw or bat a ball at a player they are challenging. Have them call out a teammate! The player "challenged" is to assume a good fielder's stance in between two traffic cones placed 10-15 feet apart along each baseline. Four groups work at once.

From this point, the game is simple. The hitter/thrower launches a hard grounder between the cones. If it goes through, she gets a point; if the defender stops it, even just knocks it down, they get the point. Watch the girls get dirty doing this one!

For safety: have all hitters/throwers throw outside toward the foul lines.

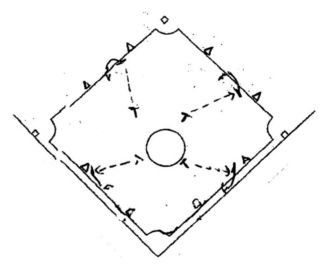

FIELDING: FUNDAMENTALS & NUANCES OF ADVANCED TECHNIQUES   "1"
"DOMINICAN DRILLS"

Few would argue with the notion that players from the Dominican Republic have transformed the game of baseball, especially with the acrobatic athleticism of their infielders. I once heard Jim LeFebvre speak of various "home made drills" that he had seen during a trip to the Caribbean. These drills can be made up on the fly. There is no set teaching pattern. They are fun and challenging for players and coaches alike. They can be done indoors as well as out. They can be worked with players as young as eight and nine years old. They can be implemented in softball, too.

A) **BACK OF THE GLOVE CATCHING:** Have the players catch every ball thrown by using only the back of their glove. Obviously, two hands must be employed. Two cautionary notes: if the glove has a finger loop, make sure that the players keep all fingers inside the mitt; also, do this drill from short distances, perhaps fifteen to twenty-five feet.

B) **SOFT HANDS & SHORT HOPS:** Players are on their knees. The glove is extended out in front of the body, "presented," as it were, pocket up. In catching each ball, the player must keep her bare hand behind her back to ensure that only the glove is utilized. The players are only about ten to fifteen feet apart, so everything is softly thrown, but insist on short hops. Throwers are to aim their throws at the knees of the receivers. Work backhand and forehand. Show them how to "give" with the ball.

In executing the short hop catch, you may wish to have the players set a marker out in front of themselves, especially if you are working with young athletes. Have them lay down at body length and place their hat on the ground where their head was. Recover to the knees and throw to the hat. You will get good short hops now.

C) **GLOVELESS CATCHES:** Arrange the players in a box formation. They are to receive each throw ball (short distances, of course) with the bare hand and then toss the ball underhanded to the next player in the square, rotating clockwise and then counter-clockwise. Insist on good footwork such as that described in the aforementioned "Box Drill."

D) **NO HANDS CATCHES:** Repeat the drill described above with only the glove used for all catches and throws. Work the underhand feed; work the backhand feed. Again, be sure to work clockwise and counter-clockwise.

E) BOUNCE CATCHES: Have the players play catch, but they must bounce the ball at their own feet prior to throwing it. Obviously the bare hand is used. This teaches recovery and "staying with the play." It works especially well indoors, but if you are working this drill on grass, there is less of a bounce, so the lesson is that players must never pick up the ball with their glove. In addition, they should stay low in returning the ball.

F) TOSS & SPIN: This is a silly drill that probably has minimal practical effect other than enhancing athleticism, but here it is: As the players play catch, they are to flip the ball in the air, spin around, relocate the ball and catch it prior to throwing.

G) "BAREHANDING:" In this drill, the thrower "leads" the fielder, throwing it at an angle in front of her. She must run it down, bare hand it and throw it—all on the run and in one motion. You can even work the backhand throw on the run, too, but obviously from a shorter distance.

Thrower X A Fielder
A - grounder thrown
B - ball fielded and thrown

H) SLIDE-N-THROW: Place a ball on the ground about twenty or twenty-five feet away. On the whistle, the fielder sprints, executes a bent-leg slide to one side of the ball (their glove side), retrieves it and throws to her partner from one or both knees. Make this a race as several players will do this drill at once. Practice this from various throwing angles.

I) RECOVERY THROWS: The fielder has just "laid out" for a ball and is flat on her belly. The ball is held in the glove. On the whistle, she must recover and throw a strike to her partner. Again, make this competitive.

J) CIRCLE TOSSES: Position two players, facing each other on the perimeter of a circle, real or imaginary. They will shuffle, facing each other all the while, in a clockwise rotation, tossing the baseball back and forth. Then rotate counter-clockwise. Then add a second ball. This drill can be laugh out loud fun as the two players in the middle are being watched, and razzed, by the rest of their team.

K) **SIDEARM ON THE RUN:** Similar to the "Slide-n-Throw" drill described above, in this drill the player sprints to a ball which has been placed on the ground about fifteen feet in front of her. She snatches the ball and without straightening up and still on the run, throws to a fielder who is placed at an angle roughly equivalent to the first baseman.

L) **TWO-HOP BOUNCE CATCHES:** Have the players "play catch," but no glove is allowed to the touch the ball. Catching the ball off to the throwing hand side, the players bare hand each ball and toss it back, bouncing ball on two hops (one-hop is acceptable, too, but this can be an easier play as the ball is more "readable.")

There are as many of these drills as the imagination can conceive. Moreover, they are excellent indoor drills and can serve to break the monotony of indoor workouts.

FIELDING: CIRCLE TOSSES

This drill primarily works your middle infielders, but it can be beneficial for first basemen tossing to pitchers covering first. Catchers can even derive a benefit by working on their tosses to a pitcher covering home. Pitchers can work on their tosses to first on bunts hit near the circle as well. Even third basemen can work on tossing underhand throws to the catcher at home on a bunt.

The drill must be executed clockwise and counterclockwise. The players should be stationary at first but can be taught to throw on the run as they get more advanced. Why not try shovel feeds with the glove, too?

One ball is generally used, but two or even three balls can liven the drill.

FIELDING: BAREHANDING & CHARGING GROUNDBALLS
"T"

Simply put, this is an excellent skill for players to learn, but it must be taught and then drilled. First, have the players charge stationary balls lying still in the grass. They are to "stab" them with a pre-set two or three fingered grip and come up throwing, all on the run. Next, toss slow-rollers at them. They must approach the ball on the throwing hand side, seize the ball with two or three fingers underneath it and again, throw on the run. The throw itself will amount to a side-arm throw. They must not straighten up as there is not enough time.

Try to set the drill with the approximate throwing angles that a shortstop, second baseman or third baseman would encounter.

Remember to incorporate your corner infielders on die-or-die underhand tosses on the run to home plate as they replicate defending the suicide bunt squeeze play.

"T"

FIELDING: QUICKNESS IN CATCHING & THROWING "RETURN THROW DRILL"

This one is an old standby that I have used for years and generally at least twice per week. Once the players have warmed up their arms with a traditional "catch," have them work on catching and releasing a throw as quickly as possible.

Insist on a few fundamental techniques: a) catch the ball with two hands extended in-front, b) catch the ball on the throwing hand side of the body with the feet aligned toward the target. Have them "pop" the ball from the glove into the throwing hand and use a "snap throw" to return the ball quickly and efficiently.

Time it. Count ten seconds and have the players yell out how many throws they completed. Repeat the drill a second time and have them work to improve the number of throws (without telling the kids, quietly "stretch" the ten-second count to ensure success).

So as to avoid gobbling up to much pre-practice time, I will alternate this drill with long toss in successive practice sessions.

THROWING: LINE DRILLS   *"T"*

In keeping with the aforementioned "Dominican Drills" described earlier, here is a series of simple throwing drills that can be practiced indoors or out.

The configuration is simple:

The variations are imaginative:
  A) Roll a grounder and the players in Line B return the ball with a glove feed;
  B) Roll a grounder and the players in Line B return the ball with an underhand feed;

C) Roll a grounder and the players in Line B, stationary and facing up field at a right angle and feeds the ball with a backhand toss;
D) Roll a grounder and the player in Line B, again facing up field and at a right angle, works on staying low and "shovel feeding" a double-play toss with a semi-underhand motion.

Players can feed each other, in other words Line A feeds line B as described above and then line B feeds Line A to keep things moving.

FIELDING: FORM & FOOTWORK "FIGURE EIGHTS"

"I"

This is an excellent indoor drill. Set two cones about ten feet apart and line your players up to the side of the cone on the left.

Roll a ball to a spot inside of the left cone. The player scrambles around the cone, fields it, tosses it back to the coach and then scrambles around the cone on the right side to field a second ball that has been rolled just inside of that one.

Utilizing your entire gym space, this drill can be done with pairs of players scattered around the gym floor.

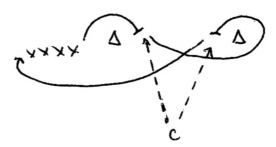

FIELDING: INFIELDERS ATTACK DRILL   "I"

This simple drill instills an aggressive approach to the ball. Stack two infielders, one behind the other. They face a coach who will roll a ball toward them, perhaps fifteen to twenty feet away. Both infielders take a step forward toward the groundball, but the player behind must circle around from behind her partner to attack the ball and catch. The player in front stops after taking only a step or two.

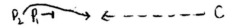

FIELDING: SIDE-TOSS PEPPER   "I"

This drill is good for pre-game or part of a batting circuit. Players divide into groups of 5: a batter, a tosser, and 3 fielders. The batter hits a real softball being short tossed from the side. Fielders work on proper techniques for groundballs. Hit five balls and then rotate. This can be done in small enclosed areas, indoors in small groups or in groups spread out across the outfield. It can even serve as a good pre-game BP if time and space do not permit a full batting practice.

Frankly, this is an excellent hitting drill, too. Your girls will learn to keep their heads down and exercise better bat control.

FIELDING: FOOTWORK & FORM "THREE BALL DRILL"   "I"

Place a cone near each side of the pitching rubber. Line up your players behind each, thus forming two lines stretching out toward the outfield. Two coaches stand near the plate. They will fungo softballs or roll out softy balls. Both lines go simultaneously.

The first ball is a slow-roller directly at each player. They field it toss it back to the coach and scramble back to the front of the line. The second ball is down the line. Again, the player fields it, tosses it back to the coach and gets back on line for a third ball, one that is thrown over their outside shoulder simulating a soft infield pop-up.

This can involve all infielders as a good indoor drill or it can be used outside for pitchers as a form of "PRP."

Players, upon completion of all three fielding drills, must switch lines.

Coaches should insist on good footwork and proper form as the players, upon fielding each of the first two balls, must set up as if they were going to make a throw to first base.

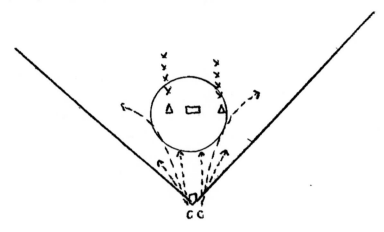

FIELDING: FORM & FOOTWORK "FOUR BALL DRILL"   "I"

While, in concept, this appears as an outfielders' drill, it is an excellent one for players of all positions except the catcher. Moreover, it can be used indoors or out of doors.

One player sets up, facing a coach who will throw softballs or indoor softy balls in succession:

- Ball One: Thrown directly over the head of the fielder. Check their foot-work. They may be required to take an over-the-shoulder catch.
- Ball Two: Thrown immediately after the player catches Ball One, the coach tosses an arcing pop fly into the "gap" to the player's right. They must run it down.

- Ball Three: A ball thrown into the gap to the player's left. Upon catching this one, however, the player must return to the original spot and face the coach.
- Ball Four: A slow-roller thrown directly at the player as a "do-or-die" play.

Note, in the diagram, that there are specific receivers to whom the fielder must throw each ball. The observant coach can again check footwork.

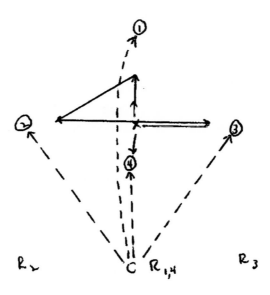

0

FIELDING: MISCELLANEOUS DRILLS TO WORK ON "THE LITTLE THINGS"   "1"

A) **LEFT SIDE COORDINATION DRILL:** Shortstops and third basemen must be able to coordinate with each other in covering the left side of the infield. How far should the third baseman range to her left, cutting in front of the shortstop to field a ball and throw to first? I like to give my third basemen this rule to begin with: "Across, but never back." Applying this simple rule, it tells the third baseman that she should allow the shortstop to take any ball in front of her. She can cut across the face of the shortstop on a line parallel with the second baseline, but she should never angle back. Let the shortstop take that ball as she is then moving in a circular route toward first base for an effective throw.

This coordination becomes something intrinsic between shortstops and third basemen who work together but I know of one coach who would actually place a cone to the left of the third baseman marking off her "territory." Frankly, repeated fungoes and application of the rule I laid down generally works well enough, but you may wish to consider the cone, especially for young third basemen.

B) **DP PIVOT DISTRACTION DRILL:** Work your middle infielders on their double-play pivots with a coach hitting short, soft fungoes or even rolling baseballs out to them for feeds and pivots. Nothing revolutionary there, I admit, but add this element. When a runner comes in, sliding hard, it can distract the pivot player, so create some sort of distraction in this most basic of drills. I know of one coach who would roll a barrel. (I actually heard him say "55-gallon drum!") across the base at the pivot man's legs. Watch her quicken her feet now! A simpler, and more controllable gimmick, is to have a coach lie on her belly and swing a fungo bat or long pole in a pendulum-like manner across the base as the pivot is being made. It is an element of fun added to a mundane drill, but one that the players indeed learn from. I know of another coach who loaded up a laundry bag with a dozen or so tennis balls. She would fling this at the feet of her pivot player.

C) **RECOVER FROM AN ERROR:** This simple drill has several levels of awareness. During infield drills, have your fielder, on an arranged call, drop or bobble or flub the ball. Why? Sports Psychologist Ken Ravizza, in his excellent book <u>Heads up Baseball,</u> suggests that the player can then practice her "mental recovery" by regaining her focus after an error and prepare herself for the next pitch. I like his book and have used his overall approach with my players, but I have doubts about the practicality of this little exercise. However, Sonny Pittano, on his contributory segment to the equally excellent book, The Baseball Drill Book, published by the American Baseball Coaches Association, uses this "Bobble Drill" to work on a player's recovery technique. He actually has them field the ball with the back of the glove and then scramble to recover, using the bare hand, and throw out a runner. He carries it a step further by loading the bases, have a player bobble a grounder and then listen for calls as to who they can then throw out.

D) **SHORT HOPS TO THE FIRST BASEMAN:** While every infielder must be adept at "picking" the ball or handling short hop throws, the first baseman must be especially good a this. One easy method of drilling this, and building confidence within the first baseman, is to simply throw short hops at a distance of perhaps twenty feet away. You can fungo them, but getting a good short hop consistently is not always easy. How about using your pitching machine to "throw" short hops? It's been done. How about this idea: if you are working with a young first baseman who insists on turning her head out of fear of the ball, put a hockey goalie mask on her.

E) **BACKHAND FLIPS & SHOVEL FEEDS (DP):** Arrange two, three or even four of your middle infielders in a circle. Rotate them counter-clockwise and as they are doing so, they are feeding softballs to each other (one ball at a time at first) as if they were beginning a double play. Have them feed with a backhand flip, an under hand toss, and then a glove-to-glove feed, all in motion. This drill is similar to the "Dominican Drill" series described elsewhere, but it is more focused on a particular middle infield skill.

G) **OVER THE SHOULDER CATCHES:** Elsewhere in this volume we describe a drill in which outfielders work on over-the-shoulder catches. Do not forget your infielders. The trajectory and arc of the ball is significantly different for an infielder making an over-the-shoulder catch, so they must work on this in a separate drill. The drill itself is simple: place all of your infielders in a line. Have one of your infielders step to the side and have her turn her back to you while looking at you over her shoulder. Toss a fly ball over her head. She runs it down and returns to the line. The beauty of a simple drill like this has distinct game advantages and when your shortstop goes out for a potentially disastrous Texas Leaguer and comes up with a game-saving over-the-shoulder catch, you will smile to yourself.

G) SHORTSTOP'S THROWS FROM THE HOLE: When this play is made it almost certainly qualifies for the highlight reel, but again, it can be practiced. You can fungo balls into the hole between short and third or use the pitching machine for greater consistency. The shortstop can make any of several types of play here:
- Backhand, plant & throw;
- Bounce throw (Ozzie Smith made this famous, but he played on Astroturf—he literally bounced or skipped the ball on one hop to his first baseman);
- "Jeter Leap"—catch the ball on the backhand, leap high in the air, spin and throw;
- Dive and throw from the knees (the least consistent technique).

H) SECOND BASEMAN'S SLIDE: Notwithstanding the artistry of the shortstop's throw as described above, there are a few truly athletic plays that the second baseman has to make as well. Fungo balls up the middle (or use the pitching machine) so that she has to slide, backhand the ball and recover to throw the runner out at first. Next, fungo balls to her left, again making her dive or slide and recover for a throw.

I) **TAG PLAYS:** As elementary as it seems, youth coaches must teach their infielders how to apply proper tags to incoming runners. This can progress into something more subtle, however, for older players. You can simply use the three infield bases and lines of players near each. There are however, four tagging techniques that need to be taught. In each case, have a feeder underhand a softly tossed ball to her partner who will be applying the tag. If possible, you may wish to add some extra portable bases arranged around the edge of the infield dirt to maximize practice time and space.

Call out each tag:
   a) "Wait & Tag"—Be sure that they tag the incoming runner's feet or ankle and not high up on the thigh. In this case the ball has arrived in plenty of time and you want to ensure an out. Minimal glove movement and perhaps two hands are to be employed. The open end of the glove should never face the runner;
   b) Slap Tag—Slap the glove down to the feet and ankles and get it out there, all in a quick motion; you may wish to use a sweeping motion here as in the old "sweep tag" technique;
   c) Running Slap Tag—Same as above, but the fielder sweeps or slaps the glove down as she is approaching the bag. This is used on a close play;
   d) "Selling the Tag"—Have the fielder slap the tag down and then triumphantly hold the ball aloft as they exit the field, selling the fact that the runner is out. This is done all in one motion and it is done with enthusiasm.

In every case, teach the infielders to "let the ball travel to them" rather than have them reach out (or worse yet, step out) for the ball.
   J) **LOOK 'EM BACK THROWS:** Teach the infielders to "look runners (leading off third) back," holding them and preventing them from scoring on a groundball. Simply fungo grounders to the left side with a runner on third. They field it, "look 'em back" and throw to first. Get creative and put pressure

on them—send the runner on occasion, either immediately or after the throw has been released. And don't forget to work on third basemen holding runners on second—"look 'em back" before they throw across the diamond. Send these runners after the throw has been released, too, and see what happens. This is the first basemen's most difficult throw.

K)THE UNKNOWN THROW: There is an infield throw in softball which is virtually unused in baseball—the second baseman throwing to third for an out. Given the shorter distances on a softball diamond; do not forget to incorporate this throw in your infield drills because it happens more often than you think. A simple drill like this one would suffice to keep the middle infielders working and still work on this vital but forgotten throw.

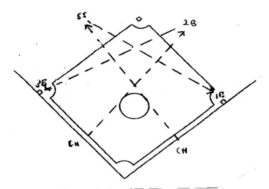

CH:coach hitting fungoes s

FIELDING: GROUNDBALL REPETITIONS "LOOKOUT DRILL"

Softball is all about repetitions, whether it is in hitting, pitching or fielding. This massed infield ground ball drill is designed to maximize repetitions.

There are four infielders stationed at the approximate locations for the first, second, third basemen and the shortstop. Note that the players situated at these positions do not have to be those specific position players; they could even be outfielders. Next, put four fungo hitters facing them across the diamond as shown. Give each of the fungo hitters (perhaps they are pitchers and catchers who are not as much in need of this drill) a "feeder" who catches the thrown balls returned from the fielders. If you still have more players, station one behind each of the fielders (or one on each side of the infield) as a back-up who chases and returns missed balls.

Give each fungo team four baseballs. Shout out a sanctified rule that no one is to go in to the infield to pick up a missed ball or stray fungo. There is a definite danger factor if they violate this rule.

Now begin to hit away. In five minutes time each infielder should see up to three dozen grounders. Maybe you wish to make this a timed sequence of seven minutes or even ten minutes. Upon the completion of whatever time sequence you have called for, rotate the players. Fielders go to back-up and back-ups come in or fielders rotate to hitter, hitter to feeder and feeder to fielder. This is your call.

Another small coaching point to keep this drill moving is to have the fielders bounce their throws in to the feeders on one hop. This minimizes not only arm wear, but also errant throws.

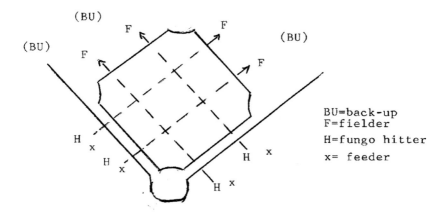

BU=back-up
F=fielder
H=fungo hitter
x= feeder

FIELDING: GROUNDERS, INFIELD THROWS & BACK-UP CONCEPTS

This drill is designed not only to impact basic fundamentals, but also to instill the concept of backing up plays, something players all too often forget even on advanced levels.

Line your players up near third base. They will get three grounders in rapid succession. On the first one, they throw across the diamond to first base. The second throw is to second base and the third is home.

Upon completion of the third throw, they are to become the new second baseman. Their predecessor slips back to a back-up position. The person who had been backing up at second rotates over to back up the first baseman while that back-up moves up to become the new first baseman. The first baseman who received the initial throw races home to back up the catcher and then becomes the catcher for the next sequence. Ultimately, the catcher runs over to join the third base line of players.

The rotation of players is diagrammed here:

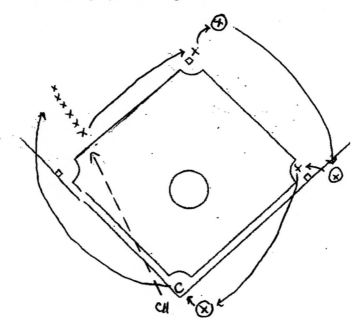

FIELDING: RELAY THROWS "RELAY DRILL"

The purpose of this drill is simple, but the skill it imparts is crucial.

Proper execution of relay throws can save a game for you. It must be taught, generally in the preseason, and once taught; it probably does not need revisiting.

Take all of your players, or just the infielders, and place them in a long line from foul line to foul line across the outfield. If you have an excess of infielders, make two parallel lines. The player at one end of the line has a ball; she begins the drill.

Once you have instructed the players as to the proper techniques of catching and throwing relays—hands up as a signal, catching the ball across the body with the glove side toward the target and using two hands in a swift and fluid exchange-step-throw sequence—let the relay begin.

If you wish you can make it competitive, use two lines; even with a single line, you can compete against the stopwatch.

Repeat the drill going back across the field in the opposite direction. Be sure to change the players at the end of the line(s) so that they get their share of work, too.

FIELDING: RELAY & CUTOFF TECHNIQUES "RELAY ROUND ROBIN"

Begin by placing two buckets or piles of softballs at the base of the outfield fence, as far away from the plate as possible. There will be a line of outfielders at modest depth in right-center and left-center. Pairs of infield relay people will line up as shown. There will be two catchers, on either side of home plate.

The infielders will do a lot of running in this drill and their relay line gets fed from an area in the outfield on each side, as indicated below.

Looking at how one line executes this drill, on a whistle, the outfielder sprints to the fence, grabs a ball and throws to the first infielder who in turn throws to the second one and then to the third infielder and ultimately to home.

More advanced players may need only two infield relay players for this drill, given arm strength what it is.

Note now the drill rotates the personnel: IF-1 sprints, after her throw, to become the next IF-2 and then to IF-3. After completing her final throw, she jogs to the outfield feeder line. Catchers simply rotate in and out if you have more than two and outfielders simply return to their feeder lines after throwing. Also, have the catchers call out the assignments: "right, right!" and "left, left, left!"

Since everything begins with a whistle, this can be made into a very competitive drill as both lines work against each other. Efficiency will always win out.

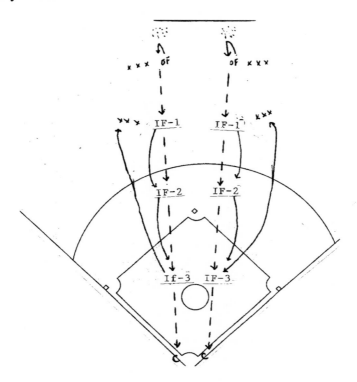

FIELDING: OUTFIELDERS THROW-THRU

Line your outfielders across the edge of the outfield grass as shown. Each outfielder has three softballs. There is a catcher at the plate. Have each OF'er place a ball on the grass perhaps ten feet in front of them. In sequence across from left field to right, each OF'er in turn charges that ball, scoops it up and in one fluid motion, crow-hops and hurls a strike to the plate. Catchers apply the tag using proper techniques. The next ball is tossed in the air by each OF'er. The "move through the ball" as if the runner is tagging up, and then they throw a strike to home. The third ball is rolled in front of them. They run it down, scoop it up, crow-hop and throw home. Three balls, three different techniques. All good.

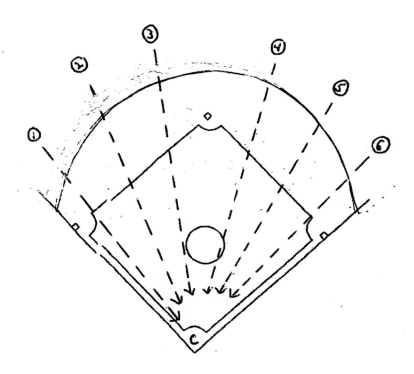

TEAM DEFENSE: ONE-THROW RUN-DOWN DRILLS

This drill was taken, with modification, from Baker and Cole's <u>Winning Softball Drills.</u> It is excellent.

Position three pitchers around the circle. Position a "trapped" runner in between first-to-second, second-to-third, and third-to-home. Use your infielders in their appropriate positions, but be sure to switch them up in order to get work as both a chaser and a receiver.

All three run-downs can be executed at once or in succession.

DRILL OPTION #1: The pitcher throws to an infielder in front of the trapped runner who then runs the base runner back toward the base they came from. One throw and a tag is put down.

DRILL OPTION #2: The pitcher runs at the trapped runner at an angle that forces them back to the base they came from. Again, one toss, a tag and an out.

DRILL OPTION #1:   DRILL OPTION #2:

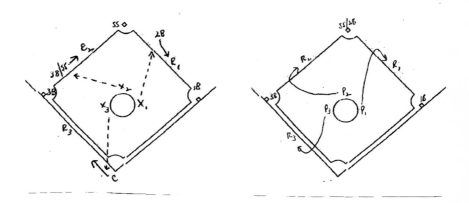

FIELDING: RUN-DOWNS "PICKLE DRILL"   *"I"*

When you trap a runner in a run-down, or a "pickle" as the kids like to call it, the play must result in an out.

First, establish some rules and guidelines for your players:

    a) run the trapped base runner back to the base he or she came from;

    b) hold the ball high, out of his glove and visible to the receiver;

    c) I allow only one "pump fake" so the receiver knows that the ball will be thrown with the next arm action.

There are two schools of thought on how best to execute the run-down. One is to have the baseman anchor on the bag from which the runner was trapped. The other fielder(s) simply run the trapped base runner back to the bag where the fielder is awaiting the throw. The other technique is to have the fielder "shorten the distance" and follow the fleeing runner after she has thrown the ball. With younger players, it is simpler and easier to anchor the rear baseman (i.e.—the first baseman if the runner is picked off first—she stays on the bag, receives the throw and swipes the tag). With older players and more savvy runners, having the rear baseman follow her throw is not a bad idea, but I have seen even major leaguers mess this up.

Here is a way to drill all this: place a set of bases along the right field line and another set sixty feet away. Three players will be involved, designated here as A, B and C. Player A, stationed along the line, has the ball, player B is in the middle and in effect, "picked off." Player C is the far-base receiver.

On the whistle, player A throws to player C and then player C runs player B back toward player A, in accordance with first of the three rules cited above. When player B is within one-and-one half body lengths away from player A's base, C throws the ball. The trapped runner should be tagged out in two throws.

By setting ups several sets of bases and trios of players, you can work your run-downs with maximum efficiency. I have seen coaches use only one or two actual (and parallel) baselines on a real diamond, but too many players are left standing around when you do this. Never use all four baselines on a diamond as too many thrown balls are crisscrossing and potential injury results.

Make it a game—see what players take the shortest time to complete their run-down and tag. It is easy to do this as all groups are working simultaneously. In addition, since all players need to work on this, including outfielders, rotate them all through the drill. A moves to B; B becomes C and C jogs over to become A.

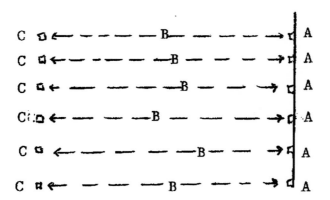

FIELDING: INFIELD & OUTFIELD FLYBALLS & CALLS "DROP ZONE DRILL"

Without describing a particular system, I always incorporated this drill in my preseason "do list." I would first teach drop zone responsibilities on an erasable diagram board. Then I taught a "call system" (the fielder coming in on a ball can ALWAYS call off a fielder going out for a ball). Having done that, I would run a complete outfield and infield on to the diamond and proceed to hit high-pop fungoes straight up, down the lines, in the gray areas over second base and shortstop, in foul territory between the catcher and the corner infielders, in the gaps, and so on. This drill is fundamental toward effective communication. Your team will catch those high-arc flies that need to be "outs" and you will minimize the chance of collisions between players.

FIELDING: INFIELD/OUTFIELD COMMUNICATION "TEXAS LEAGUER DRILL"

To work on communication between infielders going out for a pop fly and outfielders coming for the same ball, here is a simple set of drills that can isolate on areas where accidents are most prone toward happening.

Drill #1: Middle infielders—Two coaches will hit or throw pop-ups while two sets of middle infielders will then run down as shown:

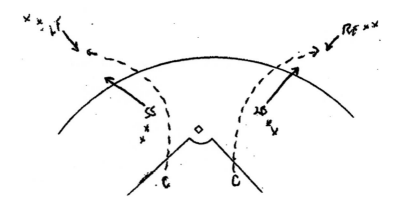

Drill #2: The Middle Infield Triangle—Work the shortstop, second baseman and center fielder in this drill:

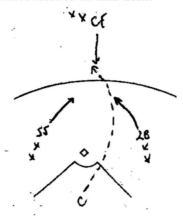

Drill #3: Down the Line—Work the middle infielder (shortstop or second baseman, depending on right or left side), the corner outfielder and the appropriate corner infielder in this drill:

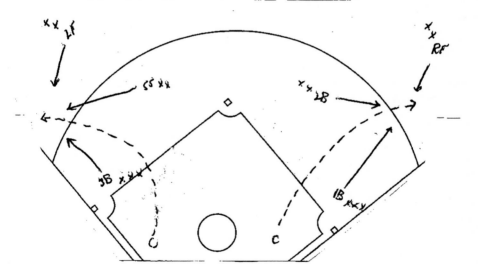

All three of these drills can be worked simultaneously if you have the personnel. Modified spatially, this drill can serve as a good indoor preseason drill as well.

Drill #4: Combinations—Have two coaches work these prescribed groups simultaneously.

Work as drop zone responsibilities and your call system as well.

FIELDING: HIT THE CUT DRILL

This drill not only instills the necessity of hitting the cutoff but it further teaches the cutoff to "telescope" in or out as she reads the depth of the ball and the strength of the fielder's arm.

Three balls will be launched. The first two by fungo bat and the third can be thrown if one desires. An entire sideline can be worked as three players are involved in each group. Group A is the outfielder; Group B is an infielder and Group C is the fungo hitter or a coach.

The first ball sails deep. As the fielder races back to retrieve it or catch it, so must the infielder race out as the cut off. The outfielder hits the cut off "in the chest" with a strong throw. The infielder, using proper body turn techniques, receives the ball and throws to the hitter.

The second fungo is of medium range and the third is a shorter fly ball that the outfielder can actually "throw through" and get it directly to the fungo hitter on a fly or on one hop.

Rotate the three groups if you wish.

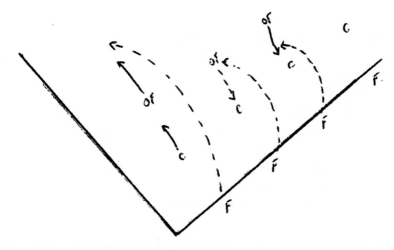

FIELDING: THROWING ACCURACY "STAR DRILLS"

This drill is elemental, fundamental and evaluative. Begin with the catcher throwing to either of the two middle infielders. Set patterns such as those diagrammed can follow or calls such as "3!", "1!", "4!" can be made. Work on quick releases after the catch, too.

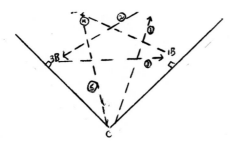

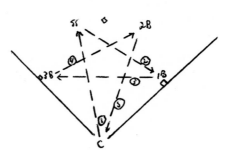

FIELDING: INFIELD "COMBO" DRILLS

Combining multiple skills in a single drill is efficient yet challenging. There is an element of choreography and timing that has to be factored in, so begin these drills slowly when introducing "Combo Drills" to your team.

SERIES 1: CORNERS & MIDDLE: Two coaches, or at least someone to roll softballs are needed; one at home and one kneeling behind the pitcher's circle. The coach at home rolls grounders to the third baseman who charges and fires across the diamond to first base. In turn, the first baseman charges slow rollers and fires across to third.

Meanwhile, the coach behind the circle is rolling grounders to the middle infielders who are working on double play pivots. You may wish to place a screen fifteen to twenty feet up the second base line with a receiver in front of it to catch balls thrown as part of this double play drill.

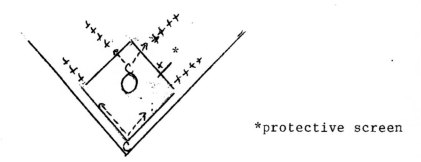

*protective screen

SERIES #2: LEFT SIDE/RIGHT SIDE: In some of the drills in this series, it helps to have two coaches, as indicated above. It is beneficial in this drill as well. Here, one coach hits ground balls to the right side where they will work on the "4-3" play and on first basemen going to second to initiate a 3-6-3 double play.

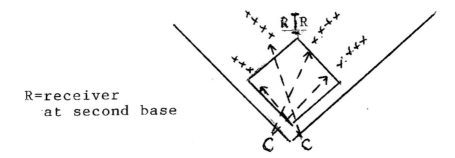

R=receiver
 at second base

On the left side, the infielders are working on 5-4 and 6-4 throws. Note that you will need to anchor a middle infielder or two on second base when you work these throws. Obviously you cannot work them simultaneously unless you use a protective screen.

SERIES #3: DOWN THE LINES: Cutoffs are essential to winning softball games and this simple drill will strengthen your team in that aspect. Whether you choose to use a "double-cut" system or a traditional single cutoff player is your option. Both are diagrammed below.

The drill itself calls for you to hit fungoes down the base lines, first and third. You will need outfielders for this phase. Your third baseman and first baseman are working on receiving the ball and alternately firing strikes to home plate. Catchers are working on their alignment calls, cut calls and tag techniques. On occasion, have the corner cutoff player throw to second to get the trailing runner.

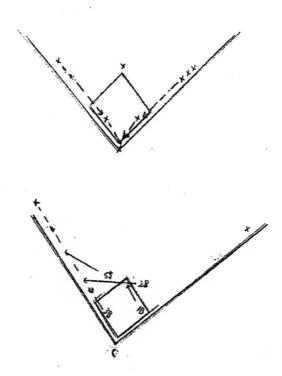

Double-Cut System—can be used on any ball that gets past an outfielder, plus balls hit into the gap. Mirror the diagram on balls hit down the RF line.

SERIES #4: DOUBLE DOUBLE PLAYS: Work your middle infielders on the standard 6-4-3 or 4-6-3 DP live and with a throw to first. You can also work the atypical "home-to-first' DP as well, but you need an additional first baseman placed at the edge of the infield cut and protected by a screen. It would look like this:

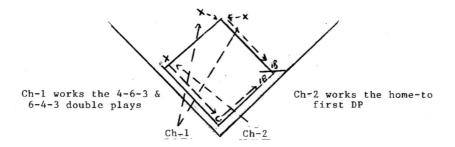

Ch-1 works the 4-6-3 &
6-4-3 double plays

Ch-2 works the home-to
first DP

Ch-1   Ch-2

SERIES #5: CENTERFIELD CUTOFFS: Your corner outfielders have already worked their cutoffs to home in Series #3, so now you need to incorporate the centerfielders. In truth, you can place all of your outfielders in CF, ensuring that they all focus on hitting the first baseman as the cut-off player. Include loud verbal calls and be sure to have the cutoff player throw to third or second once in a while to keep everyone honest. How about keeping the pitchers honest, too? Is it not infuriating when a pitcher, apparently frozen in a "brain lock," lingers in the infield and either fouls up the synchronization or fails to backup a key play at home or third? Arrange it with you catchers and third basemen that, on your signal, they are to purposely miss the ball. See if the pitcher is in place and awake.

SERIES #6: PLAYS AT HOME: Draw the infielders in and work on throwing runners out at home. Tell them that the throw MUST be a strike as "this throw goes up on the scoreboard." You may try to make it a competitive game in that coaches can try to drive a ball through the infield while the infielders will try to keep on diving and scrambling to prevent a second runner from scoring on a base hit. You may even choose to place live runners at second and third.

If you examine all of the throws made in each of these combo drills you will see that virtually every throw a fielder must make has been incorporated (except all of the catchers' and pitchers' throws but those call for more individualized drills and the old "PFP").

SERIES #7: Despite the statement that the first six series described here allows you to work on virtually every throw your fielders will need, here is yet another "combo drill" which I took from Cliff Ainsworth's elementary yet solid book, <u>Complete Book of Drills for Winning Baseball.</u> He has three drills incorporated in one:

A) Middle infielders work on DPs;

B) Catchers and third basemen work on throws to home and throws to third (bunts, slow-rollers & picks);

C) Pitchers and first basemen work on bunt overage and pitchers covering first.

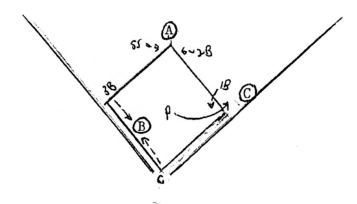

SERIES #8: Another drill from the Ainsworth book involves this combination of skills:

A) Pitchers throw live from the mound and work on bunt coverage to first or home;

B) Middle infielders and third basemen work on DPs;

C) First basemen work on tosses to pitchers covering first.

Note that there are two fungo hitters on or near each on-deck circle. The entire drill is run in phases, so the coach will shout out sequences like these:

"5-4...3-1...6 just field (no throw)"

"2-5...4-6...3 just field"

"1-3...2-5...6-4"

"1-2...6-5...4-3"

Obviously you are using the numbers employed in game scoring. Also keep in mind the various throwing lanes, so you may have to remind certain players NOT to charge a slow-roller as they may enter a throwing lane.

There are a lot of different combinations that can be built into this drill, so be creative, but with an eye toward safety.

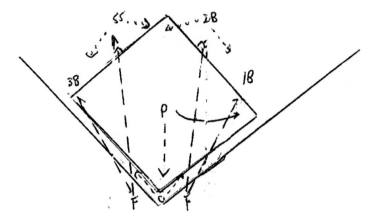

SERIES #9: I took this one from another of Ainsworth's books, <u>Drills for Winning Baseball.</u> Look closely at the diagram to see how many individual and combination skills are being worked. He has players hitting off batting tees set up on the right and left side of the infield, but I would prefer fungo hitters. Other that that, here it is, with modification:

A) Catchers receive live pitches from pitchers throwing from the circle; they work on framing and fielding bunts, although without any live throws. You can add a passed ball sequence with the pitcher covering home. Keep everything within the "alley" of the circle to the home plate;
B) Pitchers will work on live throws home, perhaps even including pitch-outs, but some of them are involved in covering first on balls fungoed to the first basemen;
C) Right-side infielders will work on groundballs hit to them and then throws to first while.
D) Middle infielders will work on double-play feeds and pivots, minus a throw to first, however; they receive their feeds from the left side infielders;
E) Left-side infielders work on throws to second to initiate double-plays.
G) When you are satisfied with the double-play repetitions, you can work on live throws from the catchers down to second base, while corner infielders can work on slow rollers and throws across the diamond.

A good drill, but as with any multiple-skill drill series, establish rules and insist on safety.

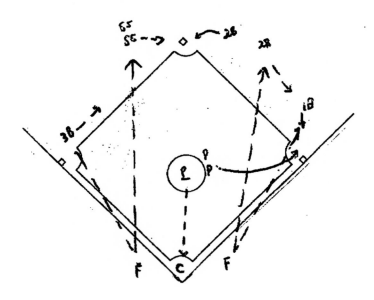

SERIES #10: As can be seen in the diagram below, pitchers work on fielding come-backers and throwing to second base, a play that can be a game-breaker if not handled properly, while corner infielders and catchers work on a variety of plays: a) foul pops, b) bunts; c) plays at the plate.

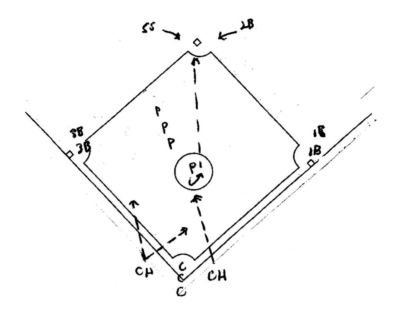

Note: The coach (CH) on the left side works with the first baseman, third baseman and catchers while the coach on the right side works the P-SS-2B combination. If you decide to work on pop fouls, consider the safety implications—be sure that the coach is skilled with the fungo bat or they must throw the pop-ups. You may also wish to consider switching sides of the diamond to hit them to the first baseman and then the third baseman.

SERIES # 11: Sequence—
1. Pitcher throws to catcher
2. Catcher throws to shortstop at 2B
   (replicating steal)
3. SS throws to first base
   (replicating double-play)

4. First baseman clears the line & throws to second

(force play)

—note: Pitcher moves third base foul line for back-up

5. Catcher throws to third base as in a pick-off

(or roll a ball out for a bunt play)

6. Third baseman throws to second for a DP

7. Second baseman throws home: P backing the play up

Diagram #1: Throws 1-4   Diagram #2: 5-7

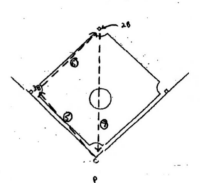

INFIELD/OUTFIELD COMBO DRILL:

This drill works in defending against the steal and in cutting runs off at the plate.

Line a series of runners at first base. They will steal second on a live pitch from the pitcher. The catcher then throws them out at second. The runner must slide and out or safe, they remain at second. The coach hits a line drive or groundball single to the outfield. The runner on second rounds third attempting to score while the outfielder throws through to get the runner at the plate or in a run-down if the throw is way ahead of the runner. The pitcher goes to her back-up position between third and home; she reads the play and backs up appropriately. Next runner.

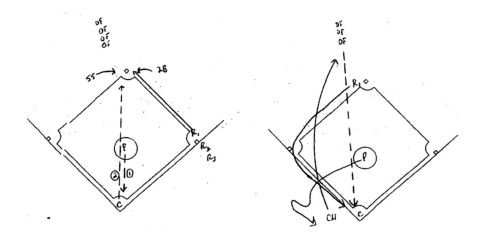

Some coaches may wish to employ a cutoff in the infield.

FIELDING: OUTFIELDERS' APPROACHES

A coaching website known as www.myteam.com offers drills in many sports, including softball. This drill teaches young outfielders how to approach a fly ball. They call it "Glide, Toss and Jet."

Line the players up facing you, the coach. The lead player steps out. On your command, they begin running at ¾ speed in the direction you point. Then you throw a fly ball upon saying the command "Jet" wherein they sprint for the ball, obviously increasing their speed. You can make this challenging by gradually increasing the distance they have to sprint. This drill can be good for increasing range.

What has been described above is actually a modification of the "team" drill. Here it is. Line the players up along a foul line; each has a ball. The first command, "Glide!", they jog out at ¾ speed. The second command, "Toss!" tells them to throw their own pop fly out in front of them. This is followed by "Jet!" which makes them speed up to run under the fly ball.

FIELDING: OUTFIELD SKILLS "AN OUTFIELDERS' DRILL SERIES"

Defensive softball has four major blocks of unique skill sets: pitchers, catchers, infielders and outfielders. Within each of these four blocks can be found distinct nuances and skill packages relevant to each position. First and third basemen, for instance, have to master skill packages that middle infielders do not, and vice-versa. What follows is a skill development series for your outfielders.

Always bear in mind that simply hitting fly balls to the outfielders is not enough, in fact 70% of what they handle in games are groundballs. Their skills, techniques and approaches must be broken down, taught and drilled.

"I" Drill #1: OUTFIELD FADES (footwork): This drill is an excellent indoor drill, but it can obviously be worked out of doors as well. I stole it from the football coaches—it is a linebacker drill. The fielder faces you in a ready position. You point over one shoulder. She opens her hips and with cross-over steps, goes back for the ball, always with her eyes on you. Do not let her back-pedal. After about ten steps, change direction by pointing over the other shoulder. The outfielder must plant her foot, open her hips once again and cross-over going in the other direction. She will, in effect, be fading back at roughly 45-degree angles. Tell her that she is working to "get behind the ball." You may wish to actually throw a softball that she must "run down" and catch. In another aspect of outfield footwork, you can point to the ground. This is the signal for the outfielder to again plant her foot and come back in for a line drive that has, imaginarily, died.

"I" Drill #2: ROUNDING GROUNDERS: Remember, outfielders are confronted with more groundballs than fly balls, so do not neglect this portion of their game. Moreover, they field a grounder differently than an infielder does. Teach them to "round" the ball, that is, get behind the ball by taking the proper angle so that when they arrive at the point of actually catching the ball, their shoulders are squared up to the relay or cutoff player. To drill this is simple—fungo grounders to their right and then to their left. Place the outfielders in a line and work all of them to the right. After the outfielder fields the ball they trot over to the other side of the field, form a new line and then you will fungo balls hit to their left. Diagram A shows the "rounding" concept. Diagram B shows an alternative way to drill this.

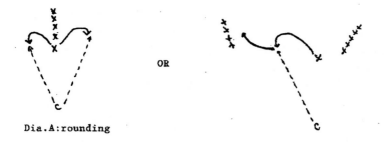

OR

Dia.A:rounding

Diagram B: each OF'er in line fields a grounder to her right, then trots over to her right beginning a new line. The coach (C) hits grounders to their left.

Variations of these drills are as follows. THE CONE DRILL

Place a line of outfielders, as shown in the diagram, facing a fungo hitter. Two cones are set beside and slightly behind the line of outfielders. The coach hits a groundball just outside the cones to either side. The outfielder must attack the ball, not directly, but by circling around behind the cone. In this way she will square up to the flight path of the ball and be in a solid position to throw runners out and/or get the ball to the proper base or cutoff.

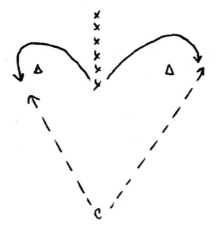

"I" **Drill #3: "DO OR DIE"** (Hard charging the ball): This technique, in practice and in game reality, is over-rated and players will often over-use it. Nonetheless, it must be taught because there will be times when the game is on the line and the runner has to be thrown out at the plate, or at the very least the ball must be returned to the infield as quickly as possible. In this technique, the ball has been hit more or less directly at the outfielder. She charges the ball, approaching it on her glove side. She will actually catch it one-handed and near the glove-side foot. With the next step, she opens the toe as if to pivot much like a baseball pitcher would do against the rubber. She pulls up, transferring the ball into her throwing hand and then launches the ball to her cutoff or target. It is all done in one fluid yet rapid motion. This is only technique and is ONLY used when a runner is on base and probably in scoring position.

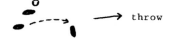 throw   (shown here is a right-handed outfielder)

Step #1: Catch ball on glove side and by the near foot
Step #2: Open the toe on the next step
Step #3: Launch throw with good body momentum and overhand action

The drill to teach this technique can be seen in Diagram A for Drill # 2. Simply hit groundballs at a line of outfielders.

This drill can be used to teach the "Crow Hop" technique as well.

Drill #4: "LEFT/RIGHT & AT 'EM": Utilize the schematic diagrams shown in Drill #2 to work fly balls at your outfielders. Line them up on one side as in Diagram B and send fly balls to their left. For line drives at them, perhaps the toughest read for an outfielder, use the same drill set-up. Teach them to take a "drop step" with one foot retreating backwards to get a side-long perspective in reading a line drive hit directly at them. If you wish to challenge your outfielders, use your pitching machine for this drill. You will find that in "reading" the machine, they will tend to get a late jump and while this is not inappropriate in and of itself, it can prove frustrating for more experienced outfielders. I have placed a manager or spare player off to one side of the machine, had them swing a fungo bat (no ball) and feed the machine at the appropriate instant to provide a better sense of timing.

The right-left segment of this drill is a standard one for pregame "I/O", or infield/outfield drills.

A coaching point for coaches: I have coached teams in tournaments where the games are played on artificial turf, something that every player needs to get used to, especially the outfielders. Hit your requisite amount of fly balls at them to be sure, but do not forget to line them up deeper than usual and hit line drives at them. They need to be able to judge the high hops off the bouncier, springier surface.

Drill #6: "BALL IN THE GAP DRILL": This is an old favorite of mine, especially in the preseason. Place two lines of outfielders perhaps one-hundred and fifty to two-hundred feet apart. Designate one as a "centerfield" line since the centerfielder in most systems has the "preferred call" and the option to get to every ball she possibly can. This drill is primarily designed to enhance communication between your outfielders and to minimize the chances of those horrific, crowd-gasping collisions.

Having aligned the OF'ers as shown below. Hit fly balls in the gap between them. The one who calls it must run it down and catch it while the other outfielder goes to a back-up position. Ground balls and line drives are appropriate for this drill as well. If both outfielders call for the ball, the CF line has preference and the other line MUST defer and retreat to back-up. (Some coaches allow the player on the "glove side" to have preference).

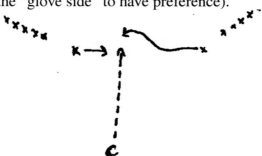

On occasion, in combination with a pre-arranged signal such as a sudden and late whistle, allow the fielding outfielder to purposely miss the ball just to see if the back-up is alert and doing her job.

Drill #7: BALL IN THE SUN DRILL: Lawsuits can emanate from the omission of this drill. It need only be taught once and in the preseason as it is an instructional drill rather than a skill drill which needs repetition. Obviously it is best to teach this on a sunny day, but frankly, the technique of how to shield the eyes and catch a ball in the sun can even be taught indoors

Simply line the players up, teach them to take a drop step to get a side-long perspective on the ball that seems to hover in the sun, get their glove up as a sun block and "stay with the ball." Next, toss softee balls or tennis balls into the air and right up into the sun. Progress to regulation softballs. Besides technique, this is largely a matter of confidence.

"I" **Drill #8: THE SLIDING CATCH:** The high trajectory "Texas Leaguer' needs to be caught. The outfielder can sell out, diving for the ball with little fear of the ball skipping past her for extra bases. How she accomplishes this is something that needs to be taught and drilled. Often, like the aforementioned ball in the sun drill, it is a matter of confidence.

Sit the players down, placing their legs tucked into a "figure 4" position. Have them toss a few short pop-ups to a partner who is also sitting in the figure four position. Note how their hands are freed up to adjust to any ball. Show them how the technique resembles sliding into a base.

Next, line them up and have a coach toss short pop-ups to them. They must time their approach so as to arrive late to the ball, thus necessitating a sliding catch. I frown on the head-long dive for a ball like this because the elbows are among the first body parts to hit the ground and thus, the hands are locked up. It is difficult to recover from this position, too.

Sliding catches can make a huge difference in the outcome of a game. They can "make the highlight film," but they must be taught and drilled. Diving and sliding for a ball does not come naturally, so this drill needs to be re-visited several times during a season.

"I" Drill #9: TAG-UP TECHNIQUE: A lazy fly ball sails into the outfield, but the runner on third base is tagging up. What was an innocuous situation now gains urgency. The outfielder must employ certain techniques to not only catch the ball, but also be able to throw a strike to the plate.

The drill phase is simple: line the players up and toss them fly balls, but have them execute the techniques you want to emphasize:

A) "STEPPING THROUGH THE BALL"—The outfielder lines up one step behind where she feels the ball would land. She catches it with two hands and on her throwing hand side. She is actually moving forward through the flight path of the ball and toward her target, either the cutoff, relay or the catcher.

B) CATCH-STEP & THROW: all in one motion. The outfielder is also transferring the ball from the glove to throwing hand during this forward movement. Too many outfielders catch the ball one-handed on their glove side and then must transfer the ball across their body to throw. This slightly excessive time factor can be the difference between safe or out. During this phase, the outfielder should also employ the "crow hop" technique in order to balance and gather momentum.

Players can actually work on these themselves with a "self-catch drill." Line up two parallel lines facing each other. One side has softballs. They will flip the ball into the air and in front of themselves. They must align their body off to the glove side, step "through the ball," catch with two hands and execute the proper throw.

"I" Drill #10: GAPPERS—A line drive has been smoked into the gap in right-center field, but your outfielders have taken the proper angles and they are able to run it down before it reaches the wall. Excellent play! What they do next, however, can determine the fate of the runner.

If the outfielder reaches that ball on a dead run to her glove side, she needs to jam on the brakes and turn over the glove side, spinning with her back to the infield briefly, in order to regain control of her body momentum. If she reaches the ball on her throwing hand side, then a few choppy "gathering steps" will be sufficient. (Hint: drop the hips as this will slow down her body momentum and enable her to recover body control before launching a good throw).

This can be drilled outdoors with a line of outfielders a coach with a fungo bat or it can be addressed indoors with thrown balls.

Drills # 7-10 are ones that need to be taught only in preseason and perhaps not re-visited unless your team is showing weakness in these areas.

The drills can all be run in this simple formation, indoors and out:

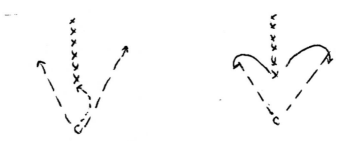

"1" Drill #11: OFF THE WALL—Outfielders need to be taught how to "play the wall." This simple drill can be employed either indoors or outdoors. Line your players up; one player steps forward. Point the ball so that she opens up toward the proper side and the races back, at an angle, toward the wall. Lob a pop fly up to the wall, just over the wall or to the base of the wall. Indoors you can use a wall of the gym; outside you can use the fence.

The basic approach I have used over the years is to teach my outfielders to retreat toward the wall with the bare hand pointing back, feeling for the wall. I allow them one glance back at the wall; no repeated swivels of the head as this can disorientate. They can use the bare hand to assist in climbing the wall or fence if need be.

You may wish to place a second outfielder near the one you are working with. This aids in communication as that second outfielder is telling her, "Ten feet!, Three feet!, You're good!" and so on. Frankly, this should be done in games as well, so add it to the drill.

Truly skilled outfielders have developed another judgmental aspect toward playing the wall. If they think that the ball may clear the fence, they will go back on their glove side so that when they leap, they can make that dramatic "homerun saving" grab over the top of the wall. This takes exquisite judgmental abilities however. The safer approach for young, emerging outfielders is to use the bare hand side.

Another consideration and something that never is formally drilled is to work with infielders playing against the fence. Theirs is a more lateral approach and bare hand side/glove side differentials would not factor in.

Diagram A (outfielders)   Diagram B (infielders)

If you are playing on a field with "quirks" such as a sloping hill leading up to the outfield fence or a fence that has weird angles, be sure to throw or fungo balls into these "quirks" so that your outfielders can grow accustomed to them and they do not become a negative factor in the game.

Outfield fences and walls have different tensile strengths producing variable rebound factors, so drill this as well. Place your outfielders up closer to you and further away from the wall. Fungo a line drive into the wall and have your outfielders learn the carom.

FIELDING: PARTNER TOSSES
This solid two-person drill can produce a lot of fly ball technique work in a brief time. Pair the players up along two parallel lines. They

face each other Line A has the softball and throws the ball over a designated shoulder (right or left done in unison to prevent collisions). The partner fades, makes the catch and throws the ball back in.

The second throw is a pop-up and the receiver works on shoestring catches, sliding catches, and tag-ups.

Repeat five times and switch lines.

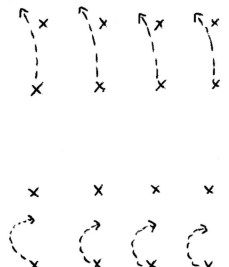

FIELDING: OUTFIELD HUSTLE DRILL

Line your outfielders up along the leftfield line. One OF'er steps out into the left fielder's position. Two fungo hitters are involved and they can hit any type of ball: line drive, pop fly or grounder. Set two infield relay players in proper position, too.

Fungo hitter A hits a ball to the OF'er who then throws to her third baseman. She then scrambles across to face the next fungo hitter.

Fungo hitter B hits a ball and the OF'er must throw to a middle infielder, either the shortstop or second baseman. She scrambles back to left field.

Hitter A hits another ball and the OF'er throws to third again. The hitter should hit a different type of ball. The OF'er next scrambles back to the centerfield position and Hitter B hits here another ball that she throws the middle infielders once again.

Four fungoes, four throws...the OF'er runs over to the right field line and begins a new line while the second OF'er steps out. It's her turn to become very tired.

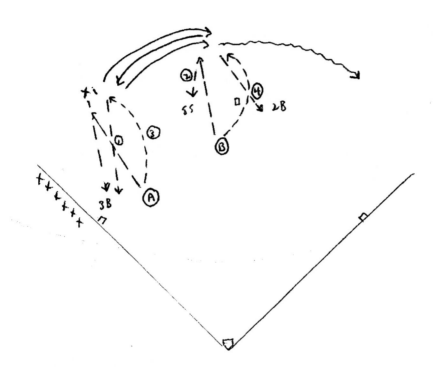

FIELDING: OUTFIELD FUNGOES "STAR DRILL" OR "CROSSFIRE DRILL"

Place outfielders in all three OF positions—right, center & left.

Place a fungo hitter and a catcher (receiver/feeder) at each base, first, second and third. They will hit fly balls in this sequence:

Fungo Team @ 1B: hits to RF
Fungo Team @ 2B: hits to CF   Sequence # I
Fungo Team @ 3B: hits to LF

Fungo Team @ 1B: hits to CF
Fungo Team @ 2B: hits to LF   Sequence # II
Fungo Team @ 3B: hits to RF

Fungo Team @ 1B: hits to LF
Fungo Team @ 2B: hits to RF   Sequence # III
Fungo Team @ 3B: hits to CF

Obviously skilled fungo hitters are necessary, so run this drill with older, experience players only.

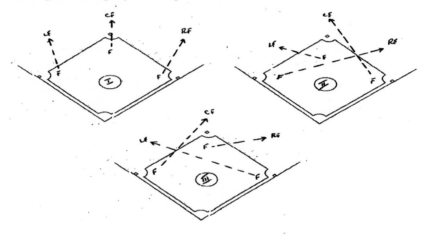

OUTFIELD PLAY: TEACHING DEPTHS, SHIFTS & ALIGNMENTS

Earlier we described how we teach the infielders about their various depths and alignments by having them stationed about the infield and observing their movement as you call out different situations and prescribed alignment. Do the same for your outfielders. Teach them your system and then, with the outfielders in normal alignment (and they can be in pairs or sets of players), call out these situations:

• "Lefty pull hitter!"
• "Righty pull hitter!"
• "No doubles"

- "Gap hitter!"
- "Throw-out position" (runner must be thrown out at the plate)
- (Specialty shift, such as one used for players like David Ortiz or Ryan Howard and is based on scouting reports or tracking charts).

OUTFIELD PLAY: SHALLOW BP

Insist that your outfielders always play shallow during team batting practice. In this way, they will work on that most difficult of skills, going back on the ball.

FIELDING: FLY BALL REPETITIONS "THREE FIELD DRILL"

In some ways, this drill is the reverse of what we described as the "Look out Drill" for infielders. In that drill, it may have been the pitchers and catchers who were doing the hitting, but more often than not, on a high school team with pitchers often being position players as well, it was the outfielders who were hitting the fungoes. In this drill the outfielders get the attention while the infielders hit the fungoes. In a practice that has a defensive theme to it, this drill is an excellent follow-up to the "Lookout Drill."

In its simplest form, the drill is set up in this way:

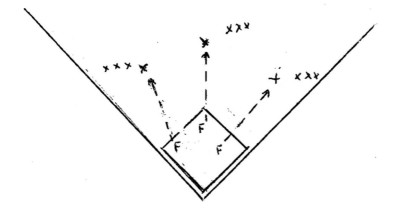

Note that there are three fungo hitters, a feeder in front of each, and the remainder of the players are fielders shagging as many flies as can be hit. There may be a desire to rotate the outfielders across all three fields depending upon time and positional specificity.

Here, however, is another variation of the same drill which would definitely call for a rotation across the outfield.

Left field is Station "A": Fungo hitters drive balls to the left and right of the fielders.

Center field is Station "B": Fungo hitters hit balls directly at the outfielders and over their heads. This is the toughest ball for an outfielder to read so coaches can make it more challenging by having the fielders play a bit more shallow than normal. This will enable them to work on "going back on the ball."

Right field is Station "C": Fungo hitters will drive ground balls to the right and left of the outfielders. The latter must work on "rounding" the ball by getting behind it and as they field it, they are squared up to their target. In addition, ground balls are hit directly at the outfielders and they must execute the one-hand pick up, "do-or-die" play.

It is a good idea to place a cutoff between the outfielders and the fungo teams so that a particular skill can be worked on as well.

FIELDING: OUTFIELD SKILLS "OUTFIELD BOX DRILL" "I"

Earlier we described the "Box Drill" for infielders' footwork. This "Box Drill" is designed for outfielders' skills and they will work to near exhaustion over a 60-second stint.

Set up four cones as shown below. An outfielder is set in the middle and she must react, sprint and catch the balls thrown by the coach (C). After each catch the fielder returns to the middle of the box.

Phase I: Throw baseballs toward cones A and B so that the fielder must make running catches in the gaps or even over her shoulder.

Phase II: Roll grounders toward cones A and B so that the outfielders practice her "rounding skills." Field and throw to spare outfielders positioned behind cones C and D.

Phase III: There are a series of options for this one: sliding catches, "do-or-die" plays, ball in the sun, catching vs. a tagging runner or even the over-the-shoulder catch. The coach can demand all of these types of catches or focus on one or two in this phase of the drill.

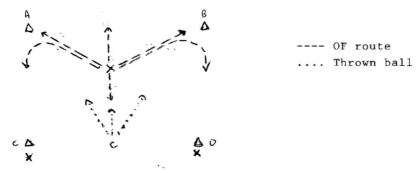

---- OF route

.... Thrown ball

FIELDING: FLY BALLS & FOOTWORK "ROUND THE CLOCK DRILL"

Place five cones around an area roughly the size of a softball infield. Station a player at each cone. They will be fielding fly balls thrown at them, over their heads and over their shoulders. Two coaches are needed.

Begin by throwing (or better yet, using one of the slingshot devices mentioned elsewhere in this volume) a fly ball to the player positioned at "Three O' Clock." They catch it and throw it back to a receiver near the coaches. Next, "One O' Clock," then "Noon," and so forth around the perimeter. However, as soon as the ball is tossed at the player in the "Noon" position, the second coach launches a ball to the player at "Three O'clock" to build as many reps into the drill as possible.

Note that the two coaches coordinate in such a way that there is an idle player in between the active fielders. This is for safety's sake. This drill can be done with players stationed at 3 o'clock, noon and nine o'clock.

You can rotate players around the perimeter, initiating them from a "feeder line" near first base. They would filter in after the second pop-up has been thrown to that particular position on the "Clock."

You can also make this a conditioning drill by using only one player scrambling around the perimeter to each cone. As soon as they catch one ball they must hustle to the next cone and set up for the next pop-up. You can feed into this drill, as described above so that a minimal amount of players are standing around waiting. Thus, two or even three players are fielding pop-ups at any given time.

"I" This drill can serve as good indoor training drill, too. Emphasize proper "tracking" techniques and proper footwork. Also stress the point about "getting behind the ball."

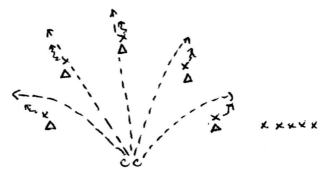

Be careful to ensure adequate space between players, for safety's sake. You may prefer to work every player with the same type of ball—everyone shags a ball thrown over their left shoulder, for example—until every round is completed before drilling another type of ball.

FIELDING: GROUNDERS, POP-UPS AND FIELDING RANGE "LATERALS"   "I"

A player stands in line, holding a softball. She throws it to her coach and then immediately breaks to the left. The coach will roll a grounder, throw a line drive or toss a pop fly and the player scrambles to receive it, often on the run. They stop, set up, throw it back and then scramble to their right. Repeat three times (six catches per player total).

Use traffic cones to mark the "set-up locations.

Make sure that the players do not cheat by breaking early. They cannot move until the ball hits the coach's glove.

Coaches can really challenge their players here and this is an excellent indoor drill with thrown balls or an outside drill with fungoed balls.

This drill can also serve as an evaluative drill and/or a conditioning drill.

The coach should mix in a variety of thrown or batted balls—line drives, fly balls, and grounders—all with a sense of conditioning, evaluation and technique.

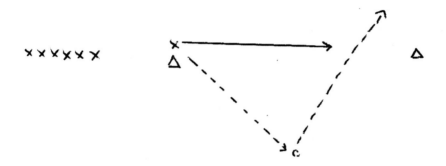

FIELDING: FLY BALLS "SHOESTRING CATCH DRILL"
"T"

Use the same drill format described above to teach outfielders how to make the "shoestring catch" on a sinking line drive or dropping pop-ups. Have the coach throw the ball (thrown is better than fungoed as it is more consistent) just inside the maximum reach of a player. You may wish to add in the semi-dive or "catch and roll" technique, but if you do, be sure to utilize mats indoors or grass surfaces out of doors.

FIELDING: OUTFIELD FLY BALLS "RUN 'EM DOWN" DRILL

Place a fungo-hitting coach on the infield out by second base. Align all of your outfielders on the right field foul line. One steps out from the line. The coach hits a fungo into the gap to the outfielder's right. She must run it down and catch it on the run. She then stops, sets up and awaits the next fungo, again to her right. Running that one down as well, the drill continues until all of the outfielders have reached the left field line and the drill then mirrors itself with fungoes to the outfielders' left.

For maximum efficiency, I have seen this drill used with two fungo hitters. As soon as one ball is caught, the next outfielder in line steps out and receives a fungo that she must run down, thus two outfielders are simultaneously involved in catching fly balls.

To keep the tempo, if the fly ball is missed and beyond the reach of the outfielder, she is instructed to let it go and set up for the next fungo. Generally, each outfielder will catch three fly balls as they race across the outfield.

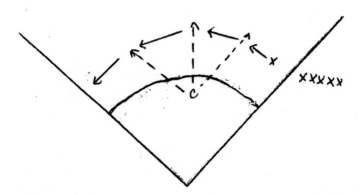

FIELDING: OUTFIELDERS' TARGET THROWS

Place a ball bucket or a chair just up the third base line near home—exactly where you want the outfielder to hit the catcher's mitt for a play at the plate. Fungo some balls to the outfielders. They are to catch, step and throw to get an imaginary runner at the plate. They must hit the target you just set up. This can be a fun drill. Perhaps work up a point system for "close" throws or add an infield cutoff person.

FIELDING: A TEAM THROWING DRILL Arm Strength, Fielding Footwork

Use the whole field and employ your entire team. They will throw in unison on the single command to designated partners.

Begin at 30-feet and gradually increase to 60-feet.

Throwing sequence:
1. Strong throws, glove-to-glove
2. Relay throws (use body turn and footwork)
3. Ground balls (charge and crow-hop)
4. Grounders right (rounding)
5. Grounders left
6. One-hoppers
7. Pop-ups (must call for it)
8. Long fly ball (over the shoulder catch)
9. Shoestring or sliding catch

This drill is a great pre-practice warm-up drill that incorporates all aspects of fielding which has been previously discussed in this section.

STATIONS! STATIONS! STATIONS!

If you haven't caught on to this yet, the idea of "teaching stations" permeates this book. Divide and conquer. Break you team down into skill groups and isolated drills to effectively teach this game. The old idea of having kids stand around is not only inefficient but also stultifying/boring.

A sample practice plan might run like this:

3-3:10: Stretching & agilities

3:10–20: Throwing, completed by quick-throw drill

3:20 -   Stations –   Group A: (pitchers/catchers) – Hitting in cage

                                     Subdivided stations – Tee

                                       (5 mins. Each)   Side-toss

                                                        Straight hitting (5 swings, rotate)

                                                        Bunt (all techniques)

Group B:	(outfielders) –	Shag
		Sliding catchers
		Vs. wall
		Do-or-die
		Ball in gap drill
Group C:	(infielders on diamond)	Star drills
		DPs
		Bunt defenses

Group A: will work on bullpen session followed by PFP

4:20 Water break
4:30 Team Defense (or Offense); (situation; 1-3 double steal Off/Def.)
5 p.m Conditioning—running rules sprints today

STATION WORK: A SAMPLE PRACTICE PLAN

Pat Barnaba observed that since there were many times in which she was the only coach on the field, she had to resort to station work to maximize practice time.

She suggested these stations in a typical practice plan:

HITTING CIRCUIT:
A) batting cage
B) soft toss into net/screen
C) hitting wiffle golf balls with broom handles
D) tee work

COLLECTIVE DEFENSE:
A) On the diamond, coach hits fungoes to outfielders to work on throws to all bases; base runners can be used.
B) OF: goes to the batting circuit while coach works the infielders are on the diamond working standard pre-game throws plus bunt defenses. Pitchers and catchers are bull penning.

C) Infielders go to the batting circuit while outfielders work on throws home and the pitchers and catchers can join them or finish their bull pen session. Pitchers can take their catchers through their position specific drills, too.

Note that the entire field complex is being used. It takes organization and it takes self-discipline on the part of the players, but it does work.

BASERUNNING & CONDITIONING

"We want to be the first team to practice and the last team to play."
Coach Dave Serrrano

This segment begins with form running and timing players.
It concludes with conditioning sprints.
In between, everything from sliding to double steals and a package of
"heads up baserunning" rules is incorporated.

CONDITIONING: TIMING PLAYERS IN THE PRESEASON

Everyone does it; the stopwatch in preseason is ubiquitous. But, why? First of all, you want to know who your fastest players are. This is obvious and it does help in formulating a lineup. You want quicker players in the top two and final spots in the batting order so as to avoid clogging the bases. You also want to know who your fastest outfielder is because if all other things are equal, the fastest should be the centerfielder.

Time all of your players in the 60-foot dash and record the data.

Next, time them from first base in a steal of second.

You must know what the numbers are. Time your players and then utilize the data.

CONDITIONING: FORM RUNNING   *"I"*

Many teams begin their practices or pregame with form running dynamic stretching drills for quick feet. There are many such drills, but here is a sampling:

   a) "Chop-Chop"—short choppy steps with plenty of arm pumping action;

b) "Step-outs"—long strides in which the back knee actually touches the ground;

c) "Butt-Kicks"—running with the back of the heel actually making contact with the leg-side buttock;

d) "High-Knees"—bounding with the knee striding as high as it can; insist on high arm pump action;

e) "Carioca"—traditionally a football drill, it involves lateral running with cross-over and cross-under steps;

f) "Backwards running"—self-explanatory

g) "Three Leaps and Run"—pliometric bounding for three distinct leaps, with plenty of arm thrust, followed by a sprint;

h) "Side Shuffle"—shuffling or slide-stepping the entire distance; keep the shoulders squared, parallel to the baseline.

The distance for these running drills is not long, perhaps 60 to 75 feet. "These drills are very effective in enhancing game performance. In addition, they help minimize muscle and joint injuries," observed Coach Barnaba.

CONDITIONING & FOOTWORK: CONE DRILLS
Creativity rules the day here. The coach can make up any combination of footwork drills that he or she wishes.

Place four traffic cones in a square perhaps 15-20 feet apart, even longer is permissible. The players will execute four different footwork drills in between each cone as they work their way around the perimeter. For example:

Cone 1-Cone 2: back peddle
Cone 2-Cone 3: side shuffle
Cone 3-Cone 4: carioca
Cone 4-Cone 1: full sprint

You can ask for standing broad jumps between cones (plyometric bounding), spins, cross-over steps, hi-knee skipping, butt kicks, and so on.

You can set the cones in any pattern you prefer. For example:

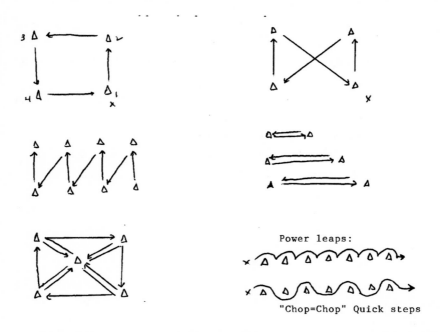

"Chop=Chop" Quick steps

Coaches may wish to purchase rope ladders or step-up platforms and create quick-feet drills relevant to these items.

CONDITIONING: MEDICINE BALL WORKOUTS   *"I"*

The "core" is often overlooked in softball as coaches and player focus on getting their arms and legs in shape. Think about it—the "core" or the center of the body's mass (i.e. torso and hips) is essential to many phases of the game: hitting, and so forth. Core strength equals body strength.

The age-old medicine ball can work the "core" quite efficiently. Using 10 or 12 pound medicine balls (relative to the age of the players, of course), exercises such as the following can be done in station work or as a team drill.

A) BACK-TO-BACK: Players stand with their backs touching each other and they pass the medicine ball around their sides, exchanging it clockwise and then counter-clockwise.

B) OVERHEAD: Line the players up and have them pass the ball over their heads to the next player in line.

C) THROUGH THE LEGS: Line the players up and have them bend over, passing the ball between their legs to the next recipient.

D) OVER & UNDER: Combine exercises B & C.

Many, many more medicine ball exercises exist, but these few can suffice to enhance core strength for your team. The number of repetitions is up to the coach.

"I"

KNEE-HIGH RUNNING: Line your players up and have half-a-dozen small hurdles (they can be purchased in most sporting goods chain stores or in a catalog—they are only about a foot off the ground) placed out in front of the line. Run over them with high knee actions. Plyometric side-hoops and two-legged bounding can also be done. All of this strengthens the lower body and particularly the fast-twitch muscle fibers so necessary in softball. Each plyometric bounding/leaping drill requires a 30-60 second recovery period, according to research.

CONDITIONING: CIRCUIT TRAINING

Oh, how I remember this well: 6 a.m. daily all through summer football camp. I played Division III football and reportedly our coach, "Nick" Nicolau wrote his doctoral dissertation on circuit training. It was exhausting, but we did come out of camp each year in top shape.

Circuit training is designed for conditioning rather than skill development, so sport-specific exercises are not as important as they might seem. Be creative in designing your circuit. You may wish to group your athletes in pairs or threesomes, no more than that. Each station may take only 15, 30 or 45 seconds but each time interval can seem like an eternity. The number of stations are up to you as a coach and is somewhat dependent upon the size of your squad and upon the facility you train in.

A typical circuit may include:

a) push-ups;
b) sit-ups;
c) squat thrusts;
d) pull-ups;
e) step-ups or short-flight stair running;
f) box jumps;
g) wall jumps (touching a piece of tape high on the wall);
h) short-length suicide sprints (side-to-side);
i) jumping rope;
j) medicine ball trunk twists (or other exercises with the medicine ball);
k) wrist-rollers with five-pound weights;
l) depth jumping;
m) "Box" drills—backwards run/carioca/side-shuffle left, side-shuffle right.

You can come up with as many stations as you wish. Be creative.

PRE-PRACTICE AGILITY SERIES

As an old football coach, I am a believer in agility drills. After completing our team stretching routine, I would have the players go through their agilities. The form running drills, which also serve as agility training, would follow. They were described earlier. Here are some suggested agility drills that I would use to train middle school and high school players:

A) GROUNDBALL CROSS-OVERS: Keeping the shoulders square to the path of the groundball, the players, as a team, execute a cross-over step to the side indicated by the coach and field an imaginary grounder, pulling it in with two hands and proper form. Next, go to two-step cross-over in which they are lowed to turn their shoulders, but square up to the ball upon arrival at the receiving point.

B) FLY BALL FADES: Described elsewhere, have them work on going back on fly balls.

C) PRE-PITCH READ STEPS: On the commands, "One!", "Two!", "Spread!" or simply have them read the coach going through an imaginary pitching motion, have them walk through their pre-pitch footwork. This, too, is described elsewhere in this volume.

D) LOWER BODY HITTING ACTION: Have them, on command, take an imaginary swing, but focus on the toe-tap load-up, the hip action and the back heel roll. This is primarily for younger players.

Next, they pair up for two-girl bat resistance drills, also described elsewhere. Two person arm strengthening resistance work can be done also. These are described in the throwing/pitching section of this book.

All this takes just three-to-five minutes, but it pays dividends in terms of sound muscle memory and proper mechanics.

BASERUNNING: A TEACHING SEQUENCE "T"

Young players have to be taught to run the bases. Here is a teaching sequence that may be helpful in doing this.

A) **RUNNING TO FIRST BASE:** Two techniques—teach them to run through the bag as if they have hit a ground ball and must beat it out. The eyes focus on the base, the head dips as the last step is taken, the near edge of the base is the one that receives the lead foot, the hips drop after the runner clears the bag, the player stays on the foul line without turning to the outside or the inside and head turns to look over the right shoulder into foul territory. And too many coaches, especially on the Little League level, just tell the kids to run...

The second technique involves the intricacies of running out a ball hit in the air, a line drive or fly ball. Teach them to "cut" the bag by flaring out on the grass in foul territory and touching the inside corner of the base. While some coaches insist on the inside foot or the outside foot—I do not care which foot lands on the bag as long as it hits the inside corner of the base. They turn toward the infield with their shoulders facing second base. In teaching this technique, I will place a traffic cone perhaps 10 to 15 feet in front of the base and on the baseline. Or, more preferably, I will literally stand with my back to the plate and on the line so that the runners must swerve to the outside to avoid me. It works.

How about this teaching gimmick? Spray paint the inside corner of an old base to provide a visual reminder for runners as to where they should step when "cutting" the bag?

In drilling these two techniques, you can apply the stop watch for the ground ball technique to add an element of competitiveness. In drilling either technique, occasionally send the runners to second just to instill the notion of aggressive baserunning.

More advanced players should be taught to read the first baseman's feet. If they come off the bag to the inside, or home plate side, the runner should slide and she can avoid being tagged by a heads-up first baseman handling an errant throw.

B) **FIRST TO SECOND/THIRD:** Teach your runner to "cut" the second base bag as well, but in this sequence, insist that they look at the third base coach. As a coach, you can wave them in or hold them up, but they must learn to look for this.

C) **SECOND TO THIRD:** I teach four basic rules (with two caveats) for runners leading off second base. These rules are to be applied off a secondary lead, or after the pitcher has released the ball.

- **FLYBALL BEHIND THEM—TAG UP!**
- **FLYBALL AT THEM OR IN FRONT OF THEM—TURN & READ**

(Hint: you can modify this one. In middle school ball or in more developmental leagues, I would teach it this way: Fly ball at them or behind them—tag up. We would challenge the center fielder's arm).

- **GROUNDBALL AT THEM OR BEHIND THEM—GO!**
- **GROUNDBALL IN FRONT OF THEM—HOLD.**

  (Hint: tell them that if the third baseman charges the ball, then they can go.

  Simply line the players up and hit fungoes; run them two at a time.

D) THIRD TO HOME: I teach three reads along with appropriate rules.

- Groundball: Either go on contact or go when the ball clears the infield.

Practice both.

- Freeze on a line drive.
- Fly ball: back to the bag.

E) TAG-UPS: Young players need to be taught this and for many of them it is a difficult concept to grasp. Little Leaguers simply do not understand that a player can advance after a ball is caught for an out, but when they do finally get it, it is a revelation and they feel that they are actually "stealing" a base.

Set players at second and third with a "feeder line" or players near second base. Hit or throw fly balls to a player or coach. As soon as the ball hits the glove, have them tag and go. Have them listen for the "Go" call if it looks like the outfielder has no shot at catching the ball, too.

More advanced players need to be taught a "Safe go" or a "Tight go" call. In the former, the outfielder catching the ball is deep and the outfielder has no chance of throwing the runner out, so teach her to delay a half-second so as to eliminate any doubt of an umpire calling her out for leaving the base early. With the latter call, and these two techniques are actually verbal calls from the third base coach, you are telling her that the play is going to be a close one so quickness, both in the read and the speed are vital.

BASERUNNING: SOFTBALL LEADS AND BREAKS   *"I"*

Leading off a base in softball is fundamentally different from that which is taught in baseball. Softball coaches generally prefer either of two techniques: the "rocker" or the sprinter's push off. Teach both; drill both. Then make the sprints which emanate from this part of your team's conditioning package.

The rocker begins with a player straddling the bag. Off first base, this means that the left foot clutches the edge of the bag while the right foot is in foul territory. (Fig. B) The player literally rocks her upper body as the pitcher begins her motion. The "sprinter's push off" technique calls for the base runner to use the edge of the bag as a sprinter's block, placing the right foot on the edge and pushing off when the pitcher releases the ball. (Fig. A) Note the position of the rear foot—it is not directly behind the bag. This helps avoid getting the foot caught up with the base when the runner breaks. It may prevent an embarrassing trip.

Without getting into the debate about the advantages and disadvantages of either technique, it is obviously valuable to teach both.

Fig.   A Fig. B   Fig. C

In drilling these techniques, there are several ways to go about it:

a) Line players up along the right field foul line, using the line itself as a imaginary edge of the base;

b) Throw several portable bases out along the right field foul line;

c) Line players up at home (use the plate itself as a base) and fill the bases with four runners, each working the technique and sprinting to the next base.

This drill can be a good indoor drill as well.

Coaching Point: Many players are now using a technique in which they hold their lead hand up in the air to simulate the timing of the pitcher's release. (Fig. C) This helps them time their break off the bag. The pitcher releases the ball—the runner brings the hand down sharply. Some suggest that it adds a bit of momentum as well.

BASE STARTS: Players can practice base starts with the coach acting as a pitcher. Players start rocking when the pitcher begins wind-up. When they see the Coach's pitching hand reach her hip, they explode off the base into a lead position. If they hear the coach clap her hands, they sprint to the next base. If the Coach continues the pitch to the "follow through" position and calls "Back," the players then dive back (this, of course, should be taught beforehand) to the base and call "Time" (this is necessary so that they get used to asking for the time out so that they can get back to standing up without the fear of being tagged out). Continue the sequence until the players wind up where they started. The players at 3rd base should sprint home and then jog to 1st base for the next start.

BASERUNNING: TEACHING PROPER SLIDING TECHNIQUES
"T"

From Little League on up, there should be at least one practice session devoted to teaching proper sliding techniques. Frankly, if not done, it can result in a lawsuit. The first question asked by a lawyer when his client sues due to an injury incurred when sliding into a base is, "Was he specifically taught how to properly slide?"

I begin by having the players sit around me in a semi-circle. I then ask them to lean back and place their legs in a figure-4 position. Tell them to slightly bend the knee of the lead leg and there you have it—the proper leg position in most slides. Still lying on their backs, have the players raise their arms and hands in the air. Call this the "Halleluiah Position." It teaches them to drop into the slide rather than jump into it. A good reinforcement is to have them grab a clump of grass in each hand and as they actually go into a slide, throw the grass in the air. This drill was seen on an old video on Little League practice organization by Al Herbeck and Al Price.

When it comes time to drill sliding, set four, five or six bases out on the outfield grass with the players lined up along the foul line. To teach the proper timing of when to go into the slide, use a rope held by two coaches. The rope is stretched out perhaps four or five feet in front of the bag and the players will slide under it. The coaches must be cognizant if potential injury, so they will raise the rope at the right moment if it looks like a slider may get "hung up" on it. I have also seen swimming pool "noodles" used as well.

With young players, I teach these basic slides:
- Bent leg straight in
- Bent leg evasive*
- Pop-up slide

With older players, it is appropriate to teach the head-first slide (remember to bunch the fists, thus protecting otherwise exposed fingers), but not with a lot of repetitions. There probably is some merit in teaching the "take-out" slide to older players as well.

Some coaches prefer to teach sliding indoors in the gymnasium or field house with the players sliding on blankets. Actual sliding pads exist too. Others prefer rainy days when the grass is wet or snow covered and an otherwise "lost day" can be turned into something productive. Whatever your preference, avoid over-teaching. Contrary to techniques taught in days gone by,

* Have coaches at each base stand to one side as if receiving a throw. In a slow-motion hand action, have them bring the "tag" down and impart the notion that the player should be sliding away from the tag.

Players do not need to be taught to slide on either hip. Also, keep the "reps" down. One slide per type is probably sufficient if the player executes it properly. Sliding is probably a bit like parachute jumping—you are only given a limited number before injury sets in, so don't use them all up in practice.

One final note—older coaches can certainly call on younger assistants or even experienced players to demonstrate. My days of doing "the demo" are long gone...

BASERUNNING: TEACHING PROPER SLIDES "4-SLIDE DRILL"

After having taught the fundamentals, one way to incorporate all, or most, of the various sliding techniques, is this multiple drill.

Line the players up at home plate near the on-deck circle. They will make their way around the bases, not in one continuous run, but on base-to-base sprints signaled by four distinct bursts of the coach's whistle.

Running from home, they will perform an evasive "slide-under" to avoid the tag from a canny first baseman who has come off the bag on an errant throw. Have the runners read the feet of either an imaginary or a real first baseman. If she comes off the bag to the "inside," their reaction should be to slide under the tag.

Leading off first in anticipation of the next whistle, they will break for second and execute an evasive bent-leg slide. Here they are seeking to avoid a tag as if on a steal. Some coaches may prefer to teach a take-out slide in this phase of the drill, but there are rules prohibiting old-school take-out slides now.

Lead off second and on the next whistle, they break for third and execute a pop-up slide.

Lead off third and on the final whistle, they slide into home with a head-first slide. (Even though they may not use this slide into unforgiving catcher's gear).

Once the drill is underway, four base runners will be going at once. With safety conditions in mind, I would not make this drill a weekly event, and I do admit, with regrets, that I have used it as a disciplinary thing for players who do not like to get their uniforms dirty.

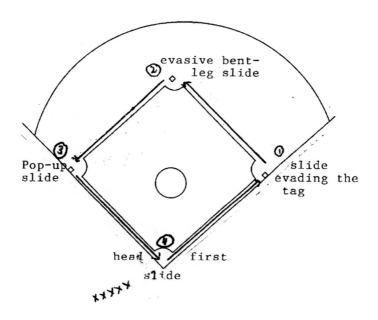

CONDITIONING: APPLYING BASERUNNING RULES "RUNNING RULES SPRINTS"

Good baserunning is one part instinct, one part speed and one part IQ. Only the latter part, the intelligence quotient, can be taught. Apply the "Running Rules" described in the teaching sequence discussed earlier in this chapter.

Use your entire team, setting four to six runners at each base and home. You are in the circle with a bag of balls. Once getting their lead, every player sprints 60 feet to the next base. Here are the reads:

You simulate a pitching motion allowing the runners, going together en masse', to time their "release" lead. Then:

- Roll the ball on the ground toward home (passed ball or dropped third strike);
- Roll the ball toward the right side of the infield;
- Roll the ball toward the third baseman;
- Roll the ball directly at the runners leading off second;
- Hold the ball straight out behind you (line drive);
- Hold the ball in the air facing toward right field;
- Hold the ball in the air directly in line with the runners leading off second base;
- Hold the ball in the air facing toward left field;

For the simulated line drives and fly balls, slam the ball to the ground after a second or two indicating that the ball has been caught and that all tagging runners should go.

The group of runners leading off third and second can apply the rules I outlined above, including the ball rolled toward home as a passed ball. The runners at the plate should run through the bag on any rolled ball and "round" or "cut the bag" on any ball in the air. They should employ solid technique in both reads.

The group of runners leading off first are to treat everything as a straight steal of second, but they should pause if the ball is hit in the air, reading it just as they would in a game. For them, when the coach slams the ball to the ground (the signal for tagging runners to break), they are to read this as a ball that has dropped in and they should advance to second.

This is a great conditioning drill and one that can make your players smarter on the base paths.

CONDITIONING: RUNNING RULES SPRINTS II: A VARIATION

Another method of instilling your baserunning rules as part of a conditioning regimen is to have the players at home fungo a ball. Somewhere, anywhere.

Place the team members around each of the bases and home as described in the previous drill. They will all run together. They will not, however, read the coach in the circle as described above. They will read the ball hit by one of the players in the group at home plate.

All reads and rules are applied by the various groups at their respective bases; all groups sprint for 60 feet.

BASERUNNING & CONDITIONING: 4-3-2-1 SPRINTS

These can be grueling, so use them selectively. Line the players up at home and blow the whistle at safe intervals (perhaps when the lead player is halfway to first). The players will run four sprints to first base, three to second, two to third and one homerun. They are to employ proper running techniques and never, ever "dog it."

CONDITIONING: BUILDING "TEAM" CONCEPTS INTO TEAM SPRINTS

New Jersey High School Hall of Fame softball coach Pat Barnaba always ended her practices with five sprints to first base. Each one would be run individually with extra sprints added if improper technique was used or someone "dogged it." She insisted, however, that the entire team run the final sprint, together spread out across the diamond. Another technique, one that I have used, is to have the lead runners, those who finish the running sequence first, act as cheerleaders "pulling the last ones in," as it were. Hoot, holler, and make noise; clap and pull for each other, especially after a difficult practice or on a hot day.

Coaching Point: During her sprints, Coach Barnaba would place one foot on the baseline, perhaps half-way to first and this would visually reinforce the idea of running in foul territory. If the runner makes contact with her, she'd add another sprint.

CONDITIONING: TRADITIONAL CONDITIONING SPRINTS:

As I describe these various types of conditioning sprints, let me insist on one thing: variety. Sprinting at the end of practice is as traditional as it is tedious, but it is also fundamentally necessary.

One way to break the tedium is to change the type of conditioning assigned each day.

In the chapter of this book on pitching, three types of sprints were described, so we will only a cursory definition here:

A) **"Poles"**—Run the warning track alternately sprinting and jogging or walking between outfield signs, light stanchions, or other markers.

B) **"Line-to-Line"**—Sprint from foul line to foul line...or at least insist on a long, hard run.

C) **"Warning Track Runs"**—Similar to what was suggested above, the players will run the warning track either back and forth in the outfield or around the entire stadium.

D) At the risk of being politically incorrect, these sprints are called "**Indian Relays**." Group your players in teams of five to eight per team. They jog, released at intervals, around the field, perhaps along the warning track. The player at the end of the line sprints to the front of the line as the line jogs along, never stopping. Each player, on reaching the end of her line, does the sprint to the front. This can be grueling. Call this, **"Run-jog-run."**

E) **"First-to-Thirds"**—a grueling drill, but an excellent conditioner. Players start from home plate, jog to first and then "turn it on" with a full-out sprint from first base to third base. They may walk from third to home as part of their recovery.

F) **"Secondaries"**—With the coach in the circle going through a simulated pitching motion, the players will break into a proper "release" lead on delivery to the plate and then break on the coach's verbal command. This is a particularly effective drill for teaching the concept of "release" leads, especially off second base.

G) **"Lead-n-Steal Sprints"**—Again with a coach in the circle, have the players take their proper stance off first base. Use as many as five to ten players at once. They all do not need a base to lead from—use the foul line. The coach will simulate players reacting properly. Remember, in softball the runner cannot leave the base until the pitcher releases the ball or, in some governances until the ball crosses the plate.

H) **"Monday Mile"**—Notwithstanding your team's practice and game schedule, I always liked to build some distance running, although not excessive, into my program. Hence, the "Monday Mile." Run the perimeter of the school grounds or a track itself, it matters not. Have the team run together as it is a good team-building concept. Back when I had sound knees, I would run with the kids, too.

I) **"Dugout Sprints"**—Tell all or your players to sit down in the dugout. They all know the positions they play. Use the traditional baseball scoring method to designate who is to sprint from the dugout to their position on the field. Yell out sequences such a "5!, 6!, 9!" or "2!, 3!, 7!". Your "utility player" is going to hate you because if any player plays multiple positions, they must respond and sprint when any of their positional numbers are called. Another point—this drill works best in open-faced dugouts with no fencing and no "gates." Admittedly, with safety concerns, these types of dugouts are becoming rare so this type of sprinting may go the way of the dinosaur.

A good variation of this drill can be conducted in this manner: place one team on the field and the remainder of your players in the dugout but with pre-designated assignments. Fungo three routine outs, grounders or flies, to the team in the field. At the conclusion of the third out, they must sprint off the field and into the dugout while the unit in waiting must sprint out to their position. Repeat the process as per need. Make it a game—the last player off the field must be in the dugout before the last player from the dugout reaches her field position.

J) **"Dirt Ball & Dropped Thirds Sprints"**—Place a coach on or near the circle and another coach behind home plate as a catcher. Line your players up near the plate. This sprinting sequence begins with a throw from the rubber and the catcher either missing it completely or dropping it. The player at the front of the line breaks for first as if it was a dropped third strike. In fact, all of the runners lined up at the plate will react this way. Sometimes, however, the coach/catcher does actually catch the ball just to keep the sprinters honest. Next, with a runner at first, they are to read the downward trajectory of the ball being thrown and break for second the moment it strikes the dirt. You are beginning to fill the bases now as there will be a runner at the plate reading the "dropped third" and runners at first and second reading "dirt balls." Eventually you will have runners at all bases including third, but that is where their reads change a bit. For the runner on third to break for home, it must be a clearly missed ball, in effect a passed ball. If it is a dropped third strike or a passed ball that does not kick far enough away from the catcher, the runner does not break. For her the drill is over and she can jog back to the line near home plate.

This is an excellent drill for instilling aggressiveness in your base runners as you always want them to look advance on every opportunity. There are some other subtle aspects to this drill that you can fit into your package of "reads" for base runners. Many coaches like to have their runners go on dirt balls that kick up the baselines, so you can have your catcher/coach flip the ball in those directions if you prefer a clearer read. Secondly, when I coached middle school ball, a standard play was for a runner on third to break for home on a dropped third strike that was thrown to first. You can add this one in as well by having the catcher/coach throw a soft overhand lob up the line to reinforce that particular read. The catcher/coach can also flip thrown balls with an underhanded toss back to the screen behind her to make the passed ball read clearer. Yet another read manifests itself on high school and middle school diamonds when the backstop is closer. In this instance you want your runners to read the carom off the fence, so the runners on the bases will hesitate at second, read the rebound angle and either go or hold. The carom is of course created by the catcher/coach once again.

K)"RECOVERY SPRINTS"—In this type of sprint, players are lying on the ground, recovering to their feet and sprinting to the next base. Think about: how many times have you needed a player to pick herself up from the dirt and break for the next base after a throw has errantly sailed wide? This sprint emanates from that premise. The player on first is lying on her belly, simulating a dive back to the bag perhaps after a caught line drive. The player at second is on the right side of the bag in a bent-leg slide position. The player on third is also lying on her belly. All three recover on the whistle and sprint to the next bag. The sprinting lines are fed from the first base coaching box.

CONDITIONING: BASERUNNING CIRCUITS

Players will run five all-out sprints during the course of this circuit drill. They will line up at home to begin the circuit. The sprints that follow are these:

- Home to first—jog back;
- Home to second—stay on second base;
- Second to home;
- Home to first—stay at first base;
- First to third—jog back in

If you wish, you can cap it off with a homerun sprint, all bases touched, but generally speaking, players are "gassed" at this point so the "homerun sprint" may be too much.

How many "circuits" you demand of your players depends upon their conditioning level, your mood as the coach or how well they played the game before...

Run the players in pairs or small groups rather than singularly. This is clearly more efficient.

Coach Barnaba often preferred adding base coaches. They would use proper signals to keep running, slide, hold-up, etc. This reinforces the practice of having the runner "pick-up the coach."

CONDITIONING: BASERUNNING TECHNIQUES "DODGER SPRINTS"

Who knows if the L.A., or even the Brooklyn Dodgers invented this drill, but it is a good one nonetheless.

Line all players up near home plate. The first two players up will occupy each batter's box, right and left.

As diagrammed below, player A in the left batter's box, sprints to first but on a "flare out" route and continues to second as she would have as if she had hit a double. Simultaneously, player B, in the right batter's box breaks and legs out an infield grounder, straight through the first base bag. This places runners at first and second as the next two players step into their respective batter's boxes.

As the next two batters/runners repeat the sprints executed by players A and B, the latter work on these running routes: A rounds third and goes home while B goes from first to third. This loads the bases for the third combination of runners.

Teaching the drill is actually easier than it reads here. Besides player B's (right hand batter's box) initial run to first, all sprinters will take two bases from where they end up. Players should, of course, switch from A's route to B's route on their next go-round.

(Note that there are slight variations of this somewhat traditional drill).

- - - - - - -   Player B
———————   Player A

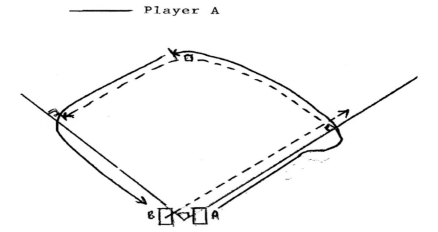

CONDITIONING: "COACH ATNIP'S HUSTLE DRILL"

Coach Don Atnip of Harding High School in North Carolina contributed this fine drill in a book entitled <u>Coaches Guide to Championship Baseball Drills and Fundamentals.</u> The book is nearly 30 years old and it is one of the first drill books that I bought for my coaching library. I have used this drill and it is outstanding.

Place an infield around the diamond in their normal defensive alignment. The drill works best with three runners at a time, but with only three running the bases it can be a bit time consuming and many players are left idle. Hence, I offer Coach Atnip's version and my own modifications.

With your runners lined up at home, their task is to make it all the way around the bases before the defense can throw the softball around the diamond two times. The throwing sequence works like this:

   a) Catcher to shortstop covering second;
   b) Shortstop to home;
   c) Catcher to first base;
   d) First baseman to second baseman on second;
   e) Second to third;
   f) Third to home;
   g) Repeat entire sequence.

My modifications have included running three runners. Another adaptation is to include your pitchers and outfielders and you can make this a competitive drill. As three runners, no matter what positions they normally play on defense, complete the circuit, they grab their gloves and take over three positions in the infield (C, 1B & 2B). The defenders come in to run. The next three will become the new SS, 3B and C, and so on through the order. I have even had the team toss their gloves in the infield to a quicker pickup.

Cautionary note: make sure that the runners are wearing batting helmets for this drill.

You can also make this competitive by challenging a unit of outfielders (running) against the infielders (throwing), thus "IF vs. OF." Specialty players such as pitchers can be filtered in as per choice by the coaching staff. Keep score for a designated set of rounds and then have the "IF" team race the bases against the "OF" squad covering the infield.

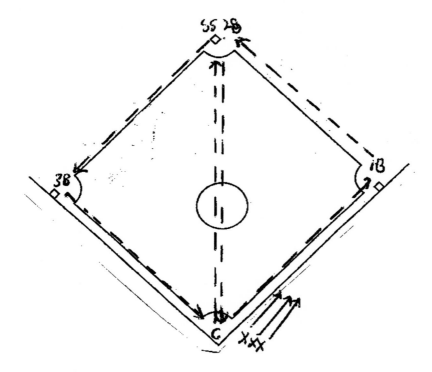

BASERUNNING: "TAKE TWO DRILL"

I took this drill from Baker & Cole's essential drill book, Winning Softball Drills. It is excellent in instilling aggressive base running. Every runner from home plate will try to stretch her base hit into a double. The coach sets an outfield in place and stands in the infield to fungo softballs into the gaps. The outfielders must run each ball down and, using the cutoff if they need it, try to gun the player down at second. It forces glove-to-glove throws. The fungo hitter must be skilled in hitting shots that the fielders can handle...or not.

CONDITIONING, FIELDING & HUSTLE: THE BARNABA HUSTLE DRILL

Coach Pat Barnaba used this intriguing drill as a change of pace. She used the full infield diamond with first and second bases as markers. The team is divided into two squads. One lines up at home and the other at third. The coach is in between the two lines, holding a fungo bat. A catcher stands on either side of them.

Line One goes first—the lead player sprints out from home to first and rounds the bag. The coach hits a fungo—fly ball or grounder. She fields it and throws to the catcher standing to the right of the coach. The moment the ball is thrown, the lead player on line two sprints out, rounds second and fields another fungo. She will throw to the catcher on the coach's left.

Repeat the drill and keep it going. There is a rotation: the fielder becomes the catcher and the catcher goes to the back of the other line.

Have the girls cheer each other on…make noise.

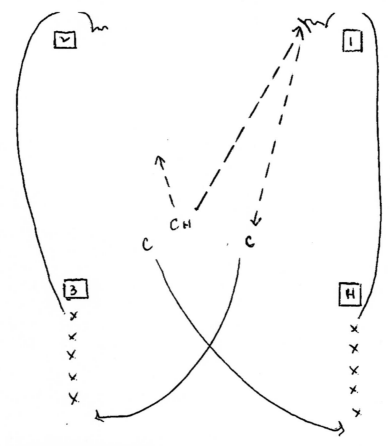

BASELINE CHASES:

Place one runner on each base and another about six-to-eight feet in front. On a whistle, all eight runners sprint to the next base. The runner from behind tries to catch the runner in front. Change positions for the next "race" from the next base.

Here is another type of baseline chase—Two teams of runners are involved, each with three girls. One "team" is at home while the other is at second. On the whistle, each team breaks for the other team's point of origin—home to second and second to home. Who wins? Their sprints are done. Put another "team" out at home or second.

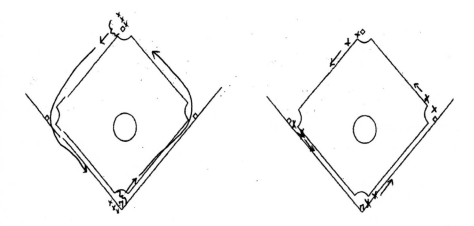

TEAM DEFENSE
COMBINATION DRILLS

"Too many kids want to be "great" without passing "good."
It's hard work and they don't seem to understand that."
Coach Jerry Stitt

This section focuses on team defense and includes everything from pre-game "I/O" to "Situation" and its various nuances. Also included is a novel idea about how to increase your "DP" reps. First and thirds are included as well. Fly ball drop zones, cutoffs and even creative ideas about how to scrimmage an opponent are all included in this innovative chapter.

FIELDING: TEACHING INFIELD DEPTHS & WORKING INFIELD THROWS

Set five players at each of the infield positions. Run a full infield, including the catcher but excluding the pitcher, out on to a regulation infield. Have a second set of infielders, perhaps even a third ready to go in the dugout.

First, teach them the prescribed infield depths that you include in your system. I would suggest these:

    a) Infield up (play at plate);
    b) Double-play depth;
    c) Corners up/middle infield halfway (between drawn in and regular positional depth).
    d) Shade the lines (corner infielders.)

Next call out each of the various depths and watch for alignment. Then fungo one groundball to any of the infielders.

The first throw automatically goes to first base, but after that it is totally up to the caller (you, as the coach, or your catcher if she is sufficiently confident). Be creative. Yell out base numbers such as "2!" then "3!" and then back to "2!" then "4!" and so on as each throw is nearing completion. After an erratic throw, it ends and the next field is run out. This drill can make for a high-tempo, competitive atmosphere. It is especially good for younger teams even veteran teams in the preseason. This drill is especially good for younger teams in the preseason. However, the second phase of the drill, the random throws around the diamond, is a very good evaluation drill for older teams during tryouts. You can even chart the errors.

FIELDING: PRE-GAME INFIELD/OUTFIELD "I/O"

Why not incorporate your regular pre-game "I/O" as a practice drill? If it is good enough to prep your players for a game, it should be good enough for practice sessions, too.

Readers will probably agree that every team warms up in a similar way, or at least within a generally recognized format. The difference, then, is how snappy and sharp is your pregame "I/O"? Does it get the attention of the other team? If so, then you have a leg up on them already.

Ten minutes is all a team needs for its infield/outfield warm-up and, under NCAA rules, ten minutes is all that is allocated. You must maximize your ten minutes.

Some teams hit grounders to the infielders while another coach hits fly balls to the outfield, usually standing along one of the foul lines.

Other teams place a coach behind the circle to hit fly balls and grounders to the outfield first, working all of the cutoff situations. Since the catchers are not involved in this segment until the end of the drill, some coaches throw balls or have the catchers do footwork drills blocking or work on bunt plays to first until the time comes for cutoff plays at the plate.

By the way, demonstrate sportsmanship. Keep your "I/O" to ten minutes. Never cut into the other team's time on the diamond. Umpires will not wait.

FIELDING: I/O VARIATION—THE TWO-BALL INFIELD DRILL

Once the outfield has finished its throwing sequence, then it is time for the infielders to put on a show. What I offer here is something that emerged from my years as a high school JV coach. We'd get off the bus, quickly stretch and then have to rush through a pre-game "I/O."

We used two balls

The first sequence is a simple "one over, nice & easy" a regular throw to first from each infielder. However, you as the fungo hitter will send the second ball out as soon as the first throw is released. The first baseman must be aware that balls are coming to him quickly and sequentially. You can rotate two first basemen if you have them. If a ball is squibbed, allow no infielder to charge into the infield as there is an injury factor in this.

Next, "one & cover." The infielder throws to first and then races to cover her bag as the first baseman, upon receiving the ball, throws home whereupon the catcher throws to the baseman covering the appropriate bag. The next throw goes to third and then home to you, but if you have one catcher, you may have to have the throw bounced to your hand.

The next series is "one & around." Throw to first again, but the first baseman goes to second with the next throw; the middle infielder, in turn, throws to third and then the ball is returned home. Note that if your initial fungo went to the shortstop, it is the second baseman who will take the throw from first and vise-versa.

"Cover corners!" is next. Roll grounders out to either side of the plate and the catcher then throws to first, followed by third. Next fungo one to the first baseman who charges and throws to third.

Finish with the infielders throwing to the plate ("Home & In") from a "drawn in" position. You may wish to incorporate slow rollers here, too one to first and then to home—if time permits. Conclude with a pop-up to the catcher(s).

Done in ten minutes. Allow the infielders to chase no errant throws or missed grounders. Get them later. Remind middle infielders to stay back and not charge any ball.

It is not revolutionary in design, but this "I/O" needs to be practiced as its timing is initially unsettling to infielders. They love it once they understand it, however.

This form of "pregame" is an excellent practice drill in and of itself. It can be extended in duration with repeated throws and grounders.

FIELDING: LITTLE LEAGUE "I/O"

I have worked with my granddaughter's softball teams these past few years and it drives me crazy to see the girl's blithely drift on to the field at 3:55 for a 4:00 p.m. game. These are 8-10 year olds, I might add, so their priorities, and those of their parents, are clearly not yours. I insist that they be on the field 45 minutes before game time.

We begin with 10 minutes of wiffleball golf ball batting practice in a corner of the outfield.

Next, ten minutes of throwing: form, regular and long-toss.

Next, it is our modified "I/O." Traditional infield/outfield pregame is not an option as there is simply too many missed throws and it takes too long. Have one coach at home plate and another near second base. The coach at home is working this sequence:

- Pitcher to home
- Pitcher to third
- Pitcher to first
- Catcher to first

Meanwhile, the coach out by second is working this series:

- Left side outfield to shortstop
- Right side outfielders to the second baseman
- Shortstop to second
- Second baseman to shortstop covering second

Finish with this:

- Middle infielders to first
- Shortstop to third.

To be sure, there are "omitted throws," but generally, these young players initially cannot throw across the diamond from third to first. Also catchers never throw down to second nor do first basemen. Remember, this is youth league girls' softball and their arms are not what they will become.

You need to modify this to the physical capabilities of your girls.

Sell them on the idea that this is a formal practice that is being conducted prior to the game. Maybe that will get them there on time, but don't bet on it.

Then it is back to the dugout to practice team cheers, get a cold drink from Mom or discuss post-game "play dates"…It's a different game. To quote a fellow coach, who played college ball and coaches hitting for advanced players in his private batting cages, "It's not about the game…it's all about the cheese fries" (after the game).

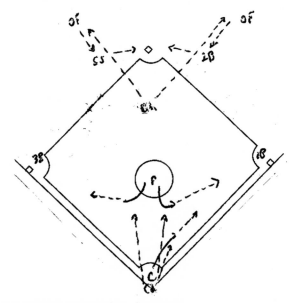

PREGAME WARMUP, D-1 STYLE

Pregame warm-ups can be completely different in softball as opposed to baseball. Here is a quick and easy one utilized by many

NCAA teams and the beauty of it is that both teams warm-up simultaneously!

You need two coaches or fungo hitters, one along the baseline nearest the dugout hitting to the infielders and the other up the line hitting to outfielders.

The infield fungo hitters alternates the balls being hit, one to the line of corner infielders and the other to the line of middle infielders as indicated in the diagram below. The first player on line steps out receives the grounder and tosses to the receiver near the fungo hitter. They then go to the end of the line. Note that their outfielders work to their left, toward the fences and receive fly balls and grounders as per necessary. They then work their way back, chasing down fly balls hit to the right.

Pitchers and catchers are warming up off to the side.

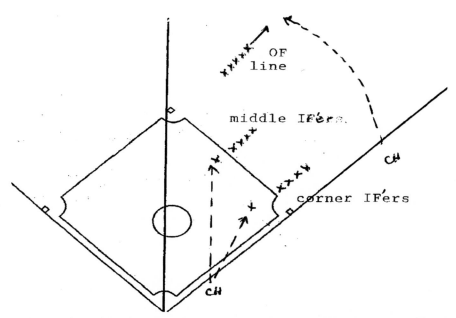

Note that the diamond is divided in half so that both teams can warm-up together. While the proper throws are not practiced, players are getting accustomed to the playing surface, which can vary greatly from diamond-to-diamond in softball. Their return throws to the fungo hitter, with a receiver standing nearby should certainly be snappy, so arms are worked.

FIELDING: SOFTBALL PRE-GAME, AN ALTERNATIVE SCHEME

Coach Pat Barnaba developed this pre-game warm-up. Outfielders are shagging flies and the pitcher-catcher battery is warming up. Her initial focus is on the infield.

Phase I: Infield fungoes—The coach works the middle infielders in their double-play combinations, 4-6-3 and 6-4-3. Then she adds the third baseman, but here's the twist. As soon as the middle infielder throw's to first, the coach hits a grounder to third who must then throw to first. The first baseman throws home. Timing is important as two softballs are flying around the infield. She will also mix in bunts to third.

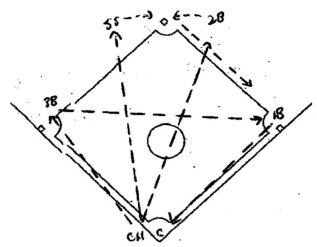

Phase II: With the outfielders and the battery still warming up, the coach shifts her focus to right side/left side combinations. Grounders are hit to the SS-3B side and they throw to second or third. In between, 2B-1B grounders are hit and they throw to the appropriate base on their side of the diamond. She may even mix in a pop fly or a "tweener" to work on communication skills.

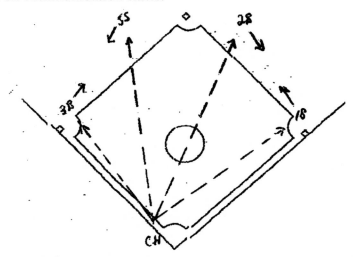

Phase III: The outfielders now jump into position. She yells out "Runner on First!", hits a fly ball or grounder and the outfielder, beginning with the leftfielder and moving across to right, throws to the appropriate base. The infield is moving and the other outfielders are backing up appropriately. Next, "Runner on Second!" and then "Runner on Third!" The outfielders throw home and jog to the dugout side baseline.

Phase IV: "Home and In" for the first baseman—she fungoes a grounder, the first baseman fields it and throws home. She follows her throw, receives a slow-roller from the catcher and throws that one home also. She then jogs to the baseline to join her outfielder.

Phase V: The pitcher joins the infielders by getting into the circle. She pitches one ball and the catcher throws down to second.

Phase VI: "Home and In" for the rest of the infielders and the pitcher. They throw a strike to the plate followed by a slow-roller which is charged and thrown home. All then report to the baseline.

Phase VII: A pop fly to the catcher. Then she bolts down the line high-fiving her teammates.

This entire warm-up can be done in 15 minutes or less and every throw necessary for the game will have been practiced, even if only one time.

FIELDING: DPS BETWEEN INNINGS

Coach Ed Cheff described a unique approach to working on backhands and double plays during a game and in between innings in an issue of "Collegiate Baseball" (September 4, 2009). He is a nationally renowned coach at Lewis & Clark State College in Idaho.

Instead of having the first baseman throw grounders to the infielder as the pitcher warms-up for the defensive half of an inning, how about this? The shortstop and third basemen each bring a ball with them. They will, each in turn beginning with the third baseman, simulate a backhand stab, with proper footwork, and throw to second where the second baseman receives the ball and throws to first. The first baseman holds the balls rather than throwing them back.

Think about it. The real purpose of between-inning throws is to loosen up the arm. Why not work on something productive as it happens? Also consider how many extra double-plays you will have worked on during the course of the season.

Once each infielder, including the first baseman has thrown to second for a double-play, the latter returns the balls to the left side infielders to repeat the process.

BETWEEN INNINGS WARM-UPS: THE SBU ALTERNTIVE

Kevin Oberto, friend and coaching colleague whose daughter Kelly went on to play D-1 and has provided excellent insights into the editing of this book, said that he saw Stony Brook University, where his daughter played, adopt this throwing sequence in between innings as the pitcher warmed up.

All throws emanate from the third baseman who positions herself near homeplate, but off to the side so as to avoid interfering with the pitcher's warm-up tosses.

The first baseman begins the sequence by rolling a grounder to the third baseman near the plate.

The third baseman rolls a grounder to shortstop who throws to first.

The third baseman rolls a grounder to the second baseman who throws to first.

The third baseman roll simulates gathering in a grounder to herself and then throws to first

The third baseman rolls a grounder to the first baseman and then scrambles to third to receive a cross-diamond throw from the first baseman.

Note that the third baseman does the traditional tossing of the grounders, but there is the key point that separates this drill—they do it from a spot near home plate. Note that they are not interfering with the pitcher's warm-up throws, but off to the side enough to create the illusion of the ball coming at them from the home plate area.

May I suggest, with all due respect, this modification?

All throws emanate from the first baseman

Throw #1: grounder to 3 B for a 5-4-3 DP

Throw #2: grounder to SS for a 6-4-3 DP

Throw #3: grounder to 2 B for a 4-6-3 DP

Throw #4: grounder to 2 B for a throw to third

Throw #5: cross-diamond throws to third, sweep tag and a throw to first.

The first baseman may not get a grounder as with Stony Brook's interpretation, but all possible infield throws are executed. My apologies—I always look at drills and look to "tweak" them…

TEAM DEFENSE: "SITUATION" & ITS VARIATIONS

Teams everywhere, in prepping for a game, play "Situation." Set a defense out on the diamond and fungo base hits, outs, hard grounders, fly balls, etc. Play an imaginary game for six, seven or nine innings. You should use spare players as base runners, but this is not totally necessary. When you do use runners, tell them to be wildly aggressive. Stretch base hits; go when you might not normally take a chance.

Some coaches like to begin each play with a pitch thrown from the mound. It does add a sense of realism and perhaps timing, but if your pitchers have thrown a lot in recent games, this is not necessary.

Some coaches like to have the players' fungo softballs out to the fielders as if they were at bat. Fine, but you cannot guarantee that certain situations your team may need to work on will arise. Other coaches have the players hit the ball off a batting tee to initiate play. Unless you want to make this a ground ball scrimmage, do not do this. It does not work. Fly balls can be produced only when the batter drops down and uppercuts her swing, something most of us do not teach.

Simply put, the best way to run a "Situation" drill is to swing the fungo yourself. You can control things more. There are, however, other types of "Situation" drills that can be developed off this simple concept.

A) **"R-2"**—Place a runner on second base for every fungo you hit. The defense will work on cutoffs, tagging runners, relays, holding runners, and so on.

B) **"R**-3"—Draw the infield in and hit your fungoes with a runner on third. Again, tag plays, holding runners, plays at the plate, etc. all emanate from this. You can work on that rare home-to-first double play, too.

C) **"21 Perfect"**—We've all been there—your team has just played a game and it was a defensive nightmare. Errors, miscues and omitted coverage punctuated the day and established your mood for the next day's practice. Almost invariably I would return to this drill, "21 Perfect." My players could almost sense that it was coming. The concept is simple: play "Situation,' but when an error is made, either physical or mental, the situation reverts back to the 'Top of the first; no one out, no one on," Pressure begins to build during this drill. Perhaps you have only made it to the fourth inning before repeated errors have brought you back "Top of the first..." Don't sugarcoat things; challenge them and insist that they record 21 outs without any errors in between (21 outs being that which would be required for a seven inning game). Pressure builds as you make it into the fifth and sixth innings. Runs are scoring because you want to work on cutoffs and bunt defenses, but that is not the issue—21 outs without an error is the goal. You enter the seventh inning, three outs to go and many of the players are praying that you don't hit it to them. You can see the inherent value in this drill. Every coach wants to infuse game pressure in his drills. This one does exactly that. It may take up 20-30 minutes of practice time…it may take hours.

D) **"21 Perfect"**—a variation: Brian Shoop, Head Coach at the University of Alabama at Birmingham referred to this one at a coach's clinic I attended. It involves only the infielders. They are split into two groups, one working on isolated and individual drills such as wall drills, Dominican Drills, etc. The other group is on the diamond and they are the ones under pressure to record 21 perfect outs (As Coach Shoop's team often plays 9-inning games; he expands this drill to "28 Outs").

If and when an error is made in the course of the 21 or 28 outs, the groups switch and the count goes back to zero. However, he does something that avoids embarrassing the player who made the error. If, for example, the shortstop booted the ball to end the streak, then immediately, the coach yells out, "Shoot Two!" and they execute a double play before switching stations.

"I"

TEAM DEFENSE: CUTOFF PLAYS "WORKING CUTOFFS WITHOUT A FUNGO"

Traditionally, coaches will stand out behind the pitcher' circle, hit fungoes to the outfield, in the gaps and down the lines working on their cutoffs, relays and double-cuts. Without describing particular systems, there is an efficient way to accomplish the teaching and reviewing of all this without hitting any ball.

Take a walk, or better yet drive the golf cart, out along the warning track. Place three softballs on the ground in each corner near the foul pole and three more in each "gap," left-center and right-center. Next,

292 Richard Trimble with Pat Barnaba

set your infield and outfield in their proper alignment. Runners are optional, although many coaches believe in their necessity.

All you have to do as a coach is stand somewhere, perhaps in the middle of the diamond, where you can be heard. On a whistle or on a clap of the hands, point to one of the areas where the balls lie. The players then scramble to retrieve one of the balls and execute the cutoff play that you wish to practice.

In first describing my cutoff system, I am a believer in the erasable dry-marker board. I like to diagram it all up and then go out on to the field to practice the system. This can be useful indoors on a rainy day. Teach the concepts before you teach the physical dynamics.

TEAM DEFENSE: BUNT COVERAGES   *"1"*

Described elsewhere, this can be done indoors on an abbreviated diamond or outdoors on a true scale. Place the infield in its proper positions and bunt away.

Perhaps you would like to make it a scrimmage between the outfielders and/or pitchers versus the infield in live situations.

Be sure to add runners and be sure to include a pitcher on the mound.

Bunt coverage in softball are virtually identical to those in baseball.

TEAM DEFENSE: BUNT COVERAGES "SPLIT INFIELD DRILL"

Andy Lopez wrote up a version of this drill in his book, <u>Coaching Baseball Successfully.</u> I merely tweaked it a bit over the years.

Set two pitchers on the mound and near the rubber. Place an infield out on the diamond. You can actually use lines of infielders if you are deep enough to have several players at each position; they will not interfere with the execution of the drill and actually serve to keep it moving more quickly.

The right side of the infield works on bunts to the right side, so you will get pitchers and second basemen covering first; first baseman, pitchers and catchers will work on fielding bunts as well. Incorporate your call system, too. Yet another dimension involves having the first baseman, catchers and pitchers throwing to second, based on your call.

On the left side, catchers and pitchers will field bunts and throw to third base. You can also incorporate the "wheel play" where the third baseman charges for the ball and the shortstop covers third or you can work the "anchor play" where the third baseman holds the bag.

You can also add in a play at the plate now and again just to keep them thinking and reacting.

The only play you really do not get to include involves the throw across the diamond from the third baseman to first or the first baseman to third. Simply conclude the drill with a round of bunts incorporating this skill.

Coverage are called by the coach who also rolls the balls out on either side; throws are called by the fielders themselves.

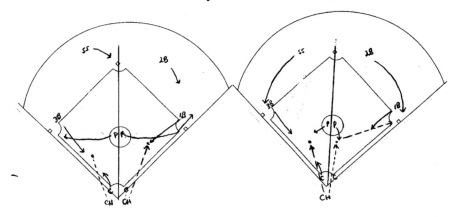

TEAM DEFENSE: DOUBLE-STEAL DEFENSES

Defending the double-steal, or "first & third" is virtually identical in softball and baseball.

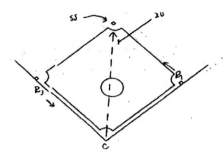

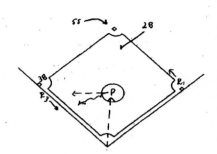

DEFENSE #1: The catcher throws through to second base while the second baseman, watching the runner on third, has the option of cutting the ball off. If the runner on third holds, she can let the ball go through to the shortstop, nailing the runner from first

DEFENSE #2: The ball is returned to the pitcher with a strong throw. The pitcher can throw to third or run at the trapped runner. Note that the pitchers run toward the runner at an angle which allows her to force the runner

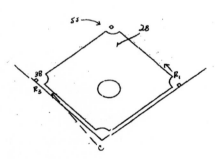

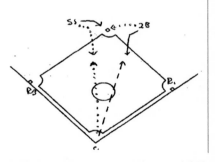

DEFENSE # 3: The catcher bluffs a throw to second and fires to third or snaps a throw to third without bluffing.

DEFENSE # 4: The middle infielder, depending on the coach's call, takes two steps toward the bag and then cuts into the infield to receive a throw from the catcher. They key the runner on third, throwing to third, home or running at them with a cutoff angle. (Both defenses are shown here—SS or 2B as the cutoff)

TEAM DEFENSE: FLYBALL DROP ZONES

Also described earlier, arrange a full outfield and infield on a diamond. Fungo fly balls and work on who covers what and where. I like to diagram the zones on a dry marker erasable broad before sending the players out on to the field. I also like to teach my verbal call system in this drill.

TEAM DEFENSE: CREATIVE SCRIMMAGING

Coaches are often too set in their ways. When they "scrimmage" against other teams, all too often it means just another game—three outs per inning, six to nine innings, play it straight. Why not add elements and situations that you need to work on? We have referred to situational scrimmaging in indirect ways throughout this book, but allow me to list and explain:

A) **First & Third Scrimmage**—cited previously, but here is another way to add vital 1-3 situations into a normal scrimmage scenario. As soon as the teams have completed their between-innings warm-up tosses, run a one-pitch do-or-die "first and third." The offense runs and the defense try to stop them. One pitch, that is it, and then move on to play ball. Think of the possibilities—your teams will work through perhaps one, two or three live 1-3 situations in the scrimmage, but here you have added nine more offensively and nine more defensively with little time added to the game.

B) **Suicide Squeezes**—Apply the format mentioned above to suicide squeezes. One pitch; do-or-die before each inning begins.

C) **Six Outs**—to keep things moving, clear the field after six outs rather than three. Of course, clear the bases after each set of three outs, but this is an effective way to maximize the number of innings in a given timeframe. Furthermore, it can help keep pitchers warm, especially if cold weather is a consideration.

D) **2-1 Counts**—If you want to use a batch of pitchers, perhaps getting them live situational work or perhaps evaluating them, use this one: each batter comes to the plate with a 2-1 count. Especially effective early in the preseason, it keeps things moving and it prevents burning out pitchers' arms. (A pitcher with a 25 pitch limit can throw three of four innings in this setting rather than a more conventional two innings).

E) **R-2 Scrimmage**—Outlined earlier, you can work on your cutoff system and, equally important, see who drives in runs with this one. Every batter has a runner on second to drive in.

F) **R-3 Scrimmage**—With this setting, you can work on cutting off runs at the plate with the infield drawn in.

G) **R-2/R-3 Scrimmage**—Work on not only cutting runs off, but also keeping the ball in the infield on a base hit, attempting to prevent the second run from scoring.

H) **Bunt Scrimmage**—outlined earlier.

I) **"Gonna Go" Scrimmage**—I once had the luxury of several viable candidates competing for the catcher position. In a scrimmage—live conditions against another team—I wanted to test their arms in combat, so I applied the one-pitch, do-or-die scenario described in sections (a) and (b) above. That runner on first was going…can you throw her out? No pitchouts allowed.

J) **Mini-Games**—Instead of traditional scrimmaging and the keeping of a score to see who wins (as if that mattered…), try this one: a seven-game series but with only the last three innings being played. You and the other coach agree to play innings seven, eight and nine, but do this five or seven times, thus garnering 15 or 21 innings of good, solid, pressurized scrimmaging. Keep a score of who wins the series, not a singular game. Ties count, too, if you wish and there is a short five or ten minute break in between "games."

K) **Multiple Opponent Scrimmaging**—Early in the preseason it is an excellent practice to bring in three or four teams to scrimmage together. In a three team tri-scrimmage, Team A and Team B will begin play while Team C is arriving late, perhaps due to travel distances. Each game is a five to seven inning affair and perhaps utilizing the "six out" or "2-1 count" approaches described earlier. When Team C arrives and is warmed up, the host team bows out and allows the other two squads to play. During the idle times extra batting practice can be taken in the cage or a team meeting held to go over mistakes. Conclude with the host team playing the late-arriving team and the other squad can depart for home.

If four teams show up, you need two fields and you can schedule an abbreviated round-robin tournament: A plays B, C plays D; then A vs. C and B vs. D wrapping up with A vs. D and B vs. C. Again, five innings suffice, but this is of course up to the coaches involved.

L) **WHITEY HERZOG'S ONE-STRIKE SCRIMMAGE—** This one will keep them hustling. Divide the squad into two teams and each "team" will keep their own score. A point is awarded for every base taken (i.e.—a single is one point, a triple is three points). The coach is the pitcher. The batter gets one strike and it is do or die. He may whiff; he may homer. Play six outs to keep things moving, but do not be afraid to call a batter out if they are not ready or assess a one-point penalty for a team not hustling on or off the field. It can be a good way to end practice. The great Cardinals manager Whitey Herzog once published this drill in a journal long forgotten. He added this rule: force outs at the plate, third base and second base do not count as outs, but must be executed nonetheless.

TEAM DEFESE: PICKOFF PLAYS

Pick plays can be worked indoors or outdoors. Not only do they add a level of sophistication to your overall defensive package, but they also add an element of fun to the game and to your practices. I always liked to add a new pickoff play before beginning a post-season tournament. We all felt that if we added a new "wrinkle" or brought something special to the "second season" we had a leg-up already.

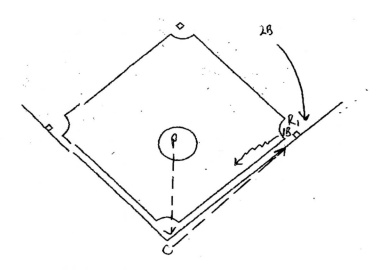

PLAY #1: Pitcher pitches the ball and the first baseman cheats in as if covering a bunt. Second baseman circles in behind and receives the throw from the catcher.

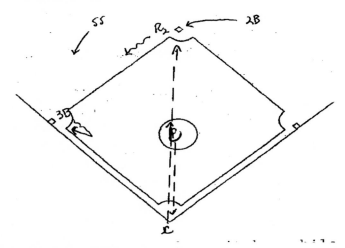

PLAY #2: Pitcher pitches while shortstop widens her position to third; catcher throws through to second baseman covering or catcher can return ball to pitcher who can wheel and throw.

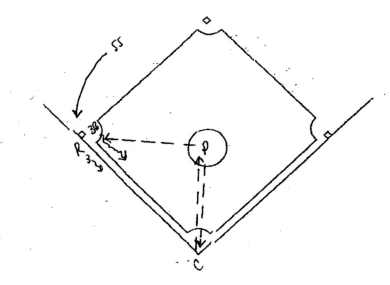

PLAY # 3: Pitcher pitches ball while third baseman cheats in as if reading bunt. The Shortstop circles behind and receives a snap throw from the pitcher who has received the ball from the catcher.

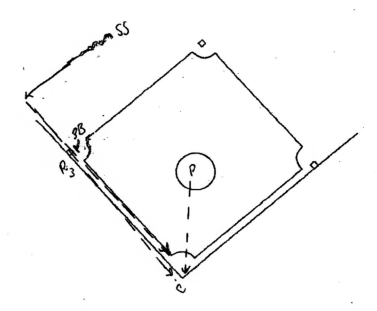

PLAY #4: Pitcher pitches ball; catcher throws to third to pick runner but intentionally overthrows the bag. SS has cheated over, receives ball and throws home or checks the runner. Third baseman holds the bag.

TEAM OFFENSE
COMBINATION DRILLS

"We forget that the big things are accomplished only by perfection of the little things."
Coach John Wooden

This segment is necessarily brief as it builds upon offensive concepts and drills described earlier in the sections on hitting and baserunning. Nonetheless, topics such as double-steal offensive plays, hit-and-run drills and even an innovative "5 Ball Scrimmage," taken from the renowned Coach Rod Del Monico, is included.

Prefacing my remarks about Team Offense, let me reiterate that in this chapter as well as in the preceding one on Team Defense, drills to enhance and develop both aspects of the game are inherent throughout the book. As the great LSU baseball Coach Skip Bertman intoned, "Synergism: the sum is greater than the parts." Implicitly, to improve the whole, each part must improve, so if each player improves her game, the team becomes better overall. These drills are written up with that sentiment clearly in mind.

Other drills for team offense can be found in the Batting Drills and in Baserunning & Conditioning. Without re-writing those drills, the reader is simply directed to review those sections.

TEAM OFFENSE: HIT-AND-RUN DRILL

Place a runner on first and tell her to steal on the pitch. The batter must deliver a bunt-and-run or slap-and-go. Help her out—pitch from an abbreviated distance and lay a short toss pitch on the outside one-third of the plate. Tell the hitter to get on "top of the ball" as hitters attempting to execute "oppo hitting" often tend to drop under the ball.

Be sure that there is a coach in the third base coaching box to either hold the runner at second or send her to third.

You may want to put a center fielder out in the outfield. Why? Center fielders don't lie. For a runner heading into second, she can get a glimpse of where the ball has been hit if she reads the center fielder. The latter will always go to the ball. Then, insist on the runner picking up the third base coach.

This drill, once your team becomes proficient at the bunt-and-run, can be a rapid-fire, high tempo conditioning drill and it will make you team better at this play.

TEAM OFFENSE: HIT OR RUN BP

A defense is positioned on the field. The remainder of the players are taking their turn at bat. Sounds familiar. Now, add this element: "deliver" or run. If the batter pops up, fouls out or hits a weak groundball, she runs; if she delivers a base hit, a gapper or even perhaps a sac-fly, she continues to hit. It sounds harsh, but this drill can serve as a conditioning drill, too.

You can choose to put runners on base to enhance the "delivery" notion of producing in game like situations.

You can temper the drill by giving the hitter five free swings first.

TEAM OFFENSE: LIVE SITUATIONAL BP "5-BALL SCRIMMAGE"

Rod Delmonico, former head baseball coach at Tennessee, described a drill that he once saw during a recruiting trip. A defense is on the field and a group of hitters are at the plate. A runner is on first while another stands by the plate, behind a protective screen and ready to break for first. A coach does the pitching.

Each batter is given five swings, but only the first one, the third one and the last ones are to be played live by the runners and the defense. The coach can call for a bunt, slap, sac-fly and so on depending on the situation that unfolds during the course of the three live swings. Even first-and-third double steal situations can be played as such.

The hitting team gets two rounds and then the defense comes in.

TEAM OFFENSE: DOUBLE STEALS OR "1ST & 3rd" "I"

Your double-steal offensive package can easily be worked on in doors as well as outdoors. In addition, I have found that the softball double steals are virtually identical to those in baseball. Here are some options:

A) STRAIGHT STEAL—The runner on first breaks as soon as the ball leaves the pitcher's hand, as per the rule book. The runner on third will break when the catcher throws to second and it is apparent that the ball will clear the pitcher's head.

B) DELAYED STEAL—The runner on first breaks when the ball reaches the plate. This gives her a late jump and one that should force a run-down between second and first. A good coaching point for the trapped runner is to not "dance" and look back at the ball. If she sprints, it will force a throw and this is what the runner on third is waiting for. That runner keys the throw, presumably from the middle infielder who has received the ball from the catcher. As soon as she releases the ball back to first, the runner on third breaks for the plate.

If however, the middle infielder holds the ball and runs the trapped 1st-to-2nd runner back to the bag, the runner on third shuffles down the line, matching the ball-holder step-for-step. She breaks when she is one third of the way home. This is risky, so it is imperative that the trapped runner (1st-to-2nd) make the middle infielder throw the ball to first by sprinting back.

C) MODIFIED DELAYED STEAL—In this sequence the runner on first breaks on the release of the ball and then stops dead in her tracks in between first and second. She forces a reaction from the middle infielder, the catcher or the pitcher, whoever has the ball. I know one coach who used to have their girls pretend that they stumbled...not bad. The runner off third applies the keys noted in (B).

D) SAFE STEAL—The runner on third has no intention of stealing home, but only bluffs a break when the ball is thrown through to second. This forces the middle infielder to cut the ball off and thereby allows the runner coming form first to take second. This steal is good when you have no outs and are trying to set up a big inning and get two runners in scoring position.

In practicing these plays, it is not a bad idea to use your sign system.

A FORMAT FOR PRESEASON PLAYER EVALUATIONS AND TRYOUTS

"…the uniform supposed say something about you. You get it for nothing, but it comes with history, so do the right thing when your in it."

NYC Firefighter Ed Schoales

In this age of accountability, coaches need to run organized preseason tryouts and document everything if they are going to "cut" players or rank players on depth charts. Simply fungoing some grounders and have players make ten cuts at the plate simply will not suffice when dealing with parents and justifying decisions. What is offered here are some challenging drills that can truly test infielders and outfielders' abilities and strengths. An overall format for indoor tryouts has been drawn up as well. As an additional thought, some coaches get involved in "showcases" and while scrimmage games serve to demonstrate players' talents, many of the drills suggested here can be utilized in showcase tournaments as well.

PRESEASON SOFTBALL TRYOUT: A SUGGESTED FORMAT "T"

The first consideration in assessing your pool of talent is equalization. The best players will stand out; so will the weakest ones. It is that large contingent of average players that needs the closest look. Hence, equalization. It is not enough to throw each kid ten pitches or have them each field ten grounders. Equalization of opportunity must go deeper than that.

First of all, think about running your tryouts indoors. Have each hitter face a designated number of pitches from a pitching machine. I would suggest a round of ten followed by two rounds of five pitches each. By using a pitching machine, everything is equalized and every pitch was a strike. By breaking up the at-bats, no player can claim that they were stuck in a rut or on a bad run.

Use your indoor facility for grounders, too. The hops will be truer. Test all candidates in balls to their right and left, slow-rollers and short-hop line drives. Work their backhand. While coaches with fungo bats are generally sufficient for this drill sequence, the hitting machine can also be used here.

You may have to take them outside for fly ball assessment. Shoot line drives into the gaps, right and left, to assess range and technical efficiency in terms of getting the ball back into the infield. Look for arm strength and accuracy. Did they hit the cutoff?

As for pitchers and catchers, check form initially. Do they have solid mechanicals? Arm strength for catchers, including footwork, can be assessed indoors. Use a stopwatch. As for pitchers do they throw strikes? Breaking balls can be assessed but it is usually enough at this point to see if they are mechanically sound and are around the plate.

The reader has probably already gleaned from this account that a good organizational approach for the tryouts is to divide the team into three groups; infielders, outfielders and pitchers/catchers. Stations can be set up in this manner:

Station A: Hitting off the pitching machine

Station B: Defensive Specialization—can be further broken down into substations such as these:

- Infielders: fungoes, backhanding, slow-rollers, range;
- Outfielders: line drives at them, going back on the ball, gappers and arm strength/accuracy (hitting the cut). You may wish to use the pitching machine for your fly ball drills to ensure consistency and to challenge;
- Pitchers/Catchers: set-ups, mechanics, arm strength.

Drills to accomplish all of this have been outlined throughout this volume.

Allow me to include a specific drill that can be helpful in the comparative aspects of tryouts, "The Shadow Drill." If you are hitting grounders to a line of infielders, have the second fielder in the line mimic and shadow the movements of the fielder in front of her as she goes through the techniques of handling grounders. Examining two players simultaneously in the same play provides interesting head-to-head comparisons.

Frankly, I would not bother to assess baserunning, although I would apply the stopwatch to time them on runs to first and from home to second. Proper baserunning is something that can be taught to your finalized team during the preseason. On another vein, some coaches prefer to use intra-squad scrimmages to assess their talent pool. While not inappropriate, individual skills might not readily emerge as the necessary situations may not arise.

However, on the college level, scrimmaging may be exactly what is needed. Colleges often use the "Fall Ball" season to evaluate talent for the upcoming spring campaign. They will take their talent pool of recruited players and walk-ons, divide them into teams, three, four or even five if available, and set up a round-robin intramural tournament. Coaches sit in the stands and evaluate these players over the course of a mini-season.

They are looking for players with the "Five Tools." Players in possession of all five "talents"—arm strength, foot speed, hitting power, hitting for average and fielding range are true gems and headed toward the professional ranks. Hence the best a high school or college coach can hope for is a player with as many of the tools as she can muster. Hall of Fame second baseman and television analyst Joe Morgan spoke of a "Sixth Tool," that being the mind—understanding the nuances, strategies and subtle tactics of the game. These become evident only in game-situations, hence the need for scrimmage at some point in the preseason (as part of the evaluation process for college coaches and part of the teaching process for high school coaches).

All this takes a lot of eyes, so do not be afraid to bring in other temporary coaches to help evaluate your players during the tryout period. There is another talent pool out there—retired coaches, respected colleagues and out-of-season coaches who can help you in this process, be it in the Fall or Spring.

One further comment in this regard: in today's world of questioning parents, you need documentation. Come up with a formal evaluation sheet, perhaps listing the "Six Tools" and a rating scale of one-to-five or one-to-ten. This is where the additional eyes can help. Solicit the input from as many evaluators as possible, because when the criticism comes down the pike, and it always does, especially on the grade school and high school level, there can be a certain "safety" in numbers. Your response to the parent "with concerns" (today's euphemism for those with complaints) is that, "five coaches all saw the same thing…"

Should the player see the evaluation? That's your call.

FIELDING: INFIELD THROWS "X"ING THE DIAMOND DRILL

Kirk Walker wrote this one up in his excellent book, The Softball Drill Book and it is an excellent evaluative drill for preseason tryouts.

Place a catcher, first baseman, shortstop and third baseman in the infield.

The catcher initiates the drill with a ball in her glove and on command launches a throw to second base. Proper footwork and base coverage is called for. The shortstop receives the throw, spins and fires to third. The third baseman throws across the diamond to first and, in turn, the first baseman fires home.

You can make this a rapid-fire, high-tempo drill by having the catcher throw a second ball to the shortstop covering second as soon as she launches the throw to third. Thus, two softballs are blazing across the infield. On a cautionary note, keep the infielders back, no drifting into the infield.

You can see who your "drill-killers" are and make judgments about who plays or who sits. You can also spot the rocket arms by means of this drill.

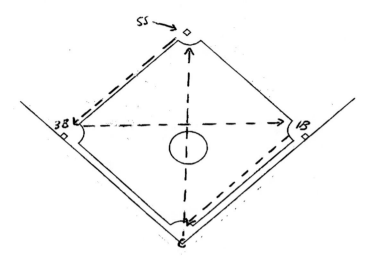

Note the absence of a second baseman. You do not need one since you are judging arm strength and footwork techniques. If, however, you elect to make this a fielding drill, add the second baseman and simply alternate the coverage at second.

FIELDING: FULL DIAMOND SHUFFLE TRY-OUTS   "I"

Baseball and softball are all about "reps." Repetitions. This drill is a good preseason drill that maximizes player involvement and groundball reps.

On the softball diamond, line your players up by each base, including home. Evenly distribute them. Set approximately three players near the baselines but inside the diamond between home and first, first and second, second and third and third and home. See the diagram below.

The players on the bases will begin the sequence. They will throw to Player #1 and shuffle down the baseline to receive a groundball which they in turn will throw to Player #2. Receive a grounder from number 2 and throw to number 3, shuffling all the way. Keep the shoulders square; pull the ball in, use proper footwork.

It can be exhausting as they work their way all around the diamond, but this serves as a good preseason evaluation drill.

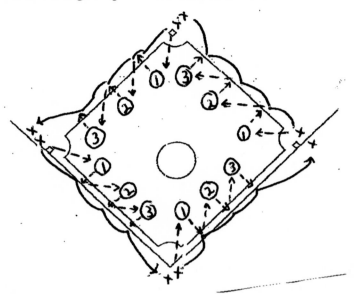

FIELDING: GROUNDBALLS "THE INFIELD LOOP"

I saw this drill written up in Kathy Veroni and Roanna Brazier's book, Coaching Fastpitch Softball Successfully. It is an excellent drill, but there is a bit of "standing around" by players since only one player is active while they complete the circuit of grounders.

This can be a good evaluative drill for the preseason, however. Begin with a player at third base. She fields a grounder and throws it to first. Then they race across the infield to field a ball lying on the infield dirt somewhere near the circle (a bunted that can be rolled out by the coach if they wish). They then sprint to the shortstop position, looping around second base. They will field two balls, one hit right at them for a throw home and the other a slow-roller, which they must charge and throw to first.

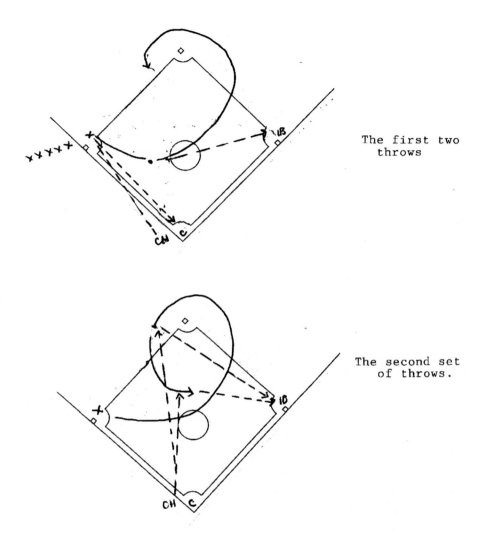

The first two
throws

The second set
of throws.

An alternative that can be developed from this drill is one that I picked up from Judi Garman's fine book, Softball Skills & Drills. She has her players line-up behind third base, execute a throw from there, and scramble over to shortstop, second and then first always throwing to first base but finishing with a throw home. As she suggests, this is an excellent evaluative drill when looking at who may be positioned where in your infield.

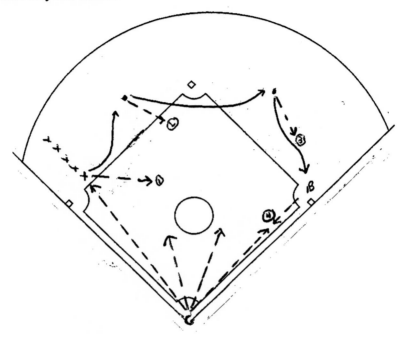

FIELDING: RANGE

Place two sets of infielders, regardless of position, around the infield as shown in the diagram. Use two fungo hitters, all hitting baseballs to the fielder's right.

You may wish to place a shagger out in the outfield behind the flight path of the groundball as many of these balls will squirt through the infield. Fungo hitters are asked to challenge the fielder by hitting the ball in the area of maximal range.

Once the fielder snags the ball or allows it to go through, she must trot to the end of the line on the other side of the infield.

Note that this is initially a counter-clockwise rotation. Remember to reverse the drill, having the players rotate clockwise.

Two fungo hitters are necessary. This is a good preseason evaluation.

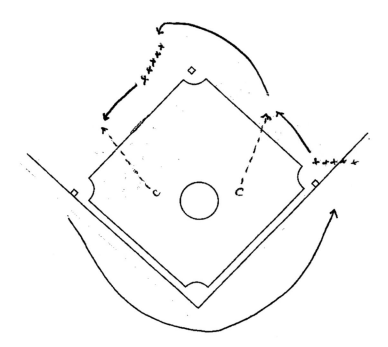

FIELDING: RANGE SCRAMBLE DRILL

This drill is not only an excellent evaluative drill, but also one that enhances range for infielders.

Place a cone on the infield dirt where an infielder would normally stand. You can "test" your middle infielders and/or corner infielders although the sense of "range" will differ for each.

One at a time, the shortstop for instance, will field a ball hit directly at them, throw across to first and then as soon as the ball is released, she will charge a slow-roller, throwing that one across to first as well. She must scramble back to the cone position, field and throw a ball hit to her left, scramble back and then field and throw one hit to her right, into the "hole," preferably a backhand.

While being a good drill, especially for tryouts or in an instructional camp session, you can actually increase the reps by having no one throw any balls, just time your fungoes so that no one is charging a slow-roller when someone else is hitting a fungo. You can use as many as four fungo hitters, but two is easier to coordinate.

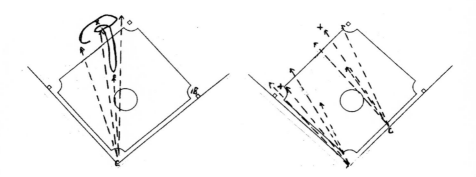

FIELDING: OUTFIELD SKILLS & CONDITIONING

Line up all of your outfielders in left field. One steps up. In a very short time, she will be exhausted.

The first play comes off a fungoed ball to the outfielder in left field. They throw it to second as in a routine play. The ball hit should be a grounder. The outfielder then sprints to centerfield where she fields a grounder or line drive and throws to a cutoff player stationed in the middle of the infield. Upon completing this throw, she sprints to right, fields another ball and throws to third. The final play is a "do-or-die" grounder in which the outfielder throws directly home.

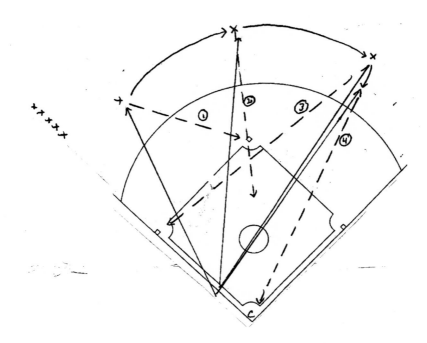

This is an excellent drill for evaluating outfielders' arms, speed, range and technique.

To re-cap:

    Throw #1: LF to 2B (grounder)

    Throw #2: CF to cutoff (grounder base hit)

    Throw #3: RF to 3B (fly ball vs. tagging runner)

    Throw #4: RF to home (grounder)

Once the line of outfielders has completed their way across the diamond, line them up on the right field foul line and hit them to their left.

ACKNOWLEDGEMENTS

In teaching The Game to our players, coaching is one part experience, one part borrowing and one part innovating. We all learn from our mentors, our colleagues, our opponents, and even players. We read; we attend coaching seminars. We learn while the players learn. The development of a coach never stops.

That is what makes it all the more difficult to recollect and mention some of the many coaches I have been fortunate enough to have known and worked with on various teams. I am certain to miss a few names, but that cannot negate the attempt.

Of the head coaches I have worked under over the years, Jake Landfried, legendary coach at Manasquan (NJ) High School, stands out. He passed on a few years ago at far too young an age, but he mentored more future coaches than he could ever imagine. I would also like to recognize Ernie Leta who gave me my chance to coach collegiate ball at Ocean County College in New Jersey. I worked under Glen Effenberger, Paul Murray and Gerard O'Donnell at Monsignor Donovan High School in Toms River, New Jersey. Lou DeSarno at the Brookdale Baseball Camp and his predecessor Paul MacLaughlin gave me a chance in their camp and kept me around for over twenty years. I would so like to recognize and thank Coaches John Musolf, Tom Weber, Art Gordon, Marty Kenney, Todd Schmidt and the late Rich Veth for asking me to join them on the staff of the prestigious Carpenter Cup teams over the years. I've learned from all of you.

Andrew Lohse looked over the section on catching and offered several key insights. Other readers who looked the manuscript included my co-author New Jersey High School Hall of Fame Coach Pat Barnaba and longtime coaching colleague Kevin Oberto. Their insights were invaluable.

All photographs were taken by the author. I would like to thank my son Andy, my granddaughters Alexandra DeForge, Emily Caccamise and a friend and coaching colleague, Jared Morris for modeling in my "photo shoots." I would also like to offer a "thumbs up" to my longtime typist, Christine Muly, on another outstanding job.

Coaches that I worked with during the course of my career include Skip Mottola, Jerry Caci, John Herbert, Bob Shafer, Ron Heile, Pete Farnum, Tom Bauer, Ed McRae, Jason Leta, Sean Cashman, Tom DeNoia, Ty Hawkins, Jared Morris, Jack Hawkins, Mike Faulhaber, Bill Fee, Greg Faria, Ed McDonald and my daughter Abby Trimble all helped me in so many different ways. I cannot thank them all enough, but I do sincerely apologize for the names I've forgotten.

Two final thoughts. One to the Moms and Dads—Coach Denny Throneburg once said, "Parents must make sure their goal is their daughter's goal, not their own."

And then there are the players...Coaches, always remember to be gracious and humble. As the axiom goes, "The horses pull the coach." Any successes we enjoy emanate from them.

Richard Trimble

ACKNOWLEDGEMENTS

As for my part of the Acknowledgements, I must point to Jack Hawkins' "Be The Best You Are Softball Coaches Clinic" held every year in Cherry Hill, New Jersey. I have clocked countless hours of attendance and participation in probably the East Coast's finest softball clinic. I have sat in the audience with the over 1000 coaches who regularly attended this event; I have also had the unique opportunity to meet, listen and soak in the wisdom of coaches like the late Dr. June Walker, Ralph and Karen Weekly, Linda Wells, Sue Enquist, and Lisa Fernandez in informal one-on-one sessions over lunch and dinner. Anyone in the family of softball coaching can appreciate the names listed and the opportunity to learn not only the game, but also the dignity of coaching, that each has exemplified.

I must also recognize the many high school coaching colleagues who, through competition, have taught me the "ins and outs" of the great game of softball.

Patricia Barnaba

SELECT BIBLIOGRAPHY

Ainsworth, Cliff, Complete Book of Drills for Winning Baseball, Parker Publishing Co., Paramus, NJ 2001.

Baker, Dianne & Cole, Sandra, Winning Softball Drills, Championship Productions Ames, IO (4th ed.) 1989

Bagonzi, John, The Act of Pitching, Hedgehoghill Press, Madison, NH 2001.

Baker, Dusty, Mercer, Jeff & Bittinger, Marv, You Can Teach Hitting, Bittinger Books, Carmel, IN, 1993.

Bennett, Bob, ed., The Baseball Drill Book, Human Kinetics, Champaign, IL 2004.

Garman, Judi, Softball Skills & Drills, Human Kinetics, Champaign, IL 2001.

Houseworth, Steven and Rivkin, Francine, Coaching Softball Effectively, Human Kinetics, Champaing, IL 1955

Joseph, Jacquie, ed., The Softball Coaching Bible, Human Kinetics, Champaign, IL 2002.

Kempf, Cheri, The Softball Pitching Edge, Human Kinetics, Champaign, IL 2002

Lopez, Andy & Kirkgard, John, <u>Coaching Baseball Successfully,</u> Human Kinetics, Champaign, IL 1996.

Mattingly, Don & Rosenthal, Jim, <u>Hitting Is Simple</u>, St. Martin's Press, New York, NY 2007.

McBee, Bob & Burgess, Tom, <u>Coaching Guide to Championship Baseball Drills & Fundamentals,</u> P.N. Thompson Printing, Burlington, NC 1982.

Perconte, Jack, <u>The Making of a Hitter,</u> Second Base Publishing, Lisle, IL 2009.

"Stony Brook (University) Softball Strength & Conditioning Program," 2006

Trimble, Richard, <u>Developing a Successful Baseball Program,</u> 2nd ed., Coaches Choice, Monterey, CA 2005.

Veroni, Kathy & Brazier, Roanna, <u>Coaching Fastpitch Softball Successfully,</u> 2nd ed., Human Kinetics, Champaign, IL 2006.

Walker, June, <u>Defensive Techniques for Championship Softball,</u> MacGregor Sports Education, 1989

Walker, Kirk, ed., <u>The Softball Drill Book,</u> Human Kinetics, Champaign, IL 2007.

INSTRUCTIONAL VIDEOS

"Baseball Excellence", Ed McRae, Shore Christian Center, Allenwood, NJ.

"Defense: The Tennessee Way," Ralph Weekly & Karen Weekly

"Hitting Fundamentals With Drills", Rod Delmoico.

"Hitting the Tennessee Way," Ralph Weekly

"Pitching Mechanics", Sue Enquist & Dee Dee Weiman, Coaches Choice, Monterey, CA.

"Pitching and Catching", Pat McMahon, Human Kinetics, Champaign, IL.

"The Towny Townsend Hitting Disc & Drill Series", Towny Townsend, HD Baseball LLC, Chesapeake, VA.

"The Tennessee Slap Attack," Karen Weekly

"USA Softball Instructional Series," Vol. 6, "Beginning Pitching," Mike Candrea & Michele Smith, Amateur Softball Assoc., 2004

"Wall Ball," John Cohen Video Masters, 2009

WEBSITES

www.myteam.com (open Sports Central Softball)

www.softballtoday.com ("Softball Today" Magazine)

www.speedbat.com

www.eteamz.active.com

ABOUT THE AUTHORS

Richard Trimble has been coaching baseball for over 40 years. He has worked with all levels of player abilities, from youth tee-ball to collegians. He is first and foremost a teacher and has spent forty years in classroom. He currently teaches History at Ocean County College in Toms River, New Jersey. He holds five college degrees and is the author of ten books. He lives with his wife Jean in Manasquan, New Jersey. They have three children and five grandchildren, all granddaughters and they have moved him into a whole new ballgame— softball coaching.

Pat Barnaba was inducted in the New Jersey Interscholastic Athletic Association's Coaches Hall of Fame in 1995. In her thirty years of coaching at Manasquan High School, she compiled a 453-115 won-loss record, seventeen divisional titles, two Shore Conference Championships, one Monmouth County Championship, and three State Group II titles. In addition, she was chosen by "The Star Ledger" as the Monmouth County Coach of the Year three times, and twice as the Shore Conference Coach of the Year by "The Asbury Park Press." According to "The Star Ledger," Pat was the first female coach in the history of New Jersey high school softball to compile 400 wins. Currently Pat serves as a certified NJSIAA umpire.

Would you like to see your manuscript become a book?

If you are interested in becoming a PublishAmerica author, please submit your manuscript for possible publication to us at:

mybook@publishamerica.com

You may also mail in your manuscript to:

**PublishAmerica
PO Box 151
Frederick, MD 21705**

www.publishamerica.com

CPSIA information can be obtained at www.ICGtesting.com
Printed in the USA
LVOW12s1658290814

401384LV00001B/80/P

9 781629 078366